A COMMENTARY ON THE
Gospel
OF
Matthew

Rev. Albert Kirk
Robert E. Obach

Paulist Press
New York/Ramsey/Toronto

Nihil Obstat: Rev. Valentine N. Handwerker, STL
            Censor Librorum

Imprimatur: Most Rev. Carroll T. Dozier, D.D.
            Bishop of Memphis

Date: January 4, 1978

The publisher gratefully acknowledges:

Scripture text © copyright American Bible Society 1966, 1971, 1976 used with permission.

Scripture and art from *GOOD NEWS BIBLE FOR MODERN MAN*, American Bible Society, used with permission.

Library of Congress
Catalog Card Number: 78-65715

ISBN: 0-8091-2173-5

Published by Paulist Press
Editorial Office: 1865 Broadway, New York, N.Y. 10023
Business Office: 545 Island Road, Ramsey, N.J. 07446

Printed and bound in the
United States of America

Contents

Preface

Since the appearance of this work as a tool in the adult study phase of the Matthew Year in the Diocese of Memphis, many of our readers have remarked on its usefulness and on their hope that it could be made available to a wider audience. We are pleased, then, to offer to believers outside our local Church a small part of the program which has renewed the enthusiasm of our people for the Word of God.

The adult study phase of the Matthew Year involved a twofold process: daily personal study of Matthew's text, utilizing the commentary; and a weekly meeting with other believers to share the word which the Lord was speaking to each individual. Although the commentary can be used in other ways, it will produce its greatest fruitfulness when used as a tool for serious personal, even daily, study of the Gospel According To Matthew, accompanied by a periodic sharing of this Good News with other believers.

The Gospel According to Matthew has been a favorite of the Church. Because of its powerful portrait of Jesus, because of its masterful literary and catechetical style, because of its continuity with Judaism, Matthew's Gospel came to have a privileged place in the liturgy of the Church and in the catechesis of the Fathers.

Above all, Matthew focuses our attention on the teaching of Jesus. He is the earliest Christian writer to take a keen interest in the sayings of the Lord. Paul, whose letters constitute the earliest "books" of the Christian Scriptures, was more interested in the significance of the Lord Jesus for human life than in the historical memory of his words. Mark, the first to use the form of writing which we call a gospel, places more emphasis on the deeds of Jesus than on his words. It is Matthew, the second evangelist, who hands on to us the teachings of Jesus.

Matthew's concern with Jesus' teaching becomes evident from the way in which he constructed the Gospel. He centers his narrative sections (the actions of Jesus) around long sermons drawn from Jesus' teaching. Matthew so writes that as Jesus speaks to his original disciples he also speaks to the believers of Matthew's day. Matthew wanted his community to understand that the Jesus who had addressed the twelve disciples decades before is the same Lord who addressed the disciples of Matthew's own day.

It is important to see that in the Gospel According to Matthew the Lord Jesus again speaks to his people. The Gospel is more than a historical record; it is a living word. The words of the Gospel are addressed to us insofar as we are disciples of the Lord Jesus in continuity with that community for whom the Gospel was first written.

This is important for us. During this Matthew Year we will be listening to the Gospel not so much as isolated individuals but as a diocese, as the Church of West Tennessee. We have a tremendous opportunity to grow together as the Body of Christ.

Our goal then is a prayerful study of Matthew's account of the Gospel. Prayerful, because it is the Holy Spirit who brings to life in each generation the words of Jesus. Without the powerful presence of the Spirit, we cannot hear the voice of the Lord speaking to us. Study, because without it the Gospel does not yield its full richness.

You are asked then to experience the Gospel, at first alone under the guidance of the Holy Spirit, and then, if possible, with others. Whether alone or with your study group, we suggest that you begin with a period of prayer; an act of faith that the Lord will speak to you and a prayer of petition for the inspiration of his Spirit.

During these eight weeks of study, we are asking you to

set aside a portion of each day to read, to reflect and to pray. (If this is not possible, perhaps two or three longer periods during the week will be sufficient.) Try to avoid a hasty reading of the scripture passages and commentary just prior to the meeting of your study group. We have divided the Gospel into forty sections, five sections for each of the eight weeks. Scripture passages and commentary readings are spaced over five days each week, allowing a sixth day for reflection and the seventh day for your group meeting.

Our first aim in producing this commentary is to provide you with a companion to the text of Matthew's Gospel. Today one is not able to open the Bible and understand its meaning as easily as one opens the newspaper and begins reading about what happened yesterday. Unlike the newspaper, the Gospel was not written yesterday.

Matthew wrote about 85 A.D. for a Christian community probably located in present day Syria. The majority of Matthew's audience were converts from Judaism, and thus familiar with the varied styles of writing in the Hebrew Scriptures. Just as the study of Chaucer or Shakespeare is enhanced by the tools of literary criticism, so our study of Matthew's Gospel will be enhanced by the tools of scripture study which have been developed over the last century. Since the magisterium of the Church has now approved them, we are happy to be able to share them with you. We are convinced that they greatly enrich our faith-filled hearing of the Gospel.

Our second goal in the commentary is to assist readers in applying the Word of the Lord to the here and now of everyday living. As Matthew took the words and deeds of Jesus and explained their significance for his own community, so we of the diocese of Memphis have the opportunity to reflect on the words and deeds of Jesus and apply them to ourselves and to the building up of our ecclesial community.

These two goals might serve to suggest a format for the

study group meetings. The first hour might deal with Matthew's message in its original context. During this time participants might concentrate on how Matthew applies the teachings of Jesus to the needs of his own day. In the second hour, participants might struggle to apply the Gospel to their own family, work and community situation. Such an approach respects the basic pattern of God's revelation. Since He has chosen to speak to us through a human author, we must accurately understand what the author is saying so that we can accurately hear the Word which God speaks to us today.

As we complete our work, we would like to express our gratitude to all of those who have supported us by their prayers and encouragement. A special word of thanks is due to Bishop Dozier, for his pastoral leadership; to Dr. Peter Ellis and Fr. Michael Barre, S.S., for serving as biblical and theological consultants; to Ray Berthiaume and Jean Jecmen, for sharing their artistic talents; to Sr. Helen Morrison, Sr. Barbara Spencer, Sr. Frances Belmonte, Mrs. Rozanne Pera, and Jack Yoste, who did our proof-reading; and to Mrs. Nam Le, Mrs. Anne Powell, and Mrs. Margaret Holcomb, who waded through our handwriting to produce the finished product; to Rose Mary Obach, for her support; and, finally, to the American Bible Society for permission to reprint the faith-filled drawings from the *Good News Bible* and various editions of *Good News For Modern Man*. Unless otherwise noted, quotations from the Hebrew Scriptures are taken from the *Good News Bible*, while quotations from the Christian Scriptures or unquoted references to particular verses refer to the third or fourth edition of *Good News for Modern Man*.

Solemnity of the Holy Trinity, 1978

Rev. Albert Kirk
Robert E. Obach

Week One

In this first week we will study the first two chapters of Matthew's Gospel, appropriately called the infancy narrative. Matthew's concern is to situate the birth of Our Lord within the history of the Jewish people. More than the other evangelists, he stresses the continuity between the chosen people of God and the disciples of Jesus of Nazareth.

It is in continuity with earlier moments of salvation history that the events of the infancy narrative take on their deepest meaning. Matthew teaches us this by frequently quoting (or alluding to) the Hebrew Scriptures. We have often meditated on the message of chapters one and two in the context of the Christmas celebrations. However, our study of these passages in the context of the history of the chosen people will greatly enrich our appreciation of the meaning of the birth of Jesus.

The events of the infancy narrative are linked with the past, but they also envision the future life and ministry of Jesus. As a prologue or introduction to the entire Gospel, Matthew's first two chapters detail "in miniature" the life, death and resurrection of Christ. With your study group, you might explore the profound theological meaning of these chapters.

Daily Study Assignment: Week One

Day	Matthew	Commentary
1	1:1 - 17	Pages 7-10
2	1:18 - 25	Pages 10-17
3	2:1 - 12	Pages 24-28
4	2:13 - 18	Pages 28-29
5	2:19 - 23	Pages 30-31

6—Reflect on chapters 1 and 2 in light of the reflection questions listed below.

7—STUDY GROUP MEETING

- Of what importance to us is Matthew's emphasis on the Jewishness of Jesus and on the continuity of his life with the Hebrew Scriptures?

- According to the practice of the times, women were not usually included in genealogies. Yet Matthew includes women who were not only Gentiles, but three of the four led less than exemplary lives. Why?

- We have seen that Matthew relates some of the events of the life of Jesus to the central experiences of the chosen people: Persecution, Exodus, Exile, Deliverance. Have you ever thought it appropriate to relate the events of your own life with the significant events in the life of Jesus?

- What is the deeper significance of the visit of the magi? of the escape to Egypt? of the slaughter of the children of Bethlehem? of the return from Egypt?

- Rank in order of significance *for your life* the following teachings contained in 1:18-25: Mary conceived by the Holy Spirit; Joseph was a man who was both obedient to the Law as well as compassionate; the child to be born will save his people from their sins; the child will be called, "God is with us"; Mary was a virgin.

The Birth and Infancy of Jesus, 1:1-2:23

OVERVIEW: Who is Jesus? Where does he come from? Matthew answers these questions in a summary manner in chapters 1 and 2, the prologue of his account of the good news of Jesus.

A. Genealogy and Birth, 1:1-25

1. The Family Record of Jesus, 1:1-17

Readers of Matthew tend to skip over the genealogy of Jesus, perhaps because we assume we know enough about the origin and identity of Jesus without our taking the time to become more familiar with the Hebrew Scriptures. Since Matthew writes this Gospel in the context of the history of God's chosen people, Matthew presumes that the readers of the Gospel of Jesus will understand it against the background of Israel's participation in God's plan of salvation. For Matthew, the Word of God contained in the Hebrew Scriptures was a living Word. Thus, God's Word was charged with the kind of meaning that spoke not only to people living centuries before, but also a Word which addressed the people of Matthew's own day. Matthew was constantly applying, constantly re-interpreting the Word of God in the light of the community's faith in Jesus.

Notice how Matthew's genealogy (1:1-17) brings us face to face with the humanity of Jesus. He was born in the midst of a particular Semitic people with their own unique history. The very first verse of the Gospel, "This is the family record of Jesus Christ, who was a descendant of David, who was a descendant of Abraham," is a summary

statement about the origin and the identity of Jesus.
Through the legal paternity of Joseph (1:16), Jesus is a
descendant of David, and a descendant of Abraham (1:1),
the pagan called by God to leave his homeland in order to
go to a new land where God would bless him (Gen 12:1).
The promise made by God to Abraham had a universal
significance:

> All the tribes of the earth shall bless themselves
> through you (Gen 12:3).

In the unfolding of the Gospel, Matthew will present
Jesus as the one who comes for the whole world, bringing
a universal salvation for both Jew and Gentile. At the very
end of the Gospel Matthew presents Jesus as giving his
authority to his disciples, sending them forth to "*all
peoples everywhere*" so that they can bring the Good News
of Jesus and his teaching to all peoples (28:18-20).

Matthew carefully divides the family record into three
sections, each containing fourteen generations (seven
being a number symbolizing fullness or completion and
therefore, $14 = 2 \times 7$). The first group of fourteen (1:2-6)
begins with Abraham (c 1800 B.C.) and ends with King
David (1000-960 B.C.). Like Abraham, David is also the
recipient of a promise from God. God told the prophet
Nathan:

> "So tell my servant David that I, the LORD Al-
> mighty, say to him, 'I took you ... and make you the
> ruler of my people Israel.... You will always have
> descendants, and I will make your kingdom last
> forever. Your dynasty will never end.' "
> (2 Sam 7:8,16)

The next group of fourteen generations (1:7-11) ends
with Josiah, the king who reigned during the terrible time

when the Babylonians destroyed Jersualem and took the survivors into the Exile (597-539 B.C.). That was the low ebb of Israel's history. From that low point of the Exile the third group of fourteen generations (1:12-16) leads to the zenith of Israel's history and the beginning of a new age:

> *Jacob was the father of Joseph, and the husband of Mary who was the mother of Jesus, called the Messiah (1:16).*

Who is Jesus and where did he come from? He came from God through his ancestors, particularly David and Abraham. He is the one in whom all the nations of the world would be blessed, the one who would secure the throne of the royal family of David forever, and the one for whom the prophets had hoped.

Matthew's account of the genealogy of Jesus contains an unusual feature: women are included in the genealogical table. Moreover, they are all Gentiles. Tamar (1:3) is the Canaanite woman who seduces Judah, her father-in-law and gives birth to Perez (Gen 38). Rahab (1:5) is the prostitute who aided the Hebrew spies and then married into the Hebrew people after the destruction of Jericho (Jos 2:1-21). Ruth (1:6) is a Moabitess whose resourcefulness brings her into the Jewish lineage of Jesus by means of her marriage with Boaz (Book of Ruth). Bathsheba (1:6), the wife of Uriah the Hittite, is the accomplice of David in adultery and murder (2 Sam 11:2-27). In the lineage of Jesus we find men and women both good and bad. Matthew's genealogy offers a summary of the Gospel: Jesus, the fulfillment of the promises of God and the hopes of Israel, comes for both Jew and Gentile, for both the good person and the sinner.

The rest of chapter one and the whole of chapter two complete the prologue or introduction to Matthew's Gospel. As we begin our study, it is important for us to realize that Matthew was a man of the first century and not of the twentieth. When Matthew wrote he did not have a twentieth century view of history as chronological sequence of events. Nor did he have the rules that govern our modern view of journalism, for example, the guidelines followed by both cub reporter and newspaper editor: "get the facts: Who, What, Where, When and Why." This difference between reporting styles in Matthew's day and ours is especially notable in the five "fulfillment passages" Matthew takes from the Hebrew Scriptures and applies to Jesus with the introductory formula, "This happened in order to make come true what the Lord had said through the Prophet," or "He did this to make come true what the Prophets had said." Matthew, in the light of his faith in Jesus, writes with a certain freedom as he reinterprets the meaning of the Hebrew Scriptures in such a way that they attest or give witness to the identity and the mission of Jesus.

2. The conception and birth of Jesus, 1:18-25.

While the evangelist Luke concentrates on Mary, Matthew places Joseph at center stage. Joseph and Mary are betrothed. To appreciate what is happening here, let us be mindful that according to the customs at the time, marriage might have three phases: a less solemn arrangement or agreement to a marriage of their children by the parents of two families; a very solemn betrothal, lasting about a year, during which the couple were regarded as legally married but without the privileges of the marriage bed; and the wedding, after which the husband takes his wife into his home. The second phase, the betrothal period was regarded as marriage. If the man died during this time, the woman would be considered a virgin and widow. To terminate the betrothal, divorce would be necessary. Mary and Joseph are in the second phase. Mary is still living at her family home.

Then,

> *before they were married, she found out she was going to have a baby by the Holy Spirit. Joseph, to whom she was engaged, was a man who always did what was right; but he did not want to disgrace Mary publicly, so he made plans to break the engagement secretly (1:18-19).*

Joseph, being "a man who always did what was right," is portrayed as the just man, that is, the man who does what the Law teaches. He finds himself in inner conflict, Mary on one side, the Law on the other.

It is important to understand what the Law is. We Christians tend to have a negative view of the Law—as if it were something oppressive or almost intolerable. But for the Jewish people, Jesus as well as Matthew, the Law or Torah is God's gift. We find the Torah/Law contained in the first five books of the Bible (the Pentateuch). The Law includes the ten commandments, but contains much more. Rather than thinking of the Law in the sense we think of "law and order," think of the Law as teaching or instruction that conveys the meaning of life itself. Accordingly, Law or Torah teaches about God's creation of the world; Torah records God's calling of Abraham (Genesis). The Law recounts the saving deeds God does on behalf of his chosen people, and it contains the expression of God's covenant will and the inspired interpretation of the events of the history of the Hebrew people (Exodus, Leviticus, Numbers, Deuteronomy).

Thus the Law was and still is the way of life for the

Jewish people. The Law enabled them to know what God wanted them to do and the way he wanted them to live. The Law/Torah gave the Jewish people their identity and enabled them to find the meaning of life throughout their entire history. The devout Jew found his greatest happiness in living out God's Law. As we shall see in Matthew's account of the Sermon on the Mount, Jesus teaches this very same idea: "Happy are those whose greatest desire is to do what God requires (5:6)." Psalm 119, a long hymn praising God's Law, begins this way:

> *Happy are those whose lives are faultless, who live according to the law of the LORD.*
> *Happy are those who follow his commands, who obey him with all their heart....*
> *LORD, you have given us your laws and told us to obey them faithfully. How I hope that I shall be faithful in keeping your instructions (Ps 119:1-5).*

Now we can appreciate the plight of Joseph: his beloved Mary on one side, on the other side is the Law, Deuteronomy 22:20-21, dealing with the situation of a woman who comes to her husband's home no longer a virgin. The Law called for the woman to be stoned to death, but at least by the first century the death penalty was replaced by a system of banning or excommunicating the guilty party. Deut 22:21, the command to "purge the evil from the midst of you," according to one interpretation, could be obeyed by divorcing the adulterous woman. Joseph decides on two actions: 1) To obey the Law and 2) To be merciful to Mary by divorcing her without accusing her of serious crime. Thus Matthew characterizes Joseph as a man who did what the Law required (the Law being the expression of God's will) as well as a man who obeyed the Law in a spirit of merciful compassion.

In this depiction of Joseph, we see a technique Matthew will use throughout the Gospel, the use of a person or event for the purpose of linking the past with what is to come. As the genealogy has indicated, Matthew wants to show the continuity of past and present, of old and new. Joseph is a descendant of David and of Abraham. There is an important parallel between Joseph, the legal father of Jesus and another Joseph the twelfth son of Jacob, whose name was changed to Israel (Gen 32:28). Like the patriarch, Joseph, the foster father of Jesus was an obedient man. Both men dreamed significant dreams (a dream being one of the ways God reveals himself and his will), and both went to Egypt (see chapters 37-50 of Genesis). But Joseph, husband of Mary, is also linked with what is to come. As foster father of Jesus, he is the legal forebear of him who will perfectly accomplish the will of the Father. Joseph also pre-figures the disciple of Jesus. As we will see, Matthew will portray the disciple as the one who hears and acts upon the teaching of Jesus. That teaching of Jesus will center upon the observance of the Jewish Law interpreted according to the principles of love, of mercy and of compassion.

As Joseph finds himself torn between his love for Mary and his desire to observe the Law that calls for separation from her, God reveals Himself to Joseph in a dream. The conflict is resolved by the revelation that the child in Mary's womb has been conceived by the Holy Spirit. Man had no role whatsoever; the initiative for the incarnation is God's alone.

At the time Matthew wrote of the creative power of God's Spirit, the faith of the Church had not yet developed to the point at which she could pray:

> *We believe in the Holy Spirit, the Lord, the giver of*
> *life,*
> *Who proceeds from the Father and the Son,*
> *With the Father and the Son He is worshiped and*
> *glorified.*

This perception of the Holy Spirit as third Person of the Trinity came to the Church only gradually. The Nicene Creed which contains the doctrinal expression of our faith in Father, Son and Holy Spirit only came to be formulated during the fourth century. Matthew understood the Holy Spirit in terms of God's creative and transforming activity. Recall that it was God's spirit that moved across the waters of chaos bringing creation into existence (Gen 1:2). It was the spirit of God's power that was given to the prophets. It was the spirit of God that brought life to the dead bones of the exiled Jewish people in Ezekiel's vision (Ezek 37:1-14). With the event of the incarnation of Jesus, Matthew tells us, God has intervened in human history in a totally new way.

Today we read Matthew with the benefit of nineteen centuries of the Holy Spirit's guidance. Through prayer and reflection our understanding has deepened. We know of the Holy Spirit as the one whom we worship and glorify along with the Father and the Son. It is as the Second Vatican Council teaches:

> *...there is a growth in the understanding of the*
> *realities and the words which have been handed*
> *down. This happens through the contemplation and*
> *study made by believers, who treasure these things in*
> *their hearts (see Lk 2:19,51), through the intimate*
> *understanding of spiritual things they experience,*
> *and through those who have received through epis-*

*copal succession the sure gift of truth until the words
of God reach their fulfillment in her (CONSTITU-
TION ON DIVINE REVELATION, #8).*

By means of an angel, (often God's revealing presence
and the role of the angel are interchangeable) God tells
Joseph to complete the marriage and take Mary into his
home. Matthew closes this section with another declaration that it was by God's action and God's action alone that
Jesus was conceived: Joseph "had no sexual relations with
her before she gave birth to her son (1:25)." (Some read this
verse and conclude that Joseph and Mary lived a typical
married life after the birth of Jesus. The fact is that Matthew
is only concerned with making clear the early Church's
belief that Jesus was conceived by the initiative of God, not
of man. The marital relationship of Mary and Joseph after
the birth of Jesus was simply not a concern of Matthew. The
Catholic Church's doctrine of the *perpetual* virginity of
Mary cannot be proved or disproved on the basis of Matthew's account of the Gospel.)

"She will give birth to a son and you will name him
Jesus—because he will save his people from their sins
(1:21)." Man contributes neither seed nor name; it is not
Joseph who names the child but God. The name "Jesus"
speaks of both the identity and the mission of Jesus. It is a
shortened form of Joshua, the name of the man who succeeded Moses and then led the Hebrew people out of the
desert into the promised land (Joshua 1:1-5). The name's
oldest meaning was "God (Yahweh) helps," but later on it
came to mean "God (Yahweh) *saves*." From this point on
the Gospel will detail the wonderful and unexpected way
in which God will save humankind. His beloved Son
comes to offer his life: "...this is my blood which seals
God's covenant, my blood poured out...for the forgiveness of sins (26:28)." His name is Jesus "because he will

save his people from their sins (1:21)."

> *Now all this happened to make come true what the*
> *Lord had said through the prophet. "The virgin will*
> *become pregnant and give birth to a son, and he will*
> *be called Emmanuel" which means, "God is with us"*
> *(1:22-23).*

This is the first of twelve fulfillment quotations contained in Matthew's writing. It is taken from Isaiah 7:14. Remember that when Matthew wrote, the Christian Scriptures were only in the process of formation. The only "Bible" that Matthew and the rest of the Christian community knew was the Word of God contained in the Hebrew Scriptures. Since the fulfillment of prophecy is a most important element in Matthew as well as in the whole of Christianity, let us take a close look at the process Matthew uses in his citation of the Hebrew Scriptures.

First of all, he interprets the Hebrew Scriptures in the light of his faith in Jesus, whom Matthew regards as the climax of God's revelation. For this reason Matthew sees no separation between Hebrew Scripture and the new age inaugurated by Jesus, Messiah and Son of God. As a matter of fact, if Matthew were to comment upon our common practice of dividing the Word of God into "Old Testament" and "New Testament," he would probably strongly disapprove. He would remind us that he wrote his account of Jesus for a community composed mainly of Jewish Christians as well as for those Jewish people who might accept Jesus as Messiah. He would point out that his intention in writing was to show the continuity between Judaism and the Church. He would tell us that to accomplish this purpose, he portrayed Jesus as both the one who fulfills Hebrew prophecy and the one who comes to affirm and complete the Mosaic Law (5:17)

Let us turn to the original context of Isaiah 7:14. Almost eight centuries earlier Judea was under severe pressure from her neighbors. In Jerusalem King Ahaz wanted to enter into an alliance with Assyria for protection. Isaiah the prophet appeared and told King Ahaz to trust in God rather than in the military strength of a pagan nation:

> *Listen now, descendants of King David, It's bad enough for you to wear out the patience of men—do you have to wear out God's patience too? Well then, the Lord himself will give you a sign: a young woman who is pregnant will have a son and will name him 'Emmanuel.' By the time he is old enough to make his own decisions, the lands of those two kings who terrify you will be deserted (7:13-16).*

Isaiah told King Ahaz that a sign, the birth of a son, would be given him. He would be named with a symbolic name, Emmanuel, because God was with his people.

Matthew applied this text to Jesus. Born also of the Family of David, Jesus is Emmanuel, that is, "God-with us." From that time when Matthew re-interpreted Isaiah 7:14 in light of his faith in Jesus, this text of Isaiah has had two meanings. The first is the meaning given by the original context in which Isaiah made his prophecy. The second meaning is the later interpretation given the text of Isaiah 7:14 by Matthew: the child conceived in Mary by the Holy Spirit is the ultimate saving sign, the incarnate presence of God who will forever be with his people. Thus, Matthew begins the Gospel with God's promise in Mary's womb (1:23). He will end the Gospel with this promise of the risen Jesus:

> *I will be with you always, to the end of the age (28:20).*

B. The Messiah's Infancy, 2:1-23

OVERVIEW: This chapter is perhaps the most familiar and the most complex chapter in Matthew's work. We find in it a blend of literary forms. There are theological affirmations, citations of the Hebrew Scriptures, parallels drawn between Jesus and the events of Israel's history, references to Jewish midrash, and details that foreshadow the final days of Jesus—his final entry into Jerusalem, rejection, trial, passion and death.

To read this chapter as if it were a mere reporting of a sequence of events taking place during the infancy of Jesus, then, is to fail to appreciate what Matthew is teaching in these twenty-three carefully written verses. If we were to insist on reading this chapter solely on the basis of the literal meaning of the words found here, we would in effect reject the teaching of the Catholic Church that the inspired writers were "true authors" who "made use of their powers and abilities" while they wrote (CONSTITUTION ON DIVINE REVELATION, #11, Second Vatican Council). To understand what Matthew is communicating to his local Church about the year 85 of our era, we need to take into account both Matthew's writing skills and the literary techniques utilized in his day. To grapple with the theological meaning of chapter two presupposes three perspectives. First, we must see this chapter in the context of the entire Gospel. Secondly, we must see the entire Gospel in the context of the Jewish-Christian community for whom Matthew is writing. Thirdly, we must see both community and Gospel in the context of the history of Israel.

At first the perspectives just mentioned seem difficult for the average Catholic to achieve. However, during the twentieth century certain methods or tools for studying Scripture have been developed that enable us to gain this triple perspective. All of the tools utilized in this study have been approved by the Church.

The first tool we can refer to is literary criticism. It is a way of discerning the process by which the gospel was put together. For example, literary criticism examines the sources used by Matthew and the stages those sources went through as they themselves were developed. Here is a rough outline of some of the sources used by Matthew and the stages they went through. The basic source of the New Testament writings is Jesus and the words and deeds of his ministry, about 28-30 A.D. After the passion and death of Jesus, the apostles experienced Jesus risen from the dead.

This brings us to the second stage, roughly between 30 and 60 A.D. After the apostles encountered the risen Jesus, they proclaimed him by word of mouth. They interpreted for others what he did and said. As the years went by, others accepted Jesus as the Christ. This second generation of believers remembered, integrated and passed on those words and deeds of Jesus which the first generation of Christians had given them.

Thus, by at least 50 A.D., the oral preaching had taken on a fixed or stereotyped form. In this way, the "traditions" about the words and deeds of Jesus circulated throughout the Mediterranean world. Literally, "Tradition" means that which is handed on. We have a glimpse of one of these traditions in Paul's first letter to the Corinthians:

> *And now I want to remind you, my brothers, of the Good News which I preached to you, which you received, and on which your faith stands firm....I passed on to you what I received, which is of the greatest importance: that Christ died for our sins, as written in the Scriptures; that he was buried and that he was raised to life three days later, as written in the Scriptures; that he appeared to Peter and then to all twelve apostles (1 Cor 15:1-5).*

By the middle of the first century, some of the oral traditions have been written down. A written collection of the sayings of Jesus circulating in the 50's was later used by both Matthew and Luke. The collection is referred to as the Q document or simply Q (from the German *quelle*, meaning source).

The third stage of the New Testament period roughly covers the last third of the first century. The four Gospels are written during this period. The first to use the Gospel form is Mark, writing about 65 A.D. A Gospel is basically a construction of the words and deeds of Jesus in narrative form. Each Gospel writer uses materials that are at hand, namely, the traditions, both oral and written.

Let us use an analogy to see how literary criticism (which includes source criticism) can help us see the process by which Matthew wrote his version of the Gospel of Jesus Christ. If one wanted to build a stone structure, the place to begin would be a quarry. From the quarry pieces of stone would be cut out and then shaped according to the function they would play in the structure. Finally, the builder would arrange the individual stones in the desired way and the building would be completed.

We can see these three stages in the formation of Matthew's Gospel. The first stage is the quarry, the words and deeds of Jesus as he spoke them and lived them. In the second stage the words and deeds of Jesus were handed on by the community of Jesus' followers. At first, these were oral traditions; later, some were written down, for example, the Q document. Matthew now has his materials before him. He then shapes, selects, and arranges his materials until the Gospel is completed.

You might imagine Matthew seated at a table, pen in hand. To his left there is a copy of Mark. Before him his writing paper. Above that rests the Q document with its collection of the sayings of Jesus. To Matthew's right we may imagine some of his own notes or his own special sources. The Hebrew Scriptures are close by. With these materials to draw upon, Matthew will be doing the work that architects and contractors do in completing the stone building. When the third stage is completed, that is, when his Gospel is finished, it is the result of slow, deliberate, and painstaking effort.

Until now, we have left out the most important factor of all: the experience of Matthew himself. God reveals himself through events. What is experienced is then interpreted in the light of faith. The difficult situation of his small community of Jewish and Gentile Christians living in the midst of a hostile Jewish majority becomes for Matthew a revelatory experience. The period is a desperate one in Jewish history. The Romans had destroyed the temple some fifteen years before, 70 A.D. In these terrible post-war years the Jewish people are themselves struggling for survival. Without temple, sacrifice and priesthood, Judaism reeled from lack of leadership and direction. We Catholics would face a similar crisis if we were suddenly deprived of all episcopal and priestly leadership and service. Into the leadership vacuum of Judaism stepped the Pharisees.

The Pharisees fought to preserve the religious identity of the Jews by rebuilding Judaism around the Law as they interpreted it. Prior to the destruction of the Temple, Judaism was a very broad religion, tolerating a wide spectrum of practices and beliefs. After 70 A.D. that pluralism vanished as the Pharisees stressed unity in belief and practice. They had to do this in order to regain a common Jewish identity. This emphasis on unity had harsh consequences for Christian Jews in Matthew's Church. They met with increasing rejection and finally persecution from the Jewish majority. This precipitated a crisis in the local Church. There was confusion, loss of morale. Members of the community hestitated, doubted. Some gave up faith in Jesus.

This is the context, the life situation, of the Church for whom Matthew began to write. It was the experience of what was happening, the memory of what took place yesterday, last week, and last month that gave Matthew his immediate motivation for writing. When he sat down, he was determined to write another Gospel, a narrative account of the life of Jesus that would encourage and guide his storm-tossed community. He wrote to restore confidence to his fellow Christians. He wrote to renew in them a sense of their identity. He wrote to show Jewish Christian believers living in the 80's that they were in continuity with the whole history of faithful Israel, because they were the disciples of Jesus who was himself the descendent of patriarchs and kings, the fulfilment of prophecy, and the ultimate interpreter of the Torah.

What we have just reviewed is the information made available to us through the use of "literary criticism." We have dealt with such areas as sources, date of writing, and historical circumstances surrounding the writing of the text. Let us glance at one more tool or method used in biblical studies, form criticism.

Form criticism is a branch of literary science that concentrates on the different types of literature—or literary forms—within a composition. It devotes its attention chiefly to the second stage of Gospel formation, that of the oral tradition. For us, its main value will be to point out the different literary forms present in Matthew's Gospel and their characteristics. Some of these literary forms are the miracle account; the controversy account; the saying of Jesus; the parable; the sermon; apocalyptic writing; parallels from the Hebrew Scriptures; and the account of prophecy fulfilled.

Because our tendency is to read the Gospel as if it were written simply as a narrative of past events, we often miss the point that Matthew is making. The Gospel according to

Matthew is not a mere narration of a sequence of events in the life of Jesus. Nor is it a biography of Jesus. Matthew's Gospel is a highly structured theological account of the early Church's faith in Jesus. To recognize the different "literary forms" Matthew uses will help us understand what he is trying to communicate about Jesus. For example, the climax of the Gospel is the death and resurrection of Jesus. The literary forms of the passion narrative in chapters 26-27 are different from the literary forms we find in the second chapter. The visit of the magi, the reaction of Herod, the flight into Egypt, the slaughter of the innocents are meant to be understood in the light of the public life, death and resurrection of Jesus. The visit of the Gentile magi, for example, has its particular meaning because the Christian community believes that Jesus died to save both Jew and Gentile.

At first the Church was cautious in allowing Catholic scholars to use form criticism. However, after several decades of scrutiny, the magisterium saw that form criticism was not corrosive to faith. Catholic leadership realized that the use of the new tools of biblical scholarship could deepen the appreciation of God's Word and thereby enrich our belief. In 1943 Pope Pius XII gave the green light to Catholic biblical scholars to use all the tools being developed by modern studies (see the encyclical DIVINO AFFLANTE SPIRITU). The Second Vatican Council's CONSTITUTION ON DIVINE REVELATION and the 1964 statement of the Pontifical Biblical Commission, "Concerning the Historical Truth of the Gospels" opened up to the whole community of Catholics the proper use of all the tools of biblical scholarship.

Composition criticism (sometimes called redaction criticism) is the third tool of biblical scholarship that we will consider. Composition criticism is a branch of literary science that seeks to understand the Gospel in its final form.

This literary tool, perhaps the most helpful of all, is concerned with finding the distinctive interpetation of the author of the Gospel. To discover the "mind" of Matthew, this method looks at the sources Matthew used and then looks at the changes he made as he adapted the material to meet the needs of his own times and place. For example, Matthew relies on the Gospel According to Mark to supply the basic narrative structure of the life of Jesus. However, in almost every instance in which Mark portrays the disciples as failing to understand, Matthew changes the negative picture of the disciples to a positive image of the disciples. We do not know if Mark's presentation is more historically accurate. We do know that Matthew has his own theological purpose in writing. He wants his community to see themselves as disciples of Jesus, and he adapts the Markan account to fit this purpose. The evangelist, while reverently using a particular tradition, nevertheless leaves on it the stamp of his own theological perspective. Thus, composition or redaction criticism asks the questions: Why is a unit of tradition included? why is it set in this context? why does the author make this change? how does this unit of tradition serve the author's purpose?

We are now ready to reflect upon the rest of Matthew's Gospel. We have looked at the sources Matthew used; we have recognized that Matthew employed different literary forms; we have taken into account the historical events leading to Matthew's decision to write a Gospel; we have sketched Matthew's purposes and we have looked at the audience for whom Matthew is writing.

1. The visit of the "men who studied the stars," 2:1-12

Jesus is born in Bethlehem, the ancestral home of David. Reigning in Jerusalem is the infamous Herod. Upon being asked by the visitors from the east for the whereabouts of "the baby born to be king of the Jews," Herod is shaken, "and so was everyone else in Jerusalem (2:2-3)." He calls together "all the chief priests and teachers of the Law" in order to determine the place where the Messiah is to be born (2:4).

In Jewish literature there is a literary form called midrash. Midrash is the meditative process of creating a story to illustrate or teach more clearly a point contained in sacred scripture. Matthew seems to be making a parallel between Herod's reaction to the information brought by the magi and a Jewish midrash account dealing with the birth of Moses. In this account the birth of Moses was foretold by one of the priestly scribes of Pharaoh. As a result, Pharaoh and his royal court are filled with dread. Pharaoh then consulted with his advisors about what he might do. As the rest of chapter two unfolds, Matthew will continue to make comparisons between Moses and Jesus.

The men from the East tell Herod, "We saw his star when it came up in the east (2:2)." The idea of a new star appearing to herald the birth of a great man was commonly accepted by the mid-eastern peoples. In another midrashic tradition there is an account of a star appearing to King Nimrod and his royal court as an omen concerning Abraham's birth. It is possible that Matthew intended to draw a parallel between Abraham and Jesus by means of the star's appearance. Read the Balaam story in Numbers 22-24 and note the mention of the star in 24:17.

Notice how Matthew subordinates the natural sign of the star to the Word of God contained in the Hebrew Scriptures. The Gentile magi cannot locate the newborn king through nature's star alone. They need the Scriptures to learn the specific location of the king they seek:

> *This is what the prophet wrote,*
> *'Bethlehem, in the land of Judah,*

> ...*from you will come a leader who will*
> *guide my people Israel' (2:5-6)*

By having the Jewish leaders tell the pagan magi where to find the Messiah, Matthew brings out this great paradox: although the chief priests and teachers of the Law know the Scriptures indicating the place where the Messiah is to be born, they will not come to worship the newborn king. Thus, the rejection of Jesus that will take place during his public ministry is foreshadowed in the prologue of the Gospel.

By means of the magi's visit, Matthew combines the Gentile expectation of a great leader with the Jewish expectation of the Messiah, "the leader who will guide my people Israel (2:6)." Jesus is the one for whom the whole world is waiting.

The magi leave Jerusalem and follow the star to Bethlehem where they "went into the house and saw the child with his mother Mary (2:11)." In comparing Matthew's account of the Christmas story with Luke's, we can discern the different themes belonging to each evangelist. Luke emphasizes that Jesus comes for the poor and lowly. Accordingly, there is no room at the inn and he must be born in a mere stable. In Luke an angel announces the birth of Jesus to shepherds, the lowest class of society.

Matthew has a different point to make. He stresses the universal significance of the messiahship of Jesus. Accordingly, it is not angels, but a star that proclaims the birth of Jesus to scholars in the east. They find Jesus not in a stable, but in a house (2:11).

In Luke the shepherds are empty-handed, but they publicly proclaim Jesus to all (Lk 2:18). In Matthew the travelers from the east bring symbolic gifts and then return home secretly (2:12).

In the course of centuries these two separate infancy narratives have been fused together by the Christmas crib. Both star and angels hover over models of the stable. Beneath its roof, magi line up on one side of the manger offering gifts to the Christ-child. Shepherds and lambs take up positions on the other side. Jewish shepherd and Gentile scholar meet at the manger of the child born of Mary.

"They knelt down and...offered him presents: gold, frankincense, and myrrh (2:11)." Once again Matthew reaches back into the Hebrew Scriptures in order to bring out the continuity between the history of Israel and the event of Jesus. The gift of gold and frankincense are mentioned by Isaiah:

Great caravans of camels will come, from Midian and Ephah. They will come from Sheba, bringing gold and incense (Is 60:6)

Similarly, Matthew implicitly cites Psalm 72:

Teach the king to judge with your righteousness, O God; share with him your own justice, so that he will rule over your people with justice and govern the oppressed with righteousness.
...the kings of Arabia and Ethiopia will bring him offerings. All the kings will bow down before him; and nations will serve him (Ps 72:1-2, 10-11).

In the course of time, Christianity added certain details to the Christmas story that were not mentioned by Matthew or Luke. From an indeterminate number of magi, Christianity decided that three men were involved because three gifts were mentioned. Because kings are spoken of in Psalm 72, we came to think of the magi as three kings. In the centuries that followed, the Fathers of the Church perceived the gifts as symbols. Gold stood for the royal character of Jesus, born in the family of King David. Frankincense, since it was used in the worship rituals, represented the priestly character of Jesus, the bridge builder between God and man. Myrrh, a bitter spice, was seen by the Fathers as a symbol of the passion.

2. *The history of Israel and the passion of Jesus summed up in the infancy of Jesus, 2:13-18*

In a brief five verses Matthew parallels the key events of Israel's history with events in the young life of Jesus. Matthew's purpose is to demonstrate that Jesus is the culmination of Israel's hopes and history.

By the hasty departure of the holy family for Egypt (2:13-14) we are reminded of another journey into Egypt: that of Joseph, his eleven brothers (the twelve partriarchs of Israel), and their father Jacob, whose name had been changed to Israel (Gen 32:28). Matthew tells us that "This was done to make come true what the Lord had said through the prophet, 'I called my Son out of Egypt' (2:15)." In its original context this citation from Hosea 11:1 referred to the exodus of Israel, God's "son," from Egypt. Matthew, knowing in faith that Jesus is God's divine Son, uses Hosea 11:1 as a fulfillment text.

In 2:16 Herod's murdering of the male children in Bethlehem finds its parallel in Pharaoh's persecution of the male children of the Hebrews (Ex 1:1-15). As Moses survived the persecution of Pharaoh, so does Jesus escape the persecution of Herod. The attempt of Herod and his soldiers to take the life of Jesus foreshadows the mystery of the cross.

Matthew cites Jeremiah 31:15 immediately after the killing of the innocents:

> *A sound is heard..., the sound of bitter crying and weeping. Rachel weeps for her children...because they are all dead (2:18).*

By citing Jeremiah in the context of the murdered children, Matthew brings together the two greatest trials the Jewish people had suffered until that time: persecution in Egypt (c 1300 B.C.) and the bitter exile in Babylon (587-539 B.C.). It is Matthew's remarkable perception into the continuity of Israel's history that enables him to draw together such widely separated events. Jeremiah wrote in the sixth century before Christ. As the survivors of the destruction of Jerusalem (587 B.C.) were marched past Bethlehem (the burial place of Rachel, the wife of Jacob/Israel and mother of the twelve patriarchs) on their way to enslavement in Babylon, Jeremiah depicts Rachel, the ancestress of those killed and enslaved by the Babylonian army, weeping in her grave.

Matthew, alluding to Jeremiah, once again depicts Rachel weeping for her children, this time murdered by Herod. In three verses Matthew has sketched the history of Israel, from the days of Jacob and Rachel (c 1700 B.C.), through the time of Pharaoh's persecution of the Hebrew male children (c 1300 B.C.) and the days of the Babylonian invasion (587 B.C.), down to the time when Jesus was born. In the escape of the holy family we catch a glimpse of the mystery of the resurrection, God's providential care that protects Jesus through all.

3. The return from Egypt, 2:19-23

"While Moses was still in Midian, the Lord said to him, 'Go back to Egypt, for all those who wanted to kill you are dead' (Ex 4:19)." After Moses heard these words, he gathered his wife and sons, and returned to Egypt where he began his mission of leading his people to the promised land. After Herod dies, the angel tells Joseph:

> Get up, take the child and his mother, and go back to the land of Israel, because those who tried to kill the child are dead (2:20).

The family settles in Nazareth, the place from which Jesus will one day begin his mission of leading God's people. Matthew tells us that Joseph went to Galilee and then Nazareth for the purpose of making "come true what the prophets had said, 'He will be called a Nazarene' (2:23)."

It is difficult to say precisely which prophetic text Matthew is citing here. In Judges 13:1-7 we find the story of the conception of Samson. An angel tells the mother-to-be that

> after your son is born, you must never cut his hair, because from the day of his birth he will be dedicated to God as a Nazirite. He will begin the work of rescuing Israel from the Philistines (Judges 13:5).

There is, however, the greater possibility that Matthew is referring to the prophet Isaiah:

> The royal line of David is like a tree that has been cut down; but just as new branches [neser or nezir is the Hebrew word for branch] sprout from a stump, so a new king will arise from among David's descendants.

The spirit of the Lord will give him wisdom and the
knowledge and skill to rule his people (Is 11:1-2).

Since Matthew is so fond of symmetry, it is likely that he
wanted to parallel the first fulfillment prophecy (Is 7:14)
with the last fulfillment prophecy of the infancy narrative
(Is 11:1). If so, 1:23, "he will be called Emmanuel," is
balanced out by 2:23, "He will be called a Nazarene." If we
follow this arrangement, the first citation of Isaiah 7:14
refers to the birth and identity of the child: he is Emmanuel, God-with-us. The second citation of Isaiah 11:1-2
then refers to the mission and destiny of the child: Jesus is
the royal heir of David, the one led by the Spirit of God, the
one who comes to rule the Lord's people.

Matthew thus brings the prologue of his Gospel to a
close. The reader knows the answer to the questions, Who
is the Messiah? From whence does he come? The Messiah
is the descendant of Abraham and the descendant of
David. The Messiah is God's own son. The Messiah is
Jesus of Nazareth!

Week Two

In an attempt to present chapters three through seven as a specific unit of Matthew's Gospel, we have combined weeks two and three in the commentary. In your own study (and in the progress of your study group) you may wish to take more or less in the second week than the daily assignments suggest.

Chapters three and four prepare us for the first major discourse of Our Lord, the Sermon on the Mount (chapters 5-7). Matthew seems to have written a "catechetical Gospel," that is, one in which the major emphasis falls on the teachings of Jesus. This emphasis is clearly seen in this lengthy sermon, to which Matthew gives a central place in his Gospel.

Although we are familiar with many of the passages in the sermon, a study of the entire sermon will bring out the meaning of Jesus' words with a fresh clarity. Today the Church is concerned with the area of doctrine. A study of the Sermon on the Mount will provide an excellent summary of the teaching, i.e., doctrine, of Jesus. With your study group you might explore the impact these teachings should have on our lives.

Daily Study Assignments: Week Two

Day	Matthew	Commentary
1	3:1 - 12	Pages 37-42
2	3:13 - 4:11	Pages 42-49
3	4:12 - 25	Pages 49-54
4	5:1 - 12	Pages 54-60
5	5:13 - 20	Pages 60-62

6—Reflect on 3:1 - 5:20 in light of the reflection questions listed below.

7—STUDY GROUP MEETING

- The words of Jesus, "in this way we shall do all that God requires" (3:15), express the basic orientation of Jesus as he lived his life. In our own culture, many "philosophies of life" compete with each other: "looking out for #1"; "helping others"; "business is business"; "having it my way"; etc. What words would you use to express the basic orientation of your life?

- Satan suggests that Jesus use his powers to achieve a certain kind of success. Jesus rejects Satan by referring to passages of Scripture that speak of dependence upon God and obedience to his will. Our culture often places us in the position of choosing between two kinds of achievement, the one measured by society's values, the other by the Word of God. How are Jesus' responses (4:4, 7, 10) helpful to you in expressing your own measurement of success?

- Which of our American values do you find called into question by the beatitudes?

- In 5:20 and 5:48 Jesus is asking his followers to whole-heartedly strive to do the Father's will. The aim of "just getting by," of doing the minimum, is not sufficient. In what ways are we tempted to be satisfied with a mediocre discipleship?

The Proclamation of the Kingdom of Heaven, 3:1-7:29

OVERVIEW: Having presented a miniature portrait of the whole Gospel in chapters one and two, Matthew focuses our attention on the period of Jesus' public ministry. Matthew's structure for the rest of the Gospel will be a series of similar patterns: narrative material (actions of Jesus) followed by sermon material (discourses of Jesus). Thus, chapters three and four are narration leading into a discourse section (5-7). At the end of each major teaching section or discourse, Matthew places a concluding formula: "When Jesus finished saying these things....(7:28)," or "When Jesus finished giving these instructions....(11:1)." In all, there are five major discourses of Jesus, each ending with this formula. Each discourse is preceded and is followed by a narrative section, unite the harmonious whole of Matthew's book is complete.

In order to appreciate Matthew's organization, do not let our present structuring of the Gospel into chapter and verse confuse you. The division of Matthew into twenty eight chapters was imposed during the middle ages for the purpose of more easily locating specific passages. Unfortunately, the division of Matthew into chapter and verse is often misleading; breaks are made where they should not be. It is better to see the Gospel this way:

N ←--→ D ←--→ N ←--→ D ←--→ N ←--→
(3-4)   (5-7)   (8-9)   (10)   (11-12)
D ←--→ N ←--→ D ←--→ N ←--→ D ←--→ N
(13)   (14-17)   (18)   (19-22)   (23-25)   (26-28)

N means narrative section; D, a discourse section; ←--→indicates that there is no abrupt break between narrative and discourse. Each section both points ahead to what is to come and refers back to what has already been written. Chapters 5-7 teach the Sermon on the Mount. Chapter 10 is the apostolic discourse. The parables of Jesus are gathered in chapter 13. Chapter 18 is the discourse on the way the community of believers should live together. Chapters 23-25 contain a criticism of the Pharisees and the apocalyptic discourse.

A. Narrative Section, 3:1 - 4:25

1. *The Preaching of John the Baptist, 3:1-12*

"John the Baptist came and started preaching in the desert of Judea. 'Turn away from your sins because the Kingdom of heaven is near!' (3:1-2)" If one wants to reach a large audience, the desert is an unlikely place to begin preaching. Yet the people came from all over to hear John (3:5). Why? They came because of his location and his message. The desert (3:1) was the long-recognized place where God entered into a covenant relationship with his people (Ex 24:3-8). The desert symbolized the ideal relationship of God with his people, the "honeymoon period" of Israel's history.

John's message (3:2) is a prophetic message: Repent. Turn from your sins! Go back to doing God's will as expressed in the Torah (covenant)! Since the covenant was the link between God and his people, the observance of the covenant was at the heart of the prophet's concern. For several centuries there had been no prophet sent to Israel. Now there was John the Baptizer.

Matthew includes a significant detail, the description of John's garb: "clothes made of camel's hair, a leather belt around his waist (3:4)." Matthew thus links John with one of Israel's greatest prophets, Elijah. We read in 2 Kings 1:1-18 a story of one of Israel's faithless kings, Ahaziah. One of his messengers returned to him with God's word of judgment. Ahaziah asked:

> *"What did the man look like?". . . . "He was wearing a cloak made of animal skins, tied together with a leather belt." "It's Elijah!" the king exclaimed (2 Kgs 1:7-8).*

"The people confessed their sins and he baptized them in the Jordan (3:6)." This speaks of the fitting response to the Baptist's call for repentance. "Repent" is an extraordinary word. It means both going back and going beyond. On the one hand, "repent" is the prophetic call to go back to God, to return to the observance of his will as expressed in the covenant. On the other hand, "repent" means to go beyond oneself by re-ordering one's priorities, by reorganizing one's life and putting ultimate values in first place. Jesus' teaching, "be concerned above everything else with God's Kingdom and with what he requires (6:34)," is an exact expression of the two-fold meaning of the word "repent."

The citation of Isaiah 40:3, "Someone is shouting in the desert, 'Get the Lord's road ready for him. . . .' (3:3)," is another example of the early Church's practice of re-interpreting the Hebrew Scriptures in the light of their faith in Jesus. Since John the Baptist did preach about the critical nearness of God's Kingdom, the Christians saw him in the role of the herald or messenger of God announcing the arrival of Jesus, the divine Son of God. Matthew neatly situates John at the end of one era and at the beginning of another era, the new age, the dawning of the Kingdom of God in Jesus of Nazareth. For this reason, Matthew will point out that John is Elijah, the prophet whom tradition said would return some day to announce the beginning of the new age.

> When John saw many Pharisees and Saducees coming..., he said to them, 'You snakes—who told you that you could escape from God's wrath that is about to come?...' (3:7).

Note that Matthew writes "many Pharisees and Saducees (3:7)," not all. Note also that Matthew does not distinguish between Pharisee and Saducee. This is probably a reflection of the bitter conflict taking place between the Jewish synagogue and the young Jewish Christian community of Matthew's day: all Jewish leadership is opposition. So that we can keep a more balanced perspective, keep in mind that the Pharisees were a movement of devout, reform-minded Jewish laymen. They devoted themselves to the study of Torah and were zealous for the Law's faithful observance.

The Saducees were made up of the aristocratic Jewish families, from whose ranks the temple priests were chosen. The Saducees accepted only the first five books of the Hebrew Scriptures, while rejecting the wisdom writings and the Prophets. They did not accept the idea of resurrection, whereas the Pharisees did. From what we can gather, the Saducees were not especially pious, following the path that was most politically or economically expedient.

Historically, Pharisees and Saducees did not get along with one another. When the Pharisees became the leaders of Judaism after the destruction of the temple, they virtually excommunicated the Saducees, declaring them heretics for not believing in the resurrection of the body. To lump Pharisees and Saducees together is analogous to lumping Roman Catholics together with backwoods snake handling sects because both groups believe in Jesus.

We can now see that Matthew is using the Saducees and Pharisees as a symbol of the type of person who assumes he or she has no need to repent. Such a self-righteous person considers himself or herself assured of salvation. In the case in point, the Pharisees and Saducees are depicted as laying claim on salvation because they are descended from Abraham. John, however, shatters their false security by declaring that racial and religious pedigree alone means nothing:

> *I tell you that God can take these rocks and make descendants for Abraham (3:9).*

It seems that some Pharisees and Saducees had been coming to be baptized by John not to express their repentence but for some other self-centered motivation. John blasts them for going through the motions without the intention to change their lives. He calls them "snakes" and challenges them to

> *Do the things that will show you have turned from your sins (3:8).*

This theme is continued with the declaration that the tree that does not bear "good fruit," i.e., doing God's Law, "will be cut down and thrown in the fire (3:11)." It is by doing the good deeds of the Law that one demonstrates authentic repentance. John declares that in their non-repentant complacency these Pharisees and Saducees will soon find God's judgment hard against them:

> *The ax is ready to cut down the trees at the roots; every tree that does not bear good fruit will be cut down and thrown into the fire (3:10).*

To gain a sharper perspective on the Baptist's prophetic

teaching, let us look at the preaching of another prophet of judgment, Amos of Tekoa. Eight centuries before, God had sent Amos to Israel with this message:

> *Go to the Lord, and you will live. If you do not, he will*
> *sweep down like fire on the people of Israel....You*
> *are doomed, you that twist justice and cheat people of*
> *their rights!...Make it your aim to do what is right,*
> *not what is evil, so that you may live. Then the Lord*
> *God Almighty really will be with you, as you claim he*
> *is....How terrible it will be for you who long for the*
> *Day of the Lord! For it will be a day of darkness and*
> *not of light (Amos 5:6-18).*

Both Amos and John spoke of God's coming. It will bring deliverance for those who are faithful to God's Law, but it will bring doom and judgment for those whose deeds are not the expression of God's will:

> *You snakes—who told you that you would escape*
> *from God's wrath that is about to come! (3:7)*

There will be no escape:

> *I baptize you with water to show that you have*
> *repented; but the one who will come after me will*
> *baptize you with the Holy Spirit and fire (3:11).*

We may hear John the Baptist saying something like this: "You may come to me for the wrong purpose, and you may get away with it by merely stepping in the river. But there is another kind of baptism on the way. When that baptizer (Jesus the Son of God) gets here you will be surrounded by God's whirlwind (the Holy Spirit) and you will be immersed in the smelting fire. Then you will be recognized for what you are, and there will be no way out."

The description of Jesus as the one "who is greater than I (3:11)" subordinates John the Baptist to Jesus. The description of Jesus as the one who comes to baptize "with the Holy Spirit and fire (3:10)" characterizes him as the ultimate judgment of God. Matthew is writing for a Church under intense pressure, a Church that was making critical decisions about salvation now and in eternity. While Jesus is above all compassionate and forgiving, he is also tough. He comes not to hand out warm fuzzies and free lunches, but to be the crisis of the believer's life. In confronting Jesus, we must make a decision. In the Gospel according to Matthew any scene involving separation is a scene of judgment, and Jesus is the razor edge of separation:

> *He has his winnowing shovel with him to thresh out*
> *all the grain; he will gather his wheat into his barn,*
> *but burn the chaff in a fire that never goes out (3:12).*

Judgment in Matthew is always twofold. On one hand, judgment is destructive: the ax separates root from tree; the fire separates the metal from the slag; the goats, the fruitless tree, and the chaff go into the fire. On the other hand, judgment is redemptive: the fruit bearing tree is saved; the grain is gathered into the barn; the sheep, the righteous and the keepers of the Law, enter everlasting life (see 25:46).

2. The Baptism of Jesus, 3:13-17

At first glance the narrative seems simple enough. Jesus comes to be baptized and John tries to talk him out of it. Jesus insists, is baptized, and receives a revelation that he is the Son who pleases his Father. For the Jewish Christian reading Matthew, this seemingly simple passage is a network of avenues extending back into the history of God's chosen people and forward into the messianic age. Note how Matthew reworks his Markan source:

Mark 1:9	Matthew 3:13-15
Not long afterward Jesus came from Nazareth in the province of Galilee, and was baptized by John in the Jordan.	At that time Jesus went from Galilee to the Jordan and came to John to be baptized by him. But John tried to make him change his mind. "I ought to be baptized by you," John said, "yet you come to me!" But Jesus answered him, "Let it be so for now. For in this way we shall do all that God requires." So John agreed.

Only in Matthew do we find this dialogue between John the Baptist and Jesus. Reading between the lines, it seems that Matthew was addressing a problem faced by the Jewish Christians of his day: if Jesus is the sinless Son of God, why did he submit to John's baptism of repentance? Matthew makes two points in the dialogue between John and Jesus. First, John recognizes the superiority of Jesus: "I ought to be baptized by you (3:14)." Secondly, the answer of Jesus indicates that he did not come to repent of his sins but to fulfill the will of God: ". . . in this way we shall do all that God requires (3:15)."

Since these are the very first words of Jesus that Matthew records, we know that there is great significance in them. Matthew tells us that from the very beginning Jesus comes to do his Father's will. Doing God's will is obeying the Law; Jesus comes to affirm, to validate, and to bring to completion the Law of Moses and the teachings of the prophets (5:17). Doing God's will brings salvation, and the very name of Jesus means God saves (1:21). Jesus is Emmanuel, God-is-with-us (1:23). When Jesus came to John to be baptized, a transition took place. The Kingdom of God becomes manifest in Jesus because he does and will do all that God requires (3:15).

As Jesus steps out of the water, the messianic era has begun:

> *As soon as he was baptized, Jesus came out of the water. . . . he saw the Spirit of God coming down like a dove and lighting on him (3:16).*

The dove, symbol of God's power, recalls the image of God's spirit brooding over the waters of chaos at the first creation (Gen. 1:2). Later, as the destructive waters of the flood receded, the dove brought Noah an olive leaf to symbolize the beginning of another epoch in human history (Gen 8:11). And now the dove appears at the beginning of the ultimate era: God's Kingdom has come in the person of Jesus:

> *And then a voice said from heaven, "This is my own dear Son, with whom I am well pleased (3:17)."*

The words of this theophany (manifestation of God) are taken from two places in the Hebrew Scriptures, Psalm 2:7 and Isaiah 42:1. Psalm 2 speaks about God's annointed king:

> *I will announce . . . what the Lord has declared. He said to me: "You are my son; today I have become your father. Ask, and I will give you all the nations; the whole earth will be yours (Ps 2:7-8)."*

This psalm introduces another theme that Matthew will develop throughout the rest of the Gospel, the theme of the authority of Jesus. The Father is the one who gives Jesus all power and authority (11:27).

The citation of Isaiah underscores the kind of Messiah Jesus will be:

> *The Lord says, "Here is my servant, whom I strengthen—the one I have chosen, with whom I am pleased. I have filled him with my spirit, and he will bring justice to every nation (Is 42:1)."*

This citation of Isaiah is of the greatest importance for it contains the key to the identity of Jesus the Messiah: Jesus is the Suffering Servant with whom God is pleased (3:17). The citation from Isaiah 42:1 is taken from the opening line of the first of four poems or hymns depicting the rejection and trials of a mysterious servant through whom God will

save his people. These four servant hymns are contained in chapters 42 through 53 of Isaiah. For the most part they were ignored by Israel, the idea of redemption through suffering being as repugnant then as it is in our day. Read the fourth servant poem, Isaiah 52:13-53:12. This poem speaks of God's servant being rejected by the people, enduring pain, and taking upon himself the punishment others deserve for their sins:

> *He was treated harshly, but endured it humbly; he never said a word. . . . He was put to death for the sins of our people (Is 53:7-8).*

3. The Temptations of Jesus, 4:1-11

The nature of Jesus' vocation is becoming clearer. Heaven "was opened to him (3:16)," and he saw the dove and heard the voice of his Father. The call to be God's Suffering Servant as foretold by Isaiah must have seemed a terrifying mission for Jesus. He seeks a place to pray and prepare. The Spirit leads him into the desert (4:1). Mark stated that the Spirit *pushed* or *drove* Jesus into the desert. Matthew, with a greater sensitivity to the relation between Jesus and the power of God, depicts the Spirit *leading* Jesus.

Mark tells us nothing more than the fact that Jesus was tempted by Satan (Mark 1:13). Luke and Matthew, using the Q source, record three temptations. Each temptation is an attempt to have Jesus abandon the role of the Suffering Servant and take another kind of messianic mission. In effect, then, this desert experience of Jesus is the crossroads of his life. Here is the crisis, the decision he must make: two roads spread out before him. To the left, a broad and well travelled road that represents conformity to the popular expectations of the Jewish people. They are looking for security, independence from the Romans, political power and prosperity. To travel this road would mean acceptance, acclaim and the guarantee of a certain kind of success. To the right, hardly a road at all. Untravelled and rocky, this road demands that he be the Suffering Servant who does the Father's will. To journey down this road is to confront people with a clash between common sense values and values that demand a reversal of the usual human ways of thinking and perceiving. To travel this road entails probable rejection and a guarantee of a certain kind of failure.

It is suggested to him that he take the road to the left, bringing the prosperous times symbolized by making bread on the table as plentiful as rocks in the desert (4:3). Jesus remembered the Word of God. The only real security is dependence upon God:

> *Remember how the Lord your God led you on this long journey through the desert these past forty years, sending hardships to test you, so that he might know what you intended to do and whether you would obey his commands. He made you go hungry, and then he gave you manna to eat. . . . He did this to teach you that man must not depend on bread alone to sustain, but on everything the Lord says (Deut 8:2-3).*

It is suggested that Jesus take himself to the tower of the temple from which the priest calls the people to prayer at the beginning of each day (4:5). A spectacular descent would surely gain a large following as he fulfilled the passage in Psalm 91 which declares that God's angels will protect his servant. Jesus refuses, again holding to his Father's will as the priority of his life:

> Do not put the Lord your God to the test, as you did at Massah. Be sure that you obey all the laws that he has given you (Deut 6:16-17).

A third time Jesus is tempted to abandon the role of the Suffering Servant of God. Satan offers Jesus absolute power and domination over the kingdoms of the world. The price to be paid is clear: abandonment of the Father's will by kneeling down and worshiping Satan (4:9). This temptation strikes us as so outrageous that we tend to simply dismiss it. To do so, however, would be to miss much that this temptation tells us about Jesus and the times in which he lived. This is the third and ultimate temptation. It invites Jesus to reject the role of the Suffering Servant destined to redeem his people from their sins (Is 53:5,8; Mt 1:21).

Given the history of Israel, with such warrior leaders as Joshua, Gideon, King David and the Maccabees, given the popular messianic expectations of the people, given the harsh Roman military occupation, and given the work of such nationalistic underground groups as the zealots, it is possible to see how a gifted leader could bring back the kind of independence and power Israel had under King David. Popular support, nationalism, and the feeling that "God is on our side," could have given the right man an army of keenly disciplined, highly motivated patriots. It could have been a new era in Israel's secular history, and in its center could have been the nationally acclaimed messiah, Jesus of Nazareth! For the third and final time Jesus cited Deuteronomy:

> *Have reverence for the Lord your God, worship only*
> *him, and make your promises in his name alone. Do*
> *not worship other gods . . . (Deut 6:13-14).*

Jesus chooses to do his Father's will. He accepts the call to be God's Suffering Servant. There, in the desert, with the help of the Spirit, Jesus has chosen to do the Father's will. In doing so, he has succeeded where Israel had failed. His forty days in the desert recall the forty years Moses had led the people. In the desert they had yielded to temptation, but Jesus has remained faithful. He is ready to begin his ministry.

4. Jesus Begins His Public Ministry, 4:12-17

As the threat from Archelaus (2:22) had caused Joseph to settle in Nazareth, now Herod's imprisonment of John the Baptist leads Jesus to settle in Capernaum, a village located on the northern shore of the Sea of Galilee. Here, in heathen Galilee, a territory whose inhabitants were held in ill-regard by the Jews of Judea in the south, Matthew sees the prophecy of Isaiah fulfilled:

> *The people who live in darkness will see a great light.*
> *On those who live in the dark land of death the light*
> *will shine (4:16).*

The underlined words are those Matthew changed in order to make a point about Jesus. The passage from Isaiah 9:1-2 stated that the light *is already shining*. Matthew changes this to the future tense because the new age is just now beginning. Jesus is the light that will soon shine on the people of Galilee:

> From that time Jesus began to preach his message, "Turn away from your sins, because the Kingdom of heaven is near (4:17)."

Notice that the theme of Jesus' public preaching is the same as that of John the Baptist (3:2). Of the three synoptic Gospels, Matthew alone makes this identification. Since Matthew is highlighting the role of John the Baptist as both the prophet Elijah and the one who is the herald of Jesus, Matthew placed on the lips of John the very message Jesus now proclaims.

The towering center of Jesus' preaching is the Kingdom of God. (Matthew, out of respect for the name of God, uses "Kingdom of Heaven.") This symbol*, which had developed out of Israel's experience of more than a thousand years of history, is made up of two basic components. The first is rooted in the Hebrew experience of God's saving power. He had acted to save them because they were his chosen people. Notice how this perception of God's saving deeds is expressed in an ancient credal formula:

> "My ancestor was a wandering Aramean, who took his family to Egypt to live. They were few in number when they went there, but they became a large and powerful nation. The Egyptians treated us harshly and forced us to work as slaves. Then we cried out for help to the Lord, the God of our ancestors. He heard us and saw our suffering, hardship, and misery. By his great power and strength he rescued us from Egypt. He worked miracles and wonders, and caused terrifying things to happen. He brought us here and gave us this rich and fertile land (Deut 26:5-9)."

The second component of the symbol of God's Kingdom or Rule developed from Israel's borrowing of the kingly enthronement rituals practiced by their pagan neighbors. The Canaanites had the custom of greeting or enthroning the returning gods of Spring after the barren Winter. These gods, associated with the return of the soil's fertility, of warmth and of light, were ritually enthroned as kings who had conquered the darkness and chaos of the winter season.

The Hebrew people adapted this enthronement practice, at least to the extent of praising God as the King. In Psalm 96 we see the acknowledgement of God's saving deeds as well as the proclamation of God as King:

> *Sing to the Lord and praise him! Proclaim everyday the good news that he has saved us. Proclaim his glory to all the nations, his mighty acts to all peoples.*...
>
> *Say to all the nations, 'The Lord is king!*... *Be glad, earth and sky!*... *The trees in the woods will shout for joy when the Lord comes to rule the earth. He will rule the peoples of the world with justice and fairness (Ps 96:2-3, 10-13).*

The people of Jesus' day believed that just as God had acted to save their ancestors, he will again intervene in order to save them. Hopes for the coming of God burned brightest during times of hardship and oppression. Israel yearned for the "Day of Yahweh," the judgment day, the day on which God would again intervene in history on behalf of his people. They eagerly awaited the Messiah. They were waiting for God to send his Messiah King to usher in the new era. Into this climate so charged with messianic expectation, Jesus comes. He announces that God's saving initiative is about to happen (4:17). God's reign of justice, a reign characterized by right relationships between God and his people, and between each person and his/her neighbor, is about to begin. The first persons to respond to Jesus and his message are four fishermen: Peter, Andrew, James and John.

5. *The calling of the first disciples, 4:18-22*

Matthew places the calling of the first disciples immediately after the account of Jesus' first preaching. In this way he links together two inseparable themes: discipleship and the Kingdom of God. Both are God-given gifts. Both are centered on whole-heartedly doing the Father's will.

Jesus says, "Come with me and I will teach you to catch men (4:19)." Peter and Andrew respond immediately: "At once they left their nets and went with him (4:20)." Here Matthew presents two more interrelated themes: the disciple is called to make other disciples (catch men); the disciple is ready to leave all to follow Jesus. Peter and Andrew leave their nets (livelihood) behind, and James and John leave both their boats (livelihood) and their father (family) in order to answer the call to follow Jesus.

In this account (4:18-22) we have a good example of the way Matthew writes on two levels. On one level, he is putting the traditions of the words and deeds of Jesus into the gospel form in order to proclaim Jesus as the Good News. On the second level, Matthew is consciously structuring his account of Jesus to meet the needs of the people in his local church. On this second level Matthew is teaching his community what it means to be disciples of the Lord. Just as the first disciples promptly answered the invitation of Jesus to follow, so too must the members and potential members of the church of Matthew's day. Just as the first disciples were called to be missionaries, to go out and be "fishers of men," so too are the members of Matthew's community called to bring others to Jesus. Just as the first disciples left profession and family to follow Jesus, so also the members of Matthew's community must be ready to sacrifice job security, and even family, if they find themselves in a position in which they must choose between Jesus or livelihood, Jesus or family. Matthew, then, speaks also to us, telling us that the call of Jesus to follow and to be a fisher of men no matter what the cost is a call given to all Christians. It is a call given not only to the first four disciples, nor only to the first century Christians, nor only to twentieth century Christians ready to enter the convent or seminary. The call to discipleship summons each of us.

6. *A summary of the entire ministry of Jesus, 4:23-25*

"Jesus went all over Galilee, *teaching* in their synagogues, *preaching* the good news of the kingdom, and *healing* people from every kind of disease and sickness

(4:23)." In this verse Matthew summarizes chapters 3 and 4 and looks ahead to the first discourse of Jesus, the Sermon on the Mount. In these coming three chapters (5-7)

Matthew will present Jesus as the teacher, greater than Moses. In the following two narrative chapters (8-9) Matthew will depict Jesus as the healer. Jesus, both in his word as teacher and in his deeds as healer proclaims the Kingdom of God.

Matthew records the initial success of Jesus: great crowds from everywhere follow. The witnesses who attest that Jesus is God's anointed are not astonished crowds watching as angels cushion his descent from the heights of the temple (4:5-6) but rather

> *all those who were sick with all kinds of diseases, and afflicted with all sorts of troubles: people with demons, and epileptics, and paralytics—Jesus healed them all (4:24).*

B. The First Discourse: Sermon on the Mount, 5:1-7:29

1. The Setting, 5:1-2

Matthew carefully prepares us to hear this important "word" of Jesus. The setting, as it frequently does in the Gospels, takes on a theological importance. We might call it "theological geography." At the corresponding section of his Gospel (Luke 6:17), Luke notes that Jesus comes down from the mountain (where he had gone to pray and to choose the twelve Apostles) to the level ground or plain and there delivers this "great discourse." This difference in the two Evangelists indicates that Matthew sees in the mountain setting something of theological importance. (While our translation has "hill," the Greek word probably should be translated "mountain.")

Remembering the many parallels which Matthew found

between the infancies of Jesus and Moses, we are on the lookout here for another comparison. Many scholars see here a deliberate attempt to present Jesus as the New Moses. Just as Moses went up onto the mountain (to receive the Law, then shared it with his followers, so Jesus goes up the mountain) to deliver to his disciples the New Law. This would have been an important insight for Matthew's Jewish Christian readers, whose whole religious life had centered in the Law. As the Law of Sinai set the foundations for the People of Israel, so this new Law inaugurates the kingdom of God.

We may consider the Sermon on the Mount then as the principles of the Kingdom, or a description of what it means to be a disciple. It has been called the jewel of Matthew's Gospel, or the gospel within the Gospel. It has always been difficult for the Church to know what to do with this "word" of Jesus. It is the "Magna Charta" of his disciples; yet often we desire to flee its demands on us.

We cannot consider this teaching as intended only for the original disciples of the Lord; nor as meant only for a special group in the Church, those with a "special" vocation. The beatitudes are an urgent invitation, an expression of God's will for each of us. Jesus speaks here to the "disciples," which in Matthew always refers both to the original followers of the Master and also to the believers of Matthew's community in the 80's. Note that Jesus is also speaking here to the crowds (5:1 and 7:28). To anyone who even wishes to follow Jesus this sermon is addressed. Those who have already committed themselves to discipleship will listen with a special intensity.

2. *The Beatitudes, 5:3-12*

Happy, how blest are the disciples of Jesus! In the Beatitudes we encounter one of the most beautiful, most familiar and least understood passages of the Christian Scriptures. The Beatitudes are difficult for us to understand for two reasons. First, they contradict our commonsense approach to life: obviously the happy ones are those who are wealthy, have no troubles and can control their own lives! Secondly, they often contradict the values of our culture. Living in a nation whose motto is "In God we trust," we tend to assume that our cultural values are in line with the Gospel. If we examine them, though, we find that more often than not they tend to line up with what Scripture calls "the world." Some of our most cherished American values—wealth, power, independence, freedom from pain and trouble—are challenged by this teaching of Jesus.

The structure of the Greek text of Matthew seems to separate the first eight beatitudes (5:3-10) from the ninth and final one (5:11-12). Looking at the first eight, we see that the first four refer more to our attitudes toward God and the second quartet consider our relationships with one another. Let us examine several to catch the flavor of Our Lord's teaching.

"Happy are those who know they are spiritually poor!" In many ways this first beatitude encompasses them all. By inviting us to be poor in spirit, Jesus situates us at the heart of the spirituality of the "anawim." This Hebrew word describes a group of people, never numerous, who had a keen appreciation of the reality of God and of the way he was leading his people. Tempered by the Exile and the frequent failures of God's people, the "anawim" came to realize that the only authentic way to come before God was to come with empty hands. Frequently the "anawim" were materially poor, and this condition seemed to intensify their interior attitude. (Note that Luke's first beatitude proclaims God's blessing on the poor. Luke 6:20) They knew clearly how dependent on God they were, even for bread itself. They knew that they did not and could not control their own lives.

Jesus calls us to look at our lives in a new light, to learn how to expect everything from the hands of God. We are invited to grow into an attitude of confident trust in God rather than in our own goodness or virtue or independent action. To be spiritually poor is to be detached from everything that is not God: from material possessions, from our reputation and accomplishments, from the desire to be the source of our own salvation. The Kingdom of heaven—all the blessings of God—belongs to such disciples of Jesus. The Good News is this: by living in this way we are already tasting the joys of the Kingdom. In his preaching Jesus is fulfilling the prophetic words of Isaiah 61:1-2:

> *The Sovereign LORD has filled me with his spirit.*
> *He has chosen me and sent me*
> *To bring good news to the poor,*
> *To heal the broken-hearted....*

The importance of this Isaian text in the ministry of Jesus can be seen in the next beatitude: "Happy are those who mourn; God will comfort them!" In his ministry Jesus fulfills Yahweh's role as the Consolation of Israel. God is present where he is needed. To the one whose heart is broken, whether by personal suffering or by grief for the suffering of the world, Jesus brings his healing and comforting presence. Grief and troubles in themselves are not redemptive; they often impel us to complain against God and to grow bitter. It is the mourning which impels the heart to turn to God alone, which opens the heart to God's mercy and consolation, that blesses us, that becomes a grace. Only in the presence of Jesus is mourning overcome.

In the fourth beatitude we see again one of Matthew's prime concerns. He takes the Lucan "Happy are you who hunger" (Luke 6:20) and adds "for holiness, for righteousness," or as our translation beautifully puts it, "Happy are those whose greatest desire is to do what God requires!" Matthew is concerned to interpret the meaning of Our Lord's teaching for his hearers. While Luke's text seems closer to the words which Jesus actually spoke, Matthew brings out their authentic meaning more fully. Matthew saw that it was not sufficient merely to be poor, to weep, to hunger—though the Messianic blessings are directed toward such persons. It is necessary to be poor in spirit, to mourn in a way that opens one's heart to God's comfort, and to hunger and thirst that God's will be done.

Jesus calls us to a passionate desire to do the Father's will. Christian life cannot be passive; it is active obedience, a life in conformity with God's will, as was that of Jesus. Christian life is not merely staying away from mortal sin; it is a striving for fullness in doing the will of the Father. Matthew's holiness or righteousness speaks of the heart's hunger to be such as God created us and wants us to be. It is a hunger for the God who created us and calls us to union with himself and with one another. We should be careful here not to limit the meaning of this beatitude to our own individual struggle to do God's will. Our desire for holiness must have a strong social dimension, a yearning for

God's Kingdom, for the One who will bring justice to those suffering from violence, for the "new heavens and a new earth, where righteousness will be at home (2 Peter 3:13)."

We have examined three of the first four beatitudes because, dealing with our relationship to God, they are more difficult for us to comprehend. The second four envision qualities crucial to our Christian relationships with one another: mercy, purity of heart, peace-making and patience in suffering persecution. As they are more familiar to us, we will look closely only at two.

"Happy are those who are merciful to others; God will be merciful to them!" For Matthew, mercy is the focal point of Jesus' message. It is understood as an essential quality for one who prays (6:12, 14-15) as well as for leaders of the community (18:33). Mercy is common to all of the beatitudes. It gives evidence that the believer's life is not closed in upon itself but reaches out in forgiveness, in soothing pain and healing wounds. As with all the beatitudes, we do not earn God's mercy; our own mercy is both fruit of God's prior gift and condition for receiving his mercy anew.

"Happy those who work for peace!" Our world longs for peace, yet it seems ever more elusive. Today we realize clearly that peace emerges as the fruit of our struggle. The title of Bishop Dozier's first pastoral letter—"Peace: Gift and Task"—aptly summarizes the peace of the beatitudes. Peace in scripture sums up all the messianic blessings. It is not just the absence of conflict but also a positive state of harmony, mercy, self-giving. This peace is also a gift of God. The disciple of Jesus puts his person "on the line" in the difficult work of peacemaking, trusting that God will bless the world through him.

In the ninth and final beatitude Matthew shifts to the second person: "Happy are you!" when insulted and slandered for the Master's sake. This indicates to us that Matthew's church was already experiencing persecution. Already the disciples were treading the path of the Master and drinking of his cup. The paradoxical nature of the beatitudes continues: "Be glad and happy!" For the believer the moment of greatest sorrow, of seeming failure is transformed into the moment of greatest joy. This makes it clear how concretely the teaching of Jesus affects the believer's life.

The beatitudes are permeated by God's yes to those who are dependent on him, a yes which becomes reality because of Jesus' presence. Although he expects their final (should we say visible) fulfillment only at the end-time, the believer already tastes the joy and consolation of God. In the person of Jesus, God's Reign/Kingdom becomes present. As the Fathers of the Church loved to say, Jesus himself is the Kingdom!

3. Salt, Light and the Law, 5:13-20

The next passages bridge the major sections of chapter five. The teaching on salt and light describes the effect on the world of a community living by the vision of Jesus, while the teaching about the Law prepares us for Jesus' interpretation of the Law in 5:21-48 (the Antitheses). In 5:13 we hear both the effect of faithful discipleship and a warning: in following the teaching of Jesus the disciple both flavors and purifies the world. Yet if his good works are absent he becomes worthless, fit only to be thrown out. In the Greek there is a strong undertone of final damnation. The disciple's salvation is not assured without fidelity to the Lord's teaching.

Again, it is through good works that the disciples become light for the world. In this way they inherit the task of Yahweh's Servant (Isaiah 42:6 and 49:6). However, the favorable attention, the resulting praise must be directed to the Father. It is interesting to find one of the polarities which has divided Christians for several centuries already present in the Scriptures. While Paul took a dim view of any emphasis on good works, emphasizing the priority of faith, Matthew speaks often of the necessity of doing the will of the Father. As we will see in 7:21, it is not sufficient just to cry out "Lord, Lord!" The disciple must do the will of the Father. If such differing emphases were tolerable within the early Church, perhaps that should encourage us to be more open, more loving in our relationships with Protestant brothers and sisters. One of the joys of our own day is that through the gift of ecumenism we are able to view differences in our respective traditions as potential enrichment instead of as a threat.

These images of salt and light speak powerfully to us of strength in weakness. The salt is insignificant in comparison to the flour; so, often, are believers in relationship to the world. Yet how great is the effect which God's power in us makes possible! Again, this teaching on salt and light prevents a misinterpretation of the beatitudes. They emphasize poverty and dependence on God. Yet Christians are not to wallow in inferiority complexes nor to withdraw from the world. Through them the powerful God can permeate and transform the entire world.

In 5:17-20 we catch a glimpse of another controversy within the early community. The phrase "Do not think" alludes to an error which was circulating about the teaching of Jesus. Jesus had not come to abrogate the Law, as some were saying, but to bring it to fulfillment. To fully understand this passage we need a return to our Jewish "roots." As Gentiles, we have been greatly influenced by Paul's approach to the Law. Briefly, Paul taught that in Christ we have gone beyond the Law, that the Law is a bondage from which Christ has released us. Matthew retains a Jewish theology of the Law as God's gift to his people. Read again Psalm 119: your word is a lamp to my feet. If we desire with all our hearts to do the will of God, what a gift, then, is the Law, which tells us clearly and unambiguously what is pleasing to him!

There are indications that Matthew's community was troubled by certain teachings that the priority of the Law has ended, that Christians can do what they wish. In this section he clearly teaches that Jesus came not to invalidate the Law but to affirm its abiding validity. Our translation, "to make their teachings come true," indicates that he is speaking not so much of "teaching" but rather of living. We often understand this verse to mean that Jesus will go beyond the Jewish Law, leaving it behind. But the meaning of 5:17 is that he will establish the Law, actualize it by his life. In Jesus there will come true what the Law and the prophets only announced.

This same full living of the will of God must be the mark of the disciple of Jesus (5:20). Only a greater fidelity to God's will than that of the Scribes and Pharisees makes one worthy of the Kingdom of heaven. Again we meet the Greek word *dikaiosune* (holiness/righteousness/fidelity to God's will) which we saw in the fourth and eighth beatitudes. In 5:20 Matthew is contrasting the true Israel with the false one. By the time that Matthew writes, the Jewish leaders have rejected those Jews who have become Christians. Matthew thus encourages his community: the true Israel are those who actually fulfill God's will, not those who only claim to do it. *Dikaiosune* then becomes the key for understanding the important section which follows. Only Jesus provides an authentic interpretation of God's will (the Law). The true Israel then are those who follow Jesus and allow his teaching to become the norm for their lives.

Week Three

During this third week we continue our study of the Sermon on the Mount. Because it expresses the basic teaching of Jesus, the very center of our faith, we are spending two weeks on it (coupled with its narrative introduction in chapters three and four).

This week includes some of the most beautiful—and most challenging—teachings of Our Lord. The commentary endeavors to clarify the Hebrew thought patterns which lie behind many of these passages.

Jesus greatly broadens the scope of what is required of his disciples. As we find ourselves challenged by his words, we will be tempted to consider them hopelessly idealistic. Yet they constitute the "New Law" for Christians, the expression of the Father's will for us. With your group you might explore renewed ways in which you can live as twentieth century disciples of Jesus.

Daily Study Assignments: Week Three

Day	Matthew	Commentary
1	5:21 - 48	Pages 65-70
2	6:1 - 18	Pages 70-77
3	6:19 - 34	Pages 77-79
4	7:1 - 12	Pages 79-81
5	7:13 - 29	Pages 81-86

6—Reflect on 5:21 - 7:29 in light of the reflection questions listed below.

7—STUDY GROUP MEETING

In what ways can a diocesan celebration of Reconciliation throw light on Jesus' mandate "to make peace with your brother (5:24)"?

● Forbearance, the voluntary refraining from insisting on one's own rights when slighted by another, seems to be at the foundation of Jesus' teaching about turning the other cheek (5:39). In which situations of community living and working can you practice forbearance?

● In what other ways is the Lord calling me to live the teaching of the antitheses (5:21-48)?

● Jesus set the Kingdom of God in contrast with money (6:24). How can we understand and live this teaching in our money (power-status) conscious society?

● If you were to envision your life as the process of building a house (7:24-27), which three teachings of the Sermon on the Mount would you use as the foundation?

The Sermon on The Mount (continued)

4. The Antitheses, 5:21-48

In this section we hear six contrasts or antitheses. Our Lord is not contrasting an old Law with a new one. He is contrasting a Jewish interpretation of the Law with his own. In effect he is saying, You have interpreted God's Law in this way, but now I tell you....The human tendency is to reduce, to minimize God's demand on us. Over the centuries Israel's teachers had tended to water down the Law, or to substitute insignificant practices for more important ones. As in his life Jesus teaches what God desires of us, so in this section his teaching clarifies God's will. Here Our Lord teaches us what the greater fidelity of 5:20 means. It is one of the most difficult passages of the Bible, not because of difficulty in understanding it, but of living it. This teaching is radical in its truest sense: this is the ultimate meaning of the Law, these are the ultimate demands of God on us. In the antitheses we are not dealing with a contrast between the letter of the Law and its spirit. It is perhaps better to say that Jesus has spiritualized the letter of the Law. As with the beatitudes, we are often tempted to consider the antitheses as hopelessly idealistic. Thus our temptation is to water them down, to excuse ourselves from them.

a. First Antithesis, 5:21-26

In the first antithesis Jesus teaches us to fear the anger which springs up in our hearts as much as murder. For Jesus there is no sharp distinction between interior wishes and exterior acts. What we need is an entirely new heart, created by God. Whoever denounces his brother is guilty as a murderer before the court and, in the eyes of God, ripe for hell.

In 5:23-24 the duty of reconciliation is linked with the necessity of avoiding anger. According to the rabbis even the Day of Atonement would not benefit the person who refused to make peace with neighbors. Jesus teaches that the intention to honor God is authentic only if it is grounded in a state of peace and unity with other members of the community. This teaching attacks our constant tendency to ignore human duties on the pretext of the worship of God. We gladly buy ourselves freedom from difficult tasks and relationships by the flight into prayer and religion. The last verses underline the urgency of reconciliation. Hurry while time lasts, for we will soon be before the Judge.

b. Second Antithesis, 5:27-30

Again we are reminded that there can be no sharp distinction between inner desires and external actions. Jesus treats the question of adultery not in terms of asceticism or personal purity but in terms of interpersonal relationships. The disciple must avoid adultery not to preserve himself from impurity but in order not to break up another's marriage. Here we see a concrete dimension of the beatitude on purity of heart. Verses 29-30 indicate the utter seriousness of the disciple's path. The original context of this teaching would seem to be that of 19:8-9. It is perhaps placed here by Matthew because of the relationship of the eye with a covetous glance. The members of the community are enjoined by these words not merely to repeat the teachings of Jesus but to live by them.

c. Third Antithesis, 5:31-32

As this teaching is given in Chapter 19 with a fuller explanation, we will comment on it at that point.

d. Fourth Antithesis, 5:33-37

The Mosaic Law forbade only false and irreverent oaths,

which were regarded as profaning the name of God. Jesus here abolishes oaths altogether, since they are unnecessary for those who habitually speak the truth. The disciple thus moves beyond any possibility of defaming the Name of God. The evil one enters into the broad area between Yes and No. This same teaching is also found in James 5:12.

e. Fifth Antithesis, 5:38-42

This antithesis uses the language of the ancient legal system. The principle which we have come to know as the law of talion (5:38) was found in many legal codes, going back as far as that of Hammurabi. It was a restrictive law, designed to limit revenge and retaliation by fixing an exact compensation for an injury. Again Jesus extends the demand of God: take no revenge at all! Four illustrations of the new principle follow. Basically they deal with the question of the disciple's rights; he is not to insist on his personal rights, but is to await with patience God's vindication. A similar spirit is found in one of the Dead Sea scrolls: "I shall repay no man with evil: I shall pursue man with good, for with God is the judgment of all the living." The teaching of Jesus deals basically with relationships within the community, not those on a world-wide scale. Thus, absolute pacifism, as we know it, was not an issue at the time Matthew wrote the Gospel. However, this teaching of Jesus formed the basis of the Christian pacifism of the first three centuries. Moreover, this word of Jesus challenges us, his twentieth century disciples, to take a fresh look at the use of force to defend ourselves and our possessions.

The first example (5:39) refers to insulting behavior, for which the offender could be brought to court. Jesus teaches: if someone insults you, let him insult you again rather than seek vengeance in court. The second example is similar: give more than demanded. (According to Jewish law a man's cloak could not be taken, since that is his only protection against the cold night.) For the third illustration, being forced to carry a soldier's military pack, we have the example of Simon of Cyrene (27:32), who was commandeered by soldiers to carry the cross of Christ. In 5:42 the disciple is commanded to be generous to the borrower, beyond what would be normally expected.

f. Sixth Antithesis, 5:43-48

It is clear from Luke's Great Sermon (Luke 6:20-49) that both evangelists have taken the traditional material and ordered it according to their catechetical designs. Thus Matthew has deliberately placed the antithesis on love of enemies in the climactic position. As he will teach us in 22:40, the entire Law and the prophets can be summarized in the command of love.

Leviticus 19:18 taught love of neighbor as of self. The Hebrew Scriptures nowhere taught hatred of enemies. Matthew may be describing a popular opinion or thinking in terms of the enemies of God's people. (The Dead Sea community at Qumran specifically taught that the sons of darkness, whom God had rejected, were to be hated.)

The love which Jesus demands cannot be limited to a feeling. It demands positive action, a doing of good. This teaching is particularly striking when we remember that Matthew's community was being persecuted. Thus Jesus' command to pray for persecutors would have required an immediate application.

The goal of the disciple is to become like the Father in heaven. As he loves unconditionally, so must his children. Believers must imitate the lavish love of God, going beyond self-love to a love that centers on the other. This is what Matthew means by being perfect (5:48). Luke emphasizes the dimension of compassion: "Be merciful as your Father is merciful (Luke 6:36)." Matthew's focus harmonizes with his teaching on the greater fidelity (5:20). In harmony with the teachings of Leviticus 19:2, "Be holy, because I, the Lord your God, am holy," Matthew's "perfect" implies completion and wholeness of heart. The perfect disciple is the one who has directed his heart entirely toward God, who fulfills the entire will of God. According to the vision of Jesus, God is perfect not because he is aloof and totally unlike man, but precisely because he is totally devoted to man, totally faithful to his people. Thus the person who loves as God does accomplishes perfection and achieves the greater fidelity.

Such wholeness, such fidelity cannot be achieved by our desiring it; we cannot grit our teeth and accomplish perfection by sheer will power. The kind of living demanded by Jesus in the beatitudes and antitheses can be accomplished only by the grace of God. Only by opening ourselves to the life of God can we live like this. If we judge ourselves only by the Ten Commandments, we can begin to think that we are doing fairly well. It is possible to become a little smug, a little self-righteous. If, however, we judge ourselves by the beatitudes and the antitheses, there is no possibility of such attitudes. We are forced to admit that we are beginners in the task of becoming Christian. Keeping these characteristics of the Kingdom before us ensures that we remain in healthy touch with our sinfulness, with our many limitations, with our desperate need for God's mercy and forgiveness. Only then are we ready to receive his choicest blessings!

5. Teaching on the Performance of Religious Duties, 6:1-18

Our Lord demands of his disciples a greater fidelity. An important dimension of that fidelity depends on the performance of religious duties. Here again we find that a distinctively new attitude is required of the disciple. Even in the most sublime religious act the poison of self-seeking can intrude, and, if unchecked, it will entirely destroy the value of the act. Jesus' teaching in this section rules out what can become uppermost in the thoughts of a devout person: his achievement in the eyes of God. Placing his confidence entirely in God, the disciple is called to renounce all measurement of holiness that can be judged by others, even by himself.

Jesus concentrates his attention on the three fundamental acts of Jewish piety: almsgiving (2-4), prayer (5-8), and fasting (16-18). Matthew adds the Our Father (9-13) as part of the teaching on prayer. According to Jewish spirituality, almsgiving, prayer and fasting went beyond the demands of the Law, atoned for sins and could benefit others at the judgment. For Jesus the crucial element is the intention with which such good works are performed. The chapter begins with a general principle: Take care not to do your good works in public, lest you lose your reward from the Father. The principle is then applied to each of the three duties, using the same structure.

Almsgiving (2-4)	Prayer (5-6)	Fasting (16-18)

1. When you do this work, do not advertise it as the hypocrites do; they have their reward already.
2. You must do it without attracting attention to yourself.

Jesus does not condemn being seen, but acting in order to be seen.

Verses 7-8 break the pattern of teaching against hypocrisy. Now Our Lord warns against a pagan approach to prayer. In order to be sure of addressing the right god by the right name, pagans constructed lists of all the gods and their titles. They hoped to win the favor of the gods by sheer quantity, as well as by the correctness of their "incantation." The pagan seeks to weary the gods (Seneca), while the disciple of Jesus believes that, before he calls out, God answers (Isaiah 65:24).

As an illustration of the simplicity and trust which should characterize the prayer of the disciple, Matthew places here the prayer which Jesus himself taught. No words of Scripture are more familiar to us. In fact, because we have universally adopted Matthew's version, we tend to forget that Luke also includes this prayer in his Gospel (Luke 11:2-4). To study the two versions is to become aware of the freedom with which the apostolic community handed on the words of the Lord. Jesus' teachings were never handed on as a dead letter but always as applied to the life of the community. Most scholars hold that Luke's context is closer to the historical situation and that his wording is closer to the original words of Jesus. Matthew's version shows the effects of liturgical use.

Matthew 6:8-13	Luke 11:1-4
(8) "Do not be like them; your Father already knows what you need before you ask him.	(1) One time Jesus was praying in a certain place. When he finished, one of his disciples said to him, "Lord, teach us to pray, just as John taught his disciples."
(9) This, then is how you should pray:	(2) Jesus said to them, "This is what you should pray:
'Our Father in heaven: May your holy name be honored;	'Father May your holy name be honored;
(10) may your Kingdom come; may your will be done on earth as it is in heaven	may your Kingdom come.

(11) Give us today the food we need.

(3) Give us day by day the food we need.

(12) Forgive us the wrongs that we have done, as we forgive the wrongs that others have done to us.

(4) Forgive us our sins, because we forgive everyone who does us wrong.

(13) Do not bring us to hard testing, but keep us safe from the Evil One.' "

And do not bring us to hard testing.' "

We can also observe several of Matthew's themes: in heaven; your will be done; earth and heaven; deliver us from the evil one. Perhaps by design, Matthew formulates the prayer in seven petitions, of which the first three concern God and the final four look to our own needs. It also seems no accident that the Our Father is placed at the exact center of the Sermon on the Mount. As we study the prayer taught by Jesus, we might remember that in the early church it was not given to catechumens until after baptism. Through familiarity we have forgotten what a precious heritage it is. According to the *Didache*, Christians were to pray the Our Father three times daily, perhaps corresponding to the Jewish practice of praying the Eighteen Benedictions in the morning, afternoon and evening.

Our Father in Heaven

The opening greeting sets the tone for the entire prayer. It is the prayer of the Christian community, offered in filial confidence to a loving Father. Already in the Hebrew Scriptures God was regarded as a Father who warmly cared for his beloved son, Israel. (See Hosea 11:1, Deuteronomy 1:31 and Isaiah 49:15). As the centuries passed, however, so much stress was placed on God's transcendence and on observation of the Law that a sense of intimacy with God was lost. From Mark's Gospel (14:36) and Paul's letters (Romans 8:15 and Galtians 4:6) we know that Jesus (who spoke Aramaic) prayed to his Father as *Abba*, a term of familiarity and endearment, much like our words, Dad or Papa. Such intimacy with God was a revolutionary change, a tremendous gift to the Church. It seems that Matthew's community expressed its sense of wonder at this gift by adding "in heaven," so that the form of address "Our Father" would never be taken for granted.

May Your Holy Name Be Honored

The revelation of God's name, Yahweh, was refused to the patriarchs but granted to Moses (Exodus 3:13-20) as a pledge of special protection. To the Semitic mind, a name both makes present the one named and reveals his nature. Although Yahweh has revealed himself as full of tenderness and love, his people have not always responded by holding his name holy. In this first petition we ask that God himself cause his name to be honored. We find a similar petition in the Kaddish, a prayer used at the conclusion of the synagogue service: "May his name be glorified and honored as holy in the world, which he created according to his will."

May Your Kingdom Come

Again we find a parallel in the Kaddish: "May he establish his Kingdom in your lifetime and in your days and in all the ages of the whole house of Israel soon and in the near future." In the second petition we ask God to bring about the full and final establishment of the Messianic reign. This is closely connected to the first petition, since God's name will be honored when, and because, his Kingdom comes. Since God's rule has been inaugurated in the person of

Jesus, we are praying for the establishment of his authority.

May Your Will Be Done On Earth As It Is In Heaven

The third petition clarifies the meaning of acknowledging God's reign and the authority of Jesus. Only the person who in fact does the will of God is responding to God's kingship. For Matthew, "he who does the will of God" is practically a definition of the disciple. Jesus himself prayed in these same words in his hour of trial (26:42). The petition involves a strong dimension of man's fidelity to God's will. Yet the passive voice suggests that something independent of human cooperation is at stake. The same impression is given by the phrase "on earth as it is in heaven." We are praying for the accomplishment of God's purpose in history, the fulfillment of his saving plan.

Give Us Today The Food We Need

With the fourth petition we turn to human needs. The Greek word which is translated traditionally as "daily" and in our version as "we need" has puzzled scholars. It might mean "tomorrow's" bread (which stands for all our bodily needs), and/or bread "for the coming day." Since the entire prayer looks toward the end-time, Our Lord probably intended us to pray not only for bodily food but also for the food of the Kingdom, for the nourishment of the Messianic banquet (See Isaiah 25:6-9). Most commentators would not see a direct reference to the Eucharist here.

Forgive Us The Wrongs That We Have Done, As We Forgive The Wrongs That Others Have Done Us

The fifth petition takes on added significance because it

is the only one in the prayer to which Matthew appends a further saying of the Lord (6:14-15; see also 18:35). Our sins against God are envisioned as debts, which is the literal meaning of the Greek word here translated "wrongs." The Jewish Law taught that a man's generosity to his fellow believers must imitate that of Yahweh to Israel. That is what Jesus means here. It is not a question of earning God's forgiveness; our generosity to one another results from God's tenderness to us. The summons to forgive becomes a statement of how to receive God's forgiveness.

Do Not Bring Us To Hard Testing

God can lead his people into the purification of a testing (see Genesis 22:1, Deuteronomy 8:2 and Jeremiah 6:27). Jewish spirituality saw temptation as a sign of divine favor, an opportunity to demonstrate obedience. Yet Jesus teaches us both here and in 26:41 to pray that God will deliver us from such a trial. Again the petition looks to the end-time. At the end, God's people will enter into a terrifying time of trial. Humility is a characteristic of the disciple; he is not to be a religious "superstar," welcoming this final test. Instead of relying on his own strength, he seeks to be spared this trial.

But Keep Us Safe From The Evil One

In this final petition we pray to be saved from the same enemy who will oppose the final coming of the Kingdom in the last days. In some ways this is a positive re-statement of the previous petition. The disciple longs for that day when he will no longer be subject to the power of evil but in full communion with God. When the Kingdom comes in its fullness, that which is already true in the life of Jesus will be completely actualized in the life of the Church.

The Doxology

In some manuscripts we find the ending "for yours is the Kingdom and the power and the glory." The King James version followed these and it became common in Protestant usage. Most Jewish prayers ended in a doxology of this kind. Since the prayer was widely used in the liturgy, the practice soon grew of adding the doxology. We find the Matthean version, with doxology, in the *Didache*. It has been returned to our celebrations of the Eucharist as antiphonal response of the community, which is exactly the way in which it entered the Christian tradition.

The Church has always considered the Our Father as a model for the disciple's prayer. In conclusion we should note how it begins with the larger concerns of God and only then turns to our own material and spiritual needs. It begins with awareness of our personal relationship to the Father, seeks first to praise him and desire his rule and will, then prays for our material needs, forgiveness and final salvation. Its simplicity should guide us; the Father already knows our needs.

6. On Serving God and not Possessions, 6:19-34

In 6:1-18 Matthew has gathered teachings of Jesus about seeking reward in heaven rather than on earth. This naturally leads him to a series of teachings which contrast heavenly and earthly riches. These teachings are not found in Luke's Sermon on the Plain, but scattered through chapters 11, 12, and 16. Matthew, by his careful arrangement of Jesus' teachings into the sermon format, has created a powerful catechetical tool.

Earthly riches will inevitably fail us. Only heavenly treasure escapes corrosion and theft—or, today, a failing stock market. Riches will inevitably be stored; the crucial question is where, for there the heart (our most fundamental direction) will be found. To make earthly possessions our central concern is to risk losing our one chance for life with a genuine future—a life that is centered in God and his will.

The example used in 6:22-23 is thought by some to refer to generosity with possessions. However, most scholars understand it as a teaching on spiritual blindness. Just as one's life is shrouded in darkness when his eye is blind, so, too, one's life is dark when he no longer looks toward God alone, but allows himself to be distracted by earthly riches. This teaching is emphasized by the metaphor of the two masters (6:24). "Hate" and "love" here are not feelings but a decision in favor of one or the other.

In verses 25-34 we encounter one of the most familiar passages of the Gospel. Jesus does not call us beyond the human condition. We will always need food and clothing. The key to the passage is verse 33: by relying on the Father's providential care, the believer becomes free to devote his primary concern to the "Kingdom" (God's actions in human history, his sovereignty over all people) and "what he requires" (bringing our life into conformity with all that God is doing). As he did in the beatitudes,

Jesus here demands that we transcend a common sense approach to life, which he sees as the life-style of the "heathen." *They* are primarily concerned about possessions, he says. But *you*, who are salt and light for the earth, who call God "Abba" and thus recognize his tender care, must be concerned about the essential things. By his examples Our Lord is not encouraging us to idleness but to freedom from anxiety. The "heathen" do not know better; they are consumed with worry. But you, how little faith you have! This theme of "little faith" is important in Matthew's theology. The disciples are significantly different from the pagans. They have recognized what God is doing in Jesus of Nazareth and have committed their lives to him. Yet the disciples of Matthew's church have not reached a maturity of faith. Still "weak-faithed," they do not yet entirely entrust their lives to the Father. To follow Jesus is to learn such trust, such freedom from anxiety, such concern for the really important things.

7. *Teaching on Judging Others and on Prayer, 7:1-12*

Verses 1-5 are rooted in common Jewish wisdom. Even

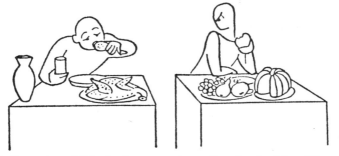

their form is rabbinic: instruction, theological justification and illustrations. Jewish tradition urged lenient judgment of others, in the spirit of our own popular saying "Don't judge another until you've walked a mile in his shoes." As he frequently does, Jesus adds a radical dimension to a common saying: don't judge at all! This teaching is closely linked with his earlier demand for forgiveness of others.

According to the rabbis, God judged the world by two rules or measures: mercy and justice. If the disciple wishes God to show him mercy, he must show mercy. Verses 3-5 are not an escape clause which allow judgment under certain conditions. They are intended to reinforce the prohibition of all judgment. Since we will never be able to rid ourselves of our own faults and sins, we will never be in a position to judge others. Verse 6 does not seem to fit here, unless it is intended to modify the absolute prohibition against judgment. In that case, it would mean that one can at least judge whether a person or group is capable of receiving Christian teaching. Originally the dogs and swine might have symbolized the Gentiles; however Matthew does not include it in this sense.

In calling us to refrain from judgment Jesus does not ask us to ignore the wrongs that others do or the evil in the world. In 18:15-17 he gives us a process for winning back an erring brother or sister. Jesus' mandate seems to be directed more toward attitudes of intolerance and contempt.

In the following section (7:7-11) we again find strong traces of rabbinic tradition: parallelism (7-8), illustrations from everyday life (9-10) and an *a fortiori* argument. Here Matthew returns to the familiar stress on the generosity and mercy of God. Again we have an illustration of the theological passive voice; it is God who gives and opens. The context of this teaching is important. It is the disciple, the one whose entire being is set upon the Lord, the one who prays as a son or daughter in the Beloved Son, whose prayer is infallibly heard. Jesus' emphasis is not a self-centered one—what will we receive?—but rather an emphasis on the joy of prayer to such a Father. If even earthly parents, for all their sinfulness, rejoice to grant the request of their children, how much more will the Father grant ours. The "good things" of verse 11 possibly refers back to the seven petitions of the Our Father. Note that in Luke's account the multitude of God's good gifts are gathered into the supreme gift of the Holy Spirit (Luke 11:13).

In Jewish tradition the "golden rule" was known in a negative form. Rabbi Hillel taught: "What is hateful to you, do not do to your fellow-creature. That is the whole Law; all else is explanation." Mention of Law and prophets links us with 5:17 and thus brings to a conclusion that part of the sermon in which Jesus reinterprets both the Law and the practice of religious duties. Jesus does not weaken the prevailing interpretations of the Law; on the contrary he makes "doing all that God requires" much more rigorous. Yet we will see in Chapters 12 and 23 that Jesus was often in conflict with the Scribes and Pharisees over the interpretation of the Law. In trying to keep the Law one can miss its heart: love of God and neighbor. The "golden rule" was known before the time of Christ, both in Jewish and in secular writing. What is new in Jesus' teaching is the measure with which we are to love others: the love with which the Father loves us. Again we see the importance for Matthew of the teaching in 5:48—be perfect as your Father is perfect.

8. *Two Ways, the True and False Prophets, 7:13-27*

In this final section we hear four brief exhortations (warnings, really) not to miss the point of the sermon. In a very Jewish manner Jesus describes contrasting ways of receiving his teachings. Again Luke knows these sayings of the Lord, but includes only two of them in his Sermon on the Plain. Examination of the parallel passages in Luke provides a good illustration of how each evangelist has taken the words of Jesus, spoken on a particular occasion and to a particular audience, and adapted them to the new situation and audience for which he was writing.

The image of the two ways was common in Jewish instruction and was taken over into Christian catechetics. The *Didache* begins: "There are two ways, one leading to life and one to death, and great is the difference between the two ways." Matthew seems to have merged two original sayings of Jesus. The first deals with the broad and narrow gates (leading either to the Kingdom of God or of Satan). The second saying speaks of the two ways: the wide (easy) way to death and the cramped (hard) way to life. In this context the narrow gate probably refers to the difficult teachings of Jesus, while the hard way signifies a life of obedience to those teachings. Speculation was widespread in Judaism on the relative numbers of saved and damned. (See Luke 13:23-24.) Jesus seems to say: don't worry about how many will be saved; your business is to find the way that leads to life. "Few" and "many" should be understood less in the strict literal sense and more as stressing that entrance through the gate and perseverance along the way are gifts of God's grace.

The Sermon on the Mount does indeed lay out a narrow and difficult path for the disciple. It is possible that the study of this section of the Gospel has discouraged us. How, we ask ourselves, can we possibly take up this burdensome life? Perhaps we should look ahead for a moment to a beautiful passage in Chapter 11. In verses 28-30 of that chapter Jesus tells us that it is precisely when we are tired and disheartened that we should come to him. For his yoke (the burden of the life of a disciple) is easy and light.

This saying of Our Lord is a paradox, and yet it is true! To follow Jesus is at the same time hard and easy, demanding and light. Happy and blessed is the person who commits himself to this path. For Jesus himself is the source of the disciple's strength. In union with him, what seems burdensome to the outsider is experienced by the disciple as joyful, fulfilling and life-giving. With this "preview of coming attractions" in mind, let us complete our study of the Sermon.

In the section on the tree and its fruit (7:15-20), we are clearly dealing with an original saying of the Lord which Matthew has adapted to the needs of his own community. In Luke's version these verses are concerned with the genuineness of personal religion; here they are applied to the problem of false prophets. Matthew is not as worried about the Pharisees or those outside the Church as he is concerned about false teachers within the community. Surprisingly, the ultimate criterion is not the orthodoxy of the teaching of the false prophets (see 1 John 2:18-27) but the "orthopraxy" of their lives. Again we have a parallel in the *Didache*: "By their behavior shall the false and the true prophets be known." The two metaphors (7:16 and 7:17-18) stress the relationship between the nature of the tree and the kind of fruit it bears. The disciple's behavior emerges from the center of his being, his heart. If there is true conversion to the person and values of the Master, then the life of the disciple will manifest it. Matthew teaches his community to refuse a hearing for any prophet/ teacher, however brilliant and persuasive, who does not live the narrow way of the Sermon on the Mount.

In verses 21-23 Matthew adds a similar saying of the Lord, one of the most devastating of the Scriptures. Again he has adapted the original context, which is probably seen in Luke 6:45, placing a heavy emphasis on the final judgment. Matthew's church was probably experiencing difficulties with powerful, specially gifted believers who worked miraculous signs in Christ's name. Such deeds do not prove that those who performed them are true disciples. Again, the only proof of fidelity to Jesus is that of obedience to the Father's will, which is clearly revealed in the teaching of his Son. As we saw in 5:17-7:12, fidelity to the Father's will is founded on love of neighbor. The same Greek word for evildoers (literally, workers of lawlessness) appears in 13:41 and 24:12, both times in the context of the final judgment. In 24:12 the spread of lawlessness causes the love of many to grow cold. It seems clear then that disciples will be rejected at the judgment not only for positive evil deeds but also for failure to love. (In 23:28 Jesus accuses the Pharisees, who slavishly observe the Law, of being full of lawlessness.) That some of these will have been prominent church-goers, even those who worked deeds of power, gives us pause for much reflection.

Throughout this section Matthew has been concerned with doing the will of God. In his closing verses the verb "to do" continues to be the central word. We have here not a contrast between those who hear Jesus' word and those who refuse to hear it, but between those who hear and obey his word and those who hear and do not put that word into practice. Again we have an indication that Matthew understands this great sermon of Jesus ("these words of mine" 7:26) as God's will for all disciples; they are not merely counsel (only for those with a special vocation). Just as those sections of the Hebrew Scriptures dealing with the Law conclude with the choice of a blessing or a curse (read Leviticus 26:3-45 and Deuteronomy 30:15-20), so also Matthew's conclusion demands a decision. The question is that of the site of the disciple's foundation. Outwardly two houses might appear the same. Only when the wind and rains come—a symbol for the judgment of God—will the quality of the foundation's site be revealed. The sand in Jesus' illustration probably meant the wadi (creek bed), which in the long dry season was often grassy and abloom with flowers. Thus it offered a more attractive location than the barren, rocky soil around. Yet when the rainy season arrived, the torrents swept away anything located in the wadi. Thus durability or collapse at the judgment depends on where a disciple "settles" with his "house." We are often tempted to build on the inviting sands of the world's truths and values, but the only adequate site on which to build our lives is that of loving and faithful obedience to Jesus and his teaching.

9. *Conclusion of the Sermon, 7:28-29*

As Matthew opens his sermon, so he closes it with two verses which demonstrate his "theological shorthand." Often in Scripture a single word or a phrase carries a wealth of meaning, due perhaps to allusions to the Hebrew Scriptures or to the personal theology of the evangelist. This indicates to us the importance of studying Scripture. Without some study, the Word of God does not speak to us with its fullest riches.

The phrase "Jesus finished..." is found five times in Matthew's Gospel, each time signaling the end of one of the great discourses. (See also 11:1, 13:53, 19:1 and 26:1.) Here Matthew notes the response of the crowd (remember they are presented as a secondary audience for the discourse) to Jesus' teaching: they are amazed. While the scribes quoted previous authorities in support of their teaching, often balancing one rabbinic school against another, Jesus spoke with freshness, directness and in his own name. As with his first listeners, we can't help but hear the authority of God in Our Lord's words. The crowd reacts ambiguously. It is attracted to the *Teacher*, but refuses to make a disciple's commitment to the *Lord*. One of Matthew's literary techniques (differing here from Mark) is his use of titles for Jesus; the title "Lord" is used only by the disciples, while "Teacher" (Rabbi) is used by the uncommitted or by those hostile to him.

Hopefully, our study of Chapters 5-7 will challenge the quality of our discipleship. Are we among those attracted by the authority of Jesus and yet choosing to remain aloof from the inner circle of his disciples? Are we disciples who minimize and water down his demands on our lives? Are we disciples who fervently proclaim our fidelity while refusing to obey the will of the Father? Or, are we disciples keenly conscious of our weakness and sinfulness, yet striving and hoping and praying for that greater fidelity which the Lord requires?

Week Four

Having presented Jesus as the Messiah of the Word (chapters five through seven), Matthew now presents him as the Messiah of Deed (chapters eight and nine). In this week we will study one of the most beautiful sections of all Scripture—Matthew's account of the healing ministry of Jesus.

Jesus does far more than teach about the Kingdom of God. Through the power of his word and deeds the Kingdom becomes visible. The miracles of Jesus are thus signs that the Kingdom of God is breaking into human history. Notice how much time Our Lord spent in healing the sick, the troubled, the possessed. Explore with your study group the ways in which this healing ministry of Jesus continues in our own lives.

In chapter ten Jesus sends out twelve disciples to proclaim the Good News and to continue the powerful works of their Master. It is important to understand that these passages also refer to us, called in our baptism to make Christ present in the world.

Daily Study Assignments: Week Four

Day	Matthew	Commentary
1	8:1-17	Pages 90- 94
2	8:18-34	Pages 94-100
3	9:1-34.	Pages 100-110
4	9:35-10:15	Pages 110-117
5	10:16-11:1	Pages 117-126

6—Reflect on chapters 8 through 10 in light of the reflection questions listed below.

7—STUDY GROUP MEETING

- When do we see the healing ministry of Jesus in the Church today?

- Would it be controversial if your pastor or associate pastor began to spend a significant amount of his time ministering to youthful drug-users, prostitutes and homosexual persons?

- How could the Pharisees remain hostile to Jesus in the face of his wonderful miracles? Why were they not converted?

- Matthew saw that the missionary instructions of Jesus had a significance for his community living some 50 or 60 years later. What might be some of the ways in which our Lord's missionary discourse can have significance for the Church today?

- Suppose that you are a Jewish person living in the 80's. You have been experiencing increasing hostility because of your affiliation with a group of people who believe Jesus is the long-awaited Messiah. Your friends are avoiding you, your family has ceased to welcome you, your little business is suffering. Last night you read for the first time the instructions of Jesus for his disciples. As you begin this day, you have a new perspective on what you are living through. Why?

- In 10:26-31 the disciple is urged to give public witness to Jesus and is counseled three times to be unafraid. In Matthew's day the members of the Church feared bodily harm and dispossession by their families. What kind of reprisals from our society do you fear in your bearing public witness to Jesus?

The Kingdom Made Visible, 8:1-11:1

A. Narrative Section: The Miracles of Jesus, 8:1-9:34

1. The Setting, 8:1

In his ministry Jesus not only spoke the authoritative word of God but also performed the powerful deeds that only Yahweh could do. Thus Matthew follows the great sermon with a section which narrates the great miracles of Jesus. Again we have much evidence of his catechetical purpose. If you notice the parallel passages, it is clear that Matthew has gathered together miracle accounts which are scattered throughout the Gospels of Mark and Luke and has again woven a beautiful tapestry. (By his choice of ten miracles Matthew may again be intending a parallel with Moses, whose ten miraculous plagues led to the deliverance of his people from Pharaoh.)

Having presented Jesus as the Messiah of the Word (chapters 5-7), Matthew now proclaims to us the Messiah of Deed (chapters 8-9). Not only has he gathered these miracle traditions together, he has also ordered them carefully, and in such a way as to enhance their meaning and power. It is instructive to notice how he adapts the basic tradition which he receives from Mark. In general, Matthew abbreviates Mark (his miracle accounts are about one-half as long as Mark's), by omitting many colorful and descriptive details. In Matthew's hand the miracle stories of the tradition become a clearer manifestation of the divine power at work in Jesus. Perhaps even more significantly, they highlight the necessity of faith.

Because of the Church's long tradition of using the miracle accounts as proofs of his divinity, we can easily overlook the purpose of miracles in Jesus' ministry. Seen in their historical context, the miracles were primarily signs of the in-breaking of the Kingdom of God upon his people. Jewish tradition realized that, since the fall of Adam, Satan had laid claim to the world and exercised a kind of dominion over it. In order then for God's dominion to enter into human history, it must throw out the rule of evil, which was always understood in terms of sickness, possession by evil spirits and the catastrophes of nature. Thus the miracles of Jesus attack, in a sense, the power of evil in exactly these areas. In addition Jesus is victorious over the final stronghold of Satan, death itself. Before men can follow Jesus and love as he commands, they must be set free from the power of evil. Jesus' miracles are thus concrete signs that the Kingdom of God is indeed near.

2. *Three Miracles and a summary, 8:2-17*

The Greek text begins with the Biblical phrase "And behold!" a term which Matthew will use several times in these two chapters. It alerts the reader that something special is about to happen, something which involves God's presence in history. The leper not only comes but also kneels before Jesus, a sign of special reverence, even adoration. A comparison with Mark 1:40-45 will show that Matthew cuts away the details of the account, especially those which mention Jesus' emotions. The emphasis is clearly on the dialogue between the leper and the Lord, especially on the threefold "clean" of 8:2-3. In this account Matthew highlights both the desire of Jesus to heal and the power of his word; the man is immediately healed.

The people of the Middle East considered leprosy a serious disease, one which excluded the sufferer from the community. Verse 4 demonstrates Jesus' faithfulness to the Law. (See Leviticus 14 for the process of purification.) Perhaps again Matthew wishes to compare Jesus with

Moses, emphasizing here that Jesus is greater than Moses. Moses could describe God's will for the exclusion of a leper and later his purification. Jesus can heal the leper! In the command to remain silent, Matthew stresses the humility of God's Servant who does not seek attention for himself. (Look ahead to 12:15-21.)

If it is significant that Matthew's initial miracle benefits a member of the chosen people, it is no less important that the second (8:5-13) is worked on behalf of a Gentile. In comparison with Luke 7:1-10, we note that Matthew highlights the faith of the Gentile officer, which contrasts sharply with Jesus' prophecy that the children of the Kingdom (the Israelites) will be excluded from their heritage.

In Matthew the centurion does not even make a request; he simply leaves it to Jesus to do what is best. Jesus' response is immediate: "I will go (8:7)." The Gentile is overwhelmed at Jesus' generosity and provides us with one of the most memorable statements of Scripture: "Lord, I am not worthy." In a similar way Yahweh's appearance to Isaiah fills him with a sense of unworthiness and he cries out, "I am a man of unclean lips (Isaiah 6:5)." For the centurion knows the power of the authoritative word. Jesus has such a word of power; his physical presence is not necessary. Say but the word!

In the presence of such faith Jesus is amazed. How near to the Kingdom is this pagan! His prophecy contains both the traditional and new. Since the time of Isaiah the Jewish people had foreseen that the Gentiles would be blessed by coming to Jerusalem, there to be included in the heritage of God's people. (See Isaiah 2:1-5.) What is unprecedented is the threat (8:11-12) that the children themselves will be excluded, thrust into darkness and weeping (symbolic of final doom). Again we remember the warning of John the Baptist in 3:9: membership in the chosen people, without faith in her Messiah, will not gain salvation. In verse 13

Jesus underlines the role faith has played in this miraculous event: what you believe, will be done.

In the healing of Peter's mother-in-law (8:14-15) we begin to understand how pervasive are the messianic blessings present in the person of Jesus. His wonderful

deeds are available to all: strangers (the leper), outsiders (the Gentile's servant) and also those within the intimate family of the Master's disciples. None of these was important in the eyes of the Jewish elite: a social outcast, a pagan slave, the mother of a simple fisherman. Yet Jesus is there for all of them. Notice a beautiful detail of Matthew's account: No one brings her illness to Jesus' attention. He seems to notice it first, and responds at once. Should we still harbor an image of God as distant and aloof, our study of this section of the Gospel will explode it.

In verses 16-17 Matthew summarizes this opening portion of his miracle chapters. As in 3:17, it is the Suffering Servant tradition of Isaiah that interprets Jesus' ministry. (It would be helpful to your appreciation of Matthew's Gospel to study all four "Suffering Servant Songs" found in Isaiah 42:1-9; 49:1-6; 50:4-11; and 52:13-53:12.) This has a profound significance: the miracles should be understood as expression of Jesus'; obedience to the Father. Jesus does not work miracles for his own glory, nor even to prove that he is the Messiah. No, he works miracles because it was the Father's will that he take upon himself the burdens of God's people. Working miracles in itself is not sufficient proof of messianic dignity. Such works of power must be coupled with a total obedience. (See commentary on 7:21-23.) The Servant's primary desire is to do God's will. Note how Matthew beautifully ties together the great sermon (which describes discipleship as doing all that God requires) and this miracle section (which demonstrates Jesus' own obedience). We are well acquainted with the fact that the Lord Jesus took upon himself the burden of our sins. This passage citing the fulfillment of Isaiah 53:4, reveals that he also heals us of our illnesses.

3. Discipleship Tested, 8:18-27

In this passage we have one of the clearest examples in the Christian Scriptures of how the tradition about Our Lord grew in richness as it was handed on from decade to decade. Matthew takes the account of a nature miracle from Mark and, gathering the rich insights of the twenty-odd years which had passed, shows us that it also taught a crucial lesson about discipleship.

Let us examine the two texts side by side.

Mark 4:35-41	Matthew 8:18-27
(35) On the evening of that same day Jesus said to his disciples, "Let us go across to the other side of the lake."	(18) Jesus noticed the crowd around him and *ordered* his disciples to go to the other side of the lake.
	(19) A teacher of the Law came to him. "Teacher," he said, "I am ready to go with you wherever you go."

(20) Jesus answered him, "Foxes have holes, birds have nests, but the Son of Man has no place to lie down and rest."

(21) Another man, who was a disciple, said, "Sir, first let me go back and bury my father."

(22) "Follow me," Jesus answered, "and let the dead bury their own dead."

(36) So they left the crowd; the disciples got into the boat that Jesus was already in, and took him with them. Other boats were there too.

(23) Jesus got into the boat, and *his disciples went with him.*

(37) A very strong wind blew up and the waves began to spill over into the boat, so that it was about to fill with water.

(24) Suddenly a fierce *storm* hit the lake, so that the waves covered the boat.

(38) Jesus was in the back of the boat, sleeping with his head on a pillow.

But Jesus was asleep.

The disciples woke him up and said,

(25) The disciples went to him and woke him up.

"Teacher, don't you care that we are about to die?"

"Save us, Lord!" they said. "We are about to die!"

(39) Jesus got up and commanded the wind: "Be quiet!" and said to the waves, "Be still!" The wind died down and there was a great calm.

(26) "Why are you so frightened?" Jesus answered. *"How little faith* you have!"

(40) Then Jesus said to them, "Why are you frightened? Are you still without faith?"

Then he got up and gave a command to the winds and to the waves, and there was a great calm.

(41) But they were terribly afraid, and began to say to each other,

"Who is this man? Even the wind and the waves obey him!"

(27) Everyone was amazed.

"What kind of man is this?" they said. "Even the winds and the waves obey him!"

Mark and Luke (8:22-25) handle this episode in basically the same manner. The focus of attention is on the historical event, with special emphasis on the miraculous power of Jesus over the forces of nature. In Mark we notice that the experience is described vividly, with an abundance of small details. The cry of the disciples displays no great reverence and the story centers on Jesus' powerful word of command.

By the time that Matthew wrote, the Church had reflected many times on this important moment in the life of Jesus and the first disciples. It is now understood not only as an event which revealed Jesus' power over the forces of nature but also as a clear example of the meaning of discipleship. Matthew enables us to see this by inserting into the traditional form of the account two sayings of the Lord about discipleship.(Luke uses them in another set of circumstances. Luke 9:57-60).

These sayings (18-22) perhaps strike us as harsh and unfeeling. Here are two men of generous spirit who seem to be rebuked by Jesus. The context clarifies the occasion for us. Jesus warns the would-be disciples that discipleship is no light matter. One should not begin to follow Jesus without knowing the price to be paid. (Here the historical circumstances become important. To follow Jesus during his ministry meant giving up the security of a home-life and taking up his itinerant life-style. Most of us are not called into this kind of discipleship. Yet the word of the Lord is also spoken to us: to follow Jesus means both renunciation as well as the acceptance of a certain joy or happiness in living that no possessions can give. See 5:3-11.) Again, discipleship comes before even the most sacred of human duties. The man (8:21) probably wants to remain with his elderly father and then join Jesus after his father dies. (Judaism placed great emphasis on the religious duty of burying the dead, especially one's own father.) The thrust of these verses on discipleship is that nothing else can have the first place in our lives because the first place belongs to the Lord. There is an urgency in these verses which should call our often complacent Christian lives into question.

The saying in 8:22 has often puzzled readers and scholars. It might mean that those who have not found the life of the Kingdom (the "dead") can attend to the burial of the physically dead.

Having been "clued in" by Matthew that this episode speaks to us about discipleship, we can notice many small changes which he introduces into Mark's account. (We have *underlined* the most important ones.) In verses 18 and 23 the relationship of the disciples to Jesus is clarified. ("Went with him" in verse 23 is actually stronger in the Greek. Matthew uses a phrase which indicates more than physical accompaniment.) He also uses a different Greek word for the "strong wind"; it now becomes an upheaval of the earth (sea). Matthew has chosen a word from the apocalyptic literature, so that the storm symbolizes the dramatic upheavals which will accompany the end-time.

In the same way, the boat has become a symbol of the Church, tossed around (as was Matthew's community) by the waves of persecution. Notice the outcry of the disciples. Mark's "Teacher, don't you care" has become a prayer in Matthew's account. It sounds like the voice of the Church's liturgy: "Lord, save us!" "Kyrie, eleison!" The most important shift of emphasis takes place in Jesus' response to the disciples' outcry. In Mark, Jesus first calms the wind/sea and then rebukes the disciples for their lack of faith. In Matthew the center of emphasis becomes the gentle chiding of the Lord: "How little faith you have!" Only then does he turn to the raging storm and subdue it.

For Matthew's community the primary need is not the proclamation of Jesus' power over nature. They knew that. A community being tested in the deep waters of persecution had need of maturity of faith. Thus in Matthew's account Jesus' first action is not to remove the danger but to call forth a deeper faith in his Lordship. He is asking if they really believe that he is Lord of nature, Lord of human history. Do they really believe that he holds the Church in the palm of his hand, even if it looks like the forces of evil are dominant?

What a beautiful example of the tradition of the Church this account gives us! As the community of believers meditated on the episode of Jesus' calming of the storm, they came to realize that this historical episode continued to speak to their own situation, endangered now not by waves of water but by those of persecution. The term "little-faithed ones"—a favorite word in Matthew's

Gospel—applied not only to the original disciples but also the members of the Church of the eighties. Thus the tradition includes not only the original memory of a day on the Sea of Galilee but also the further prayerful reflection of the Church. It is in this way that Tradition grows, adding the riches of each generation of believers. Today this deepening understanding continues. While it no longer becomes Sacred Scripture, it is no less important in God's revelation of himself to the Church of our own day.

In concluding this powerful passage we might note yet another significance of the calming of the sea. In Jewish theology the sea always represented the uncontrollable forces of nature, the forces of chaos. (See Genesis 1:1-10; Psalms 29:3 and 104:7; Job 38:8-11.) Yahweh alone was master of chaos. Psalm 93 envisions Yahweh seated in majesty above the furor of the waters of the sea. In the vision of the seer in Revelations 21:1, one of the signs of the completion of God's saving work is that the sea will be no more. By his mastery of the sea Jesus gives further evidence of his own equality with Yahweh, as well as another sign that the Kingdom of God is breaking into human history. For his followers, the age-old answer to the threatening storm remains the same: "Lord, save us!" The path of discipleship is difficult; it demands that all other values take second place. Yet Jesus rewards even in his life the sacrifices that discipleship demands. He is the Lord, ever present to rebuke the chaos, and to give us the security of his saving presence.

4. Authority Over Demons, 8:28-34

As he frequently does in these chapters, Matthew here abbreviates the tradition found in Mark (Mark 5:1-20) and Luke (8:26-39). What is stressed in Matthew is not so much the healing as Jesus' power over the demons. They fear Jesus, yet acknowledge him as the Son of God. The phrase "before the right time" in verse 29 is important. According to later Jewish theology, the demons could have power over people only until the day of judgment.

Again, the expulsion of demons is a sign that the Kingdom of God is breaking into history. In the ministry of Jesus the day of judgment is already present and the power of evil is broken. Thus in Matthew the townspeople (note that Jesus is in Gentile territory) come out to see Jesus rather than the restored man. Uncomprehending and frightened, they beg him to leave the area. We are left with the impression that the power of God threatens them (economic loss of the pigs? fear of the unknown?) rather than drawing them to the praise of God.

5. Forgiveness of sins, 9:1-7

Once again we find that Matthew has markedly abbreviated Mark's account and shifted the focus of attention. Now the healing of the paralysis falls sharply into the background. Gone are the colorful and fascinating details of the crowded house and the lowering of the man through the roof. Matthew concentrates on the question of whether the Son of Man has authority to forgive sins.

We are not told whether the paralyzed man believed in Jesus or not. (The evidence of verse 2 indicates that Jesus responded to the faith of his friends.) Nor should we think that Jesus accepted the common belief that sickness was a direct result of personal sin. (See John 9:2.) The point here is that both healing of illness and forgiveness of sins are signs of the Messiah's mission to restore all things. In forgiving the man's sins, however, Jesus lays claim to a greater than messianic dignity. Because only Yahweh could forgive sins, the scribes accuse Jesus of blasphemy. (This will be the charge for which Jesus is condemned; see 26:65.)

Knowing their thoughts, Jesus works the visible cure as proof of his power over the invisible sickness of sin. The

observers' amazement (in Mark) here deepens into fear (awe) before such divine power. (Look ahead to the accounts of the Transfiguration, 17:6 and the Resurrection, 28:5, 10.) Matthew seems to be responding to the situation of his own day when he adds that they praised God for giving *men* such authority. No longer does the incident stand as evidence only of Jesus' power to forgive sins. It now extends to the Church's claim to forgive sins by the authority and power of her Lord.

6. *The Call of Matthew, 9:9-13*

In all three synoptics the call of Matthew (or Levi according to Mark and Luke) appropriately follows the account of Jesus' healing of the paralyzed man, with its strong emphasis on the authority of Jesus to forgive sins. Thus Matthew's call becomes an illustration of the calling of sinners and of the root meaning of Jesus' ministry.

The call itself is quite similar to the call of Peter and Andrew, and of Zebedee's sons, in 4:18-22. In all three cases we are told nothing of the inner thoughts of the apostles or their reasons for responding; we learn only the immediacy of their response. In the parallel accounts (Mark 2:13-17 and Luke 5:27-32) Jesus calls Levi the tax collector to be a disciple. Since none of the lists of apostles mentions Levi (see Mark 3:18, Luke 6:15, and Matthew 10:3 and Acts 1:13), we must assume that Levi and Matthew are two names for the same person. Matthew became the name by which this apostle was best known in the Christian community. Today, the majority of scholars would differentiate between the tax collector-apostle and the author of the Gospel according to Matthew (at least in its final Greek-language form).

In order to celebrate his new vocation, Matthew the tax collector asks Jesus home for dinner, and takes the occasion to invite his circle of friends—tax collectors and sinners. The Greek word used here can be translated "sinners" but our translation, "outcasts," captures the meaning more accurately. Those who did not keep the Law in its entirety were regarded by the Pharisees as sinners; thus they were relegated to the outskirts of the Jewish community. Tax collectors were regarded with great disfavor by pious Jews, because their occupation involved them in breaking the laws regarding the Sabbath and ritual purity. (The Roman taxes were collected by tax farmers, who bid for the right to collect taxes and then extorted them to the limit. They were considered not only oppressors but also traitors to their own people, since they collaborated with the foreign power. Matthew the

Apostle probably did not work for the Romans but directly for Herod Antipas.)

That this gathering of outcasts has significance for salvation history is indicated by the Greek text. Its biblical phrases "it came to pass" coupled with "and behold!" warn us that this will be more than an ordinary meal. The question of the Pharisees provides Jesus with an opportunity to clarify the purpose of his ministry. Normally a pious Jew would not defile himself by associating with nonobservers of the Law. Yet Jesus seems very much at home with them.

Jesus' answer shows that he was not concerned with religious propriety but with his people's situation before God. "People who are well do not need a doctor, but only those who are sick (9:12)." As the healer of souls, Jesus has come to draw the alienated back into covenant relationship with his Father.

The quotation from Hosea 6:6 in verse 13 probably was added by Matthew (it is not found in Mark or Luke) in order to underline, as he had in 8:17, that Jesus' ministry is in accord with the Scriptures. Jesus associates with outcasts because that is the Father's will for him. The quotation from Hosea is important in Matthew's theology. He uses it again in 12:7 and alludes to it in 23:23. The word translated "kindness" can also be translated "mercy" or "love." Ritual observance of the Law can be dry and heartless. What Yahweh really desires is heartfelt love (the first-love of the desert wandering) and mercy (for the needs of brethren in the community). Jesus is saying, "In my actions you can discover what this passage of Hosea really means."

The passage ends with a reiteration of Jesus' purpose: "For I have not come to call the respectable people, but the outcasts." The key words can be understood in two ways. The *Good News* translation takes them in a literal sense:

Jesus has not come to call the virtuous or the righteous (those who keep the Law) but sinners (nonobservers of the Law). The translation of the *New American Bible*—"not the self-righteous, but sinners"—understands Jesus' saying in an ironical sense. Thus it not only expresses the compassion of Jesus but also strikes at the self-righteousness of the Pharisees. Those who do not recognize their illness will not summon the physician. By their refusal to recognize their sinfulness, the Pharisees place themselves outside the reconciling ministry of Jesus.

7. The Question about Fasting, 9:14-17

Again, all three synoptics place the questions about fasting after the controversy about Jesus' eating with sinners. The issue is raised both by the Pharisees (Mark and Luke) and by the disciples of John the Baptist (Matthew). We have already mentioned that Matthew's community returned to the sayings of Jesus for guidance in its controversies. So also this "word" of the Lord was probably used by the community to defend its practices against the Pharisees and John's followers, who placed a strong emphasis on the practice of fasting.

The original response of Jesus is found in verse 15a. Matthew takes the liberty of changing the "fasting" of Mark and Luke to "being sad." This is an attempt to bring out the true meaning of the controversy. Jesus' saying does not reject all fasting, only that which is an expression of inappropriate sadness and affliction. In the presence of Jesus with his disciples, the messianic age has dawned.

Thus feasting, not fasting, is the appropriate response. (Use of a marriage feast as an image of the messianic times would have been well known to Jesus' hearers.) However, when it is appropriate—when, for example, the bridegroom is taken away—then the Christian community will fast also. (Many scholars regard verse 15b as an addition of the early community, included to justify its practice of fasting.)

However, Christian fasting will be something totally new, since Jesus revolutionizes all religious practices. In verses 16-17 Jesus uses two examples to underline the newness of the Kingdom, which cannot be grafted onto Judaism. As a piece of new (unshrunk) cloth damages the old garment, and as new wine (fermenting) will burst the old skins, so the new spirit of the Kingdom cannot be contained within the old forms of Judaism. In the final phrase, "and so both will keep in good condition," we probably see Matthew's hand at work. He does not foresee the destruction of Judaism, as Mark seems to do, but its renewal and preservation.

8. The Bridegroom's Power over Sickness and Death, 9:18-26

Only in Matthew do the next two miracles follow the banquet controversies. Matthew closely links these wonderful accounts to the feasting at Levi's home, with its revelation of Jesus as the bridegroom. Again Matthew's editing—the account is about one-third shorter than its Marcan parallel (Mark 5:21-43)—has its theological purpose. He wants to highlight both the divine majesty of Jesus and the importance of faith in receiving his gifts.

In Mark the two miracles are intimately linked: the little girl, at the point of death when the official first comes, dies while Jesus is ministering to the bleeding woman. Using the tool of composition criticism, let us look first at the woman's healing (9:20-22). In contrast with the copious details of her illness in Mark, and the extremely vivid scene in which the healed woman seeks to conceal herself in the crowd (Mark 5:25-34), Matthew paints the scene in a few phrases. As we saw in 8:23-27, the miracle becomes subordinate to the saying of Jesus: "Your faith has made you well (9:22)." (The Greek word for "made well" which is used three times in verses 21 and 22, can also mean "saved.") Matthew has rearranged the traditional structure of the account in order to emphasize the conversation. Now the woman is healed not by touching Jesus' cloak but by his powerful word. The jostling crowd has dropped into the background, and one has the impression

of a solitary meeting between the woman and the Messiah.

A similar catechetical technique is likewise evident in Matthew's presentation of the raising of the ruler's daughter (9:18-19, 23-26). Matthew is not very concerned with the narration of all the details, nor even with the wonderful character of the miracle. Again he emphasizes the importance of faith. Thus he does not portray a faith which is harassed and in need of consolation (see Mark 5:22-23, 36) but one which even in the face of death itself holds firmly and confidently to Jesus. The official comes and kneels before Jesus. His grief is blotted out in the strength of his confidence in Jesus. The Master's reaction is immediate; he sets out toward the house, accompanied by his disciples.

On his arrival Jesus dismisses the musicians. (Music and lamentations were part of the burial ceremonies, and even the poorest families were expected to provide two flute players and one wailing woman to mourn the deceased.) In remarking that the girl is only sleeping Jesus does not mean that she was not truly dead, but that through his power death is not the final and absolute end which men fear. The news of this ultimate messianic sign spreads to all in the region (9:26).

9. *Jesus Heals the Blind and the Dumb, 9:27-34*

Matthew seems to have included these last two miracles in order to complete both the listing of messianic signs (11:5-6) and the Mosaic parallel of ten miraculous plagues (Exodus 7:14-12:32). The healing of the two blind men closely resembles the miracle recorded in 20:29-34 (which has its parallel in Mark 10:46-52). The conclusion of most scholars is that Matthew has narrated the same healing twice, each time with a different catechetical purpose. In chapter 20 what matters is that the royal figure, even on his way to Jerusalem to suffer, does not disdain the cry for help. In 9:27-31, as in the entire miracle section, the emphasis is on faith.

By their use of the title "Son of David," (9:27), the blind men indicate that they are requesting not sympathy but a merciful work of power. Isaiah had prophesied of the messianic days:

> *The blind will be able to see,*
> *and the deaf will hear.*
> *The lame will leap and dance,*
> *and those who cannot speak will shout for joy*
> *(Isaiah 35:5-6).*

Yet Jesus does not want to risk a misunderstanding of his ministry. He takes the suppliants to a private spot, and later forbids them ("harshly") to proclaim their healing. As we have seen so often, the conversation centers on faith: "Do you believe?" The *Good News* translation, "Yes, sir!" does not adequately reflect the Greek text. The word "Kyrios" can be rendered "sir" or "Lord." Having already used the messianic title "Son of David," it seems more probable that their response was "Yes, Lord!" as the *New American Bible* translates it. Jesus' touch precedes his authoritative word. (We heard a similar one in 8:22.) "Since you believe, your prayer is answered."

In 9:32-34 Matthew concludes his miracle section. This healing (is it also narrated twice? see 12:22-24) is placed here because Isaiah 35:5 proclaims: "...those who cannot speak will shout for joy." We have already seen the authority of Jesus over the demons. Here the emphasis falls on the contrasting reactions. The crowds are amazed, and Matthew uses biblical language ("We never saw the like in Israel!") to express the uniqueness of these events (probably all the miracles). But the Pharisees attribute Jesus' power to demonic spirits (9:34).

We can see three distinct responses to Jesus in these miracle passages. Some are awakened to faith and thus begin to share in the messianic blessings. Others, amazed at his power and authority, remain open to the person and ministry of Jesus. But the third bluntly reject him. This group is careful, even meticulous, in keeping the Law. Yet they refuse to recognize the ministry of Jesus. (He eats with sinners! He is in league with demons!) It is clear from our composition-critical study of chapters 8-9 that Matthew wrote not just to preserve the history of Jesus but to invite his readers to enter that first group, that believing in Jesus as the Messiah of God's powerful deeds they might receive his many blessings. Matthew presents, through the accounts of the earthly ministry of Jesus, a picture of the glorious Risen Christ, Lord of his Church.

The relationship between Jesus and those who need his help (quite different in Mark) is very much like that of believers to their Lord. Their continued cry is the believing prayer, "Lord, save us!" or "Lord, have mercy!" The

miracles of Jesus do not create faith. (Neither the crowds nor the scribes and Pharisees become believers.) They presuppose faith. Confident trust in Jesus' power and mercy is the almost indispensible condition for receiving his saving power. We see clearly that Matthew is a Gospel for the Church. True, there is the hope in every line that his fellow-Jews will come to faith in their Messiah. But Matthew's more immediate catechetical purpose is to stimulate the members of his church to a more mature faith. In 9:35 Matthew concludes the section which he began in 4:23-25. Having challenged the disciples to a more faithful obedience to the will of God (5-7) and to a deeper faith in his power at work in Jesus (8-9) Matthew will now teach us (chapter 10) that Jesus sent out the disciples to heal and to preach just as he did.

B. The Second Discourse: Missionary Instructions for the Apostles, 9:35-11:1

OVERVIEW: The historical background is essential for the understanding of this second discourse of Jesus. During the 80's both Judaism and the early Church were facing historical crises. Since the temple was destroyed (70 A.D.), the Pharisees have been striving to preserve the religious identity of Judaism by rebuilding that identity around the Law (Torah). The young Jewish-Christian community was also struggling to define its own identity. Both communities were claiming to be the true Israel.

Since Matthew wrote to proclaim Jesus and the meaning of his teaching for the community of believers living in the 80's, we can expect to find the same kind of process in chapter 10 that we found in chapters 5-7, the Sermon on the Mount. Matthew draws material both from Q and from Mark. Then Matthew structures these materials in such a way that the words of Jesus will encourage the storm-tossed church of his own day.

1. Introduction to the Apostolic Discourse, 9:35-10:4

Matthew summarizes the ministry of Jesus in 9:35. The compassionate concern of Jesus for the crowds and for the sick foreshadows Jesus' commissioning of the twelve apostles so that they too will heal the suffering and guide the leaderless people of Israel. In words that parallel those of the prophet Jeremiah,

Lost sheep, such were my people; their shepherds led them astray, left them wandering..., forgetful of their fold (Jer 50:6),

Matthew depicts Jesus with "heart filled with pity for them, because they were worried and helpless, like sheep without a shepherd" (9:36). For this reason, Jesus asks his disciples to pray to the Father, "the owner of the harvest," so that "he will send out workers to gather in his harvest (9:38)."

Notice three Matthean themes in the summary statement of 9:35-38. The relationship of Jesus with his Father is the first theme. The harvest (the worried and leaderless crowds) belongs not to Jesus but to his Father, "the owner of the harvest." Jesus has come to serve his Father by gathering in "his harvest." Jesus will soon hand on to his disciples the same mission.

Secondly, there is the theme portraying Jesus and his disciples as the true shepherds of Israel sent to gather the scattered flock of God's chosen people. Six centuries before, the prophet Ezekiel had spoken these words to the leaders of Israel:

"Mortal man," he said, "denounce the rulers of Israel. Prophesy to them, and tell them what I, the Sovereign Lord, say to them: You are doomed, you shepherds of Israel! You take care of yourselves but never tend the sheep.... You have not taken care of the weak ones, healed the ones that are sick, bandaged the ones that are hurt, brought back the ones that wandered off, or looked for the ones that were lost (Ezek 34:2-4)."

It is likely that Matthew has this passage in mind as he emphasizes over and over again the caring and healing ministry of Jesus. Matthew also alludes to the divinity of Jesus by portraying him as the one ultimately concerned for the sheep of Israel. The passage from Ezekiel continues:

> *"I, the Sovereign Lord, tell you that I myself will look for my sheep and take care of them in the same way as a shepherd takes care of his sheep that were scattered and are brought back together again....I will look for those that are lost, bring back those that wander off, bandage those that are hurt, and heal those that are sick; but those that are fat and strong I will destroy, because I am a shepherd who does what is right (Ezekiel 34:11-16)."*

Jesus is Lord (8:25). He will soon entrust his disciples with the mission of healing and leading, thereby giving to his disciples a share in his own power (authority).

Thirdly, there is the theme of judgment. It is implicit in the allusion to Ezekiel. Following the Lord's word that he will destroy the sheep that are fat and strong is this judgment scene:

"Now then, my flock, I the Sovereign Lord, tell you that I will judge each of you and separate the good from the bad, the sheep from the goats (Ezekiel 34:17)."

The harvest also is a symbol of judgment and the end of time. Insofar as the harvest is viewed as a "gathering in," it is indicative of the redemptive aspects of judgment. Insofar as the harvest is seen as a separating process (wheat from chaff, sheep from goats), it is an indication of the destructive aspect of judgment: "those that are fat and strong I will destroy. . . . (Ezekiel 34:16)."

Note that Jesus states that the harvest is "large" (9:34). According to these words of Jesus, there will be a great number of people gathered into the Kingdom in the final days. Yet we read earlier, "The gate is narrow and the way is hard that leads to life, and few people find it (7:14)." This paradox of the few and the many we will find all through the Gospel. Perhaps the contrasting views of the numbers of the saved are a way that Matthew reminds his readers that a person's ultimate salvation is never guaranteed. Merely belonging to the Church, merely recognizing Jesus as Lord is not enough (see 7:21-23). Salvation is basically the process of living out the teaching of Jesus "until the end" (see 10:22 and 24:13).

The works that Jesus had done he now commissions his disciples to do:

"He called his twelve disciples together and gave them authority to drive out the evil spirits and to heal every disease and every sickness. These are the names of the twelve apostles. . . . (10:1-2)."

The word "authority" is underlined to single out an important point. Recall that Matthew ended the first discourse of Jesus with these words:

> *"Jesus finished saying these things, and the crowd*
> *was amazed at the way he taught. He wasn't like*
> *their teachers of the Law; instead, he taught with*
> <u>*authority*</u> *(7:28-29)."*

As Matthew develops the gospel, the authority of Jesus becomes a central issue. Authority stands for the source of one's power. Again and again Matthew will attest that the authority of Jesus comes to him from his Father. Now, in the commissioning, Jesus gives his disciples a share in his authority (power) to exorcise, to heal (10:1) and to preach the Kingdom of God (10:7).

The number of the apostles is significant. The evangelists are more concerned with the symbolic function of twelve disciples than with the twelve individuals who were the disciples. The reason for this is that the twelve disciples represent the twelve tribes of Israel. Thus the Jewish Christians saw in the twelve disciples the renewal and continuation of the true Israel. Since the symbolic function of the twelve was of greater importance, much about the individual histories of the twelve has been forgotten. However, it is interesting to note that the early community deemed it important to pass on the memory that one member of Jesus' band was once a tax collector (10:3) and another was once a "Patriot" (10:4), i.e., a zealot, a person dedicated to the overthrow of the Roman rule. This reminds us that Jesus was able to bring together in one unity of purpose people of extremely different political positions. The former collaborator walks at the side of the political extremist, because together they follow Jesus.

2. *The Missionary Instructions of Jesus in Their Original*
   Context, 10:5-15

The instruction of Jesus begins by setting the boundaries for the ministry of the twelve: Israel alone. The restricting of their ministry to the "lost sheep of the people of Israel (10:6)," tells us that during his life-time, Jesus preached and ministered only to the Jewish people (see 15:24). Only afterwards did his followers come to understand that God wanted the Gentile peoples to share in the Good News of Jesus.

Among the instructions of Jesus, we find the admonition to travel light (10:9-10) as befits a disciple of the Son of Man having "no place to lie down and rest (8:20)." Lack of travelling expenses are no obstacle in sharing the good news they have received (10:9). They are to rely completely on God. For this reason they need not even make such preparations for the journey as the securing of an extra shirt, shoes or walking stick. Their Father will provide for them and their needs (10:10). Trust him.

The characteristics of the disciple described in the Sermon on the Mount manifest themselves again: obedience and dependence on God. There is an urgency in the instructions of Jesus: begin now! They are sent out without even the most basic requirements for a journey: money, food, walking stick, shoes. They are lacking even in a more important area: they have not received the fullness of teaching or of faith! Yet they are commissioned to go as they are, with the knowledge and faith they have. No matter what their other deficiences may be, if they have trust in their Father, they can begin.

The eleven verses of 10:5-15 capture much of the flavor of the ministry of Jesus in the years 28-30 A.D. We can see Jesus as an itinerant preacher, moving from one place to another, proclaiming the Father's will to all who would listen. Jesus preached in the prophetic style, challenging people to reform their lives in view of both the compassionate love of God and the coming of his Kingdom. Jesus proclaimed a view of God and his Law that invited all his people, the poor and the well-to-do, to know God as their loving Father.

For that reason he tells his disciples that upon entering a town they are to look for someone "who is willing to welcome you. . . ." Upon entering a home, the disciples are to pronounce a prophetic blessing, "Peace be with you (10:12)." Keep in mind that this blessing is much more than a mere wishing or hoping for peace to come to the people living in the house. In the context of the Semitic understanding, the prophetic word carries within itself the power to achieve what it says. Once the world is spoken, it has a reality, a dynamism of its own. That is why Jesus says,

> If the people in that house welcome you, let your greeting of peace remain, but if they do not welcome you, then take back your greeting (10:13).

The prophet has power over the word's existence. He can send it out and call it back; he can give it and he can take it away.

Matthew wants his readers to take nothing for granted. While it is true that Jesus comes to bring peace to the world, such peace can exist only on one condition: its free acceptance by the person invited to enter into God's Kingdom. If the people do not welcome and listen to the disciples, they must move on down the road, shaking the dust from their feet as the pious Jew would shake the dust of Gentile countyside from his feet upon returning to the soil of Israel (10:14). However, in the wake of such rejection, judgment:

> Remember this! On the Judgment Day God will show more mercy to the people of Sodom and

Gomorrah than to the people of that town! (10:15)"

3. The Instructions of Jesus as Expanded by Matthew To Meet the Needs of His Church, 10:16-42

The key to grasping Matthew's teaching in this section is the word of Jesus:

> *"No pupil is greater than his teacher; no slave is greater than his master. So a pupil should be satisfied to become like his teacher and a slave like his master. If the head of the family is called Beelzebul, the members of the family will be called by even worse names (10:24-25)."*

All the disciples of Jesus, whether they are one of the original twelve or one of Matthew's community living some 50 years later, have the same mission and identity. As Jesus was born of the family of David, they are born of the family of Jesus. As Jesus healed the sick, exorcised demons, and preached the Kingdom, they are called to heal, exorcise and proclaim the Kingdom of God. As Jesus was arrested, brought to the court of Pilate, whipped and persecuted they will be treated in the same way:

> *There will be men who will arrest you and take you to court, and they will whip you in their synagogues (10:17).*

The consolation of the disciples will be that of knowing that their Master has pioneered the path before them.

Matthew has taken the words of Jesus, perhaps first spoken in a teaching regarding the end of time (see Mk 13:9-13 and Mt 24:9,13), and has adapted them to the situation of his church. We catch a glimpse of the persecution which the Jewish Christians were suffering at the hands of their Jewish brethren. The Jews who had followed Christ had come to be regarded as heretics by the Pharisees. Accordingly, the guardians of establishment Judaism were subjecting the Jewish Christians to harassment, beatings and arrest by civil authorities. In spite of all this, Matthew tells his Christian brothers and sisters to remain steadfast in their faith. Do not worry, Matthew told them, about your defense in court:

> ...when the time comes, you will be given what you will say. For the words you speak...will come from the Spirit of your Father speaking in you (10:20).

As the source of Jesus' authority was and is the Father, so too the source of the disciple's power is and will be the Father's Spirit speaking through the disciple.

Some scholars see in the phrase, "they will whip you in *their* synagogues (10:17)," as indication that the break between Judaism and the young community of Jewish Christians has already taken place. However, other sections of this gospel demonstrate Matthew's concern to show that the Church and his beloved Judaism can coexist in peace (see 5:17; 13:24-30; 22:34-40 and 23:1-3).

Note also the growth of missionary consciousness that has taken place during the fifty years between the original instructions given by Jesus and the expanded instructions for the church in Matthew's day. Although Jesus first came for the Jews, "Do not go to any Gentile territory....Go instead to the lost sheep of the people of Israel (10:5-6)," the decades that followed saw the Good News being brought to "rulers and kings...and to the Gentiles (10:18)."

a. The disciple speaks for Jesus, 10:26-33.

Again in this section Matthew draws together sayings of Jesus and combines them into an expression of the Lord's expectation for his disciples. Even in the midst of

persecution, Jesus tells them that they are to proclaim fearlessly the Good News:

> *Do not be afraid of men.... Whatever is covered up will be uncovered.... What I am telling you in the dark you must repeat in broad daylight, and what you have heard in private you must tell from the housetops (10:26-27).*

No matter how bad things are, the disciple of Jesus is called to be a missionary, a witness to Jesus and his teachings. The insight into the mysteries of the Kingdom of heaven, at first given quietly, must be lived publicly. The disciple is to proclaim from the housetop (the traditional place from which public announcements were made) the Good News they have received from Jesus (10:27). No

doubt the believers of Matthew's community were tempted to keep a low profile, but such behavior would be
unfitting for believers who were called to be both the salt
of the earth and the light of the world (5:13-15). Salt that
had lost its flavor would be "cast out" (an image of judgment). The disciple's light (his witness to the teachings of
Jesus regarding love, mercy and forgiveness) had to have
a certain visibility if they were to lead others to praise the
Father (5:16).

The great paradox of the gospel of Jesus is once again
clearly seen in 10:26-39. At first there seems to be an un-
derlying contradiction. On the other hand we are told to
fear God who can destroy both body and soul in hell
(10:28). How are we to image God? Is he like an easy and
over-generous father? Is he like a stern and exacting
judge, sentencing people to reward or punishment on the
strict basis of what they have done or not done?

On a popular level, Christians down through the ages
have tended to choose one view of God or the other.
However, if we are to follow Matthew, both the love and
the judgment of God must be held together in tension.
The Father is both loving and just. Eternal life is promised
to those who do his will, but the end result of the refusal
to repent is eternal damnation. In Matthew's proclamation of the gospel neither Jesus nor the Father is reduced
to a wishy-washy figure who sentimentally changes his
mind in the end in order to allow everybody into the
marriage banquet of his Kingdom. Eternal loss is a possibility for all, Gentile, Jew or Christian.

Nevertheless, the caring love of the Father predomi-
nates even in the consistency of his justice. The one who
has power over both our body and our soul is none other
than our Father whose solicitude Jesus portrayed in the
Sermon on the Mount (6:35-34). If he so cares for the lilies
of the field and the sparrows of the air, how much more

does our Father care for us (10:28-31)!

At first, the words, "Do not be afraid of those who kill the body but cannot kill the soul; rather be afraid of God, who can destroy both body and soul in hell (10:28)," seem to be a threat. However, in the context of the heritage of the great prophets of Israel, these words are seen for what they are: words of encouragement. Three times in these six verses Jesus tells his disciples not to fear (10:26, 28, 31). These words occur within the overall context Jesus' commissioning of the disciples to speak in his name. It seems that Jesus has in mind a moment many centuries earlier in which the one chosen to be the Lord's spokesman first hesitated and then received encouragement for his mission:

> I answered, "Sovereign Lord, I don't know how to speak; I am too young."
>
> But the Lord said to me, "Do not say that you are too young, but go to the people I send you to, and tell them everything I command you to say. Do not be afraid of them, for I will be with you to protect you. I, the Lord, have spoken! (Jer 1:7-8)"

Being afraid of God in this prophetic context is not on the same level as the fear of men; it is the virtue of fear of the Lord (see Is 11:2), another name for piety or reverence for God. Piety enables the disciple to place his trust in God and his deliverance. Piety enables the disciple to follow in the footsteps of Jeremiah and the other prophets.

But this is not to be a reckless heroism. While the disciple is to bear witness to Jesus in spite of physical danger, the disciple is also counseled to be "as cautious as snakes and as gentle as doves (10:16)." Prudence is as necessary as gentleness in the service of others. The basic meaning of the word "martyr" is to witness, to give testimony of one's commitment by the way one lives. The words of Jesus, "when they persecute you in one town, run away to another one (10:23)," counsel prudence not cowardice. In the earliest decades of the Church such flight from persecution helped to spread the Good News from city to city.

In the verses that follow the promise of the Father's protection (10:28-31), we can see a fourfold warning. Each warning dramatizes the painful choice that must be made when circumstances are extreme:

> . . . *whoever denies publicly that he belongs to me, then I will deny him before my Father in heaven (10:33).*

> *Whoever loves his father or mother more than me is not worthy of me...(10:37).*

> *Whoever does not take up his cross and follow in my steps is not worthy of me (10:38).*

> *Whoever tries to gain his own life will lose it...(10:39).*

Because these warnings can strike us as harsh and vindictive, we may find ourselves exclaiming, "This is not encouragement; it's extortion!" But to say this is to miss the point. Matthew's church lived at the extreme boundaries of life, both physical and spiritual. The members of that community had to make radical choices in the context of life and death situations. To accept Jesus and to receive his teaching was to make a decision to accept the Kingdom of Heaven and eternal life. To reject Jesus was to refuse God's Kingdom. The stakes involved in remaining faithful to Jesus and the Church were eternal life or eternal death.

In such an intense situation, extreme choices had to be made: acknowledgement or denial of Jesus (10:32); one's family or Jesus (10:37); avoidance of suffering or Jesus (10:38); preservation/loss of one's earthly life or losing/gaining life in Jesus (10:39). It is clear that Jesus made radical demands on his disciples. Matthew collects those sayings of Jesus that called for crisis-type decisions and places them here in the missionary discourse. As the members of Matthew's community find themselves walking on the knife-edge of bodily and spiritual survival, the words of Jesus challenge them to make the same kind of radical decision that Jesus asked of his first disciples (see 4:18-22). In the 80's as well as in the years of Jesus' ministry, there was only one valid choice for the believer: Jesus of Nazareth (2:23), the Son who pleases his Father (3:17), the Lord who saves (8:25).

To deny Jesus, either by refusing to live out his teachings (see 7:21-23) or by public denial under threat of persecution (10:32), is to earn denial by Jesus before his Father. It is important to see 10:32-33 in the context of the rest of the Gospel. Even apostasy, the denial of Jesus before men, will be forgiven if it is followed by repentance. Peter's triple denial of Jesus is a prime example (see 26:69-75). The disciple is one who is called to speak for Christ. But words are never enough; the words must be always accompanied by deeds of forgiveness, mercy, love and, at times, suffering.

b. The disciple suffers with Jesus, 10:34-39

The words of Jesus, "...I did not come to bring peace, but a sword (10:34)," represent another paradox. Jesus did come to bring peace (1:22; 10:12-13). He is the Messiah, the Prince-of-Peace (see Is 9:5-7). However, by the second half of the first century Jesus has become a sword dividing family members from one another. Eight hundred years

before, the prophet Micah, commenting upon the loss of
Israel's true values, had said:

> In these times sons treat their fathers like fools,
> daughters oppose their mothers, and young women
> quarrel with their mothers-in-law; a man's enemies
> are the members of his own family (Mi 7:6).

Jesus cited these lines, declaring that it is he himself who
has come to set sons against fathers, daughters against
mothers (10:35).

Reading between the lines, we can see the terrible pressure being exerted against the Jewish Christians. They
were subject to beatings and trials (10:17). Now we see the
members of their families turning against them (10:34-35).
It is likely that Jewish Christian members of families felt
the weight of the "ban," i.e., excommunication from the
synagogue for various lengths of time. Thus, the Jewish
Christians experienced various stages of being rejected
and disowned by their families. It must have brought
tears to all concerned, especially in the light of the central
importance of Jewish family life. A glimpse of this is seen
in Tevye's response to his daughter's marriage to a Christian husband in the play, THE FIDDLER ON THE ROOF:
"I can bend, but I cannot break. She is no longer my
daughter!"

Note that Matthew places his first mention of the cross
(10:38) in the context of the suffering involved in leaving
family to follow Jesus. As Jesus suffered the cross, so too
does the disciple who suffers with Christ. The pupil becomes like his teacher, the slave like his master (10:25).

Matthew's sensitivity to the feelings of those Jewish
Christians banished by their families may be seen in his
rephrasing of the radical saying of Jesus in 10:37. Most
scholars consider that Luke 14:26 is closer to the original

saying of Jesus: "If anyone comes to me without turning his back on his father and mother,...he cannot be my follower (*New American Bible*)." Matthew softened the wording, "Whoever loves his father or mother more than me is not worthy of me" (10:37). But the meaning remains the same: in the situation where one must choose between Jesus and family, Jesus is salvation.

Once again Matthew brings us face to face with the paradox of the Gospel. Even in the loss of family relationships and family identity there is the promise of resurrection:

> "Whoever...loses his life for my sake will gain it (10:39)."

The taking up of the cross (10:38) is the prelude to risen life (10:39). Notice the parallel in the ninth beatitude:

> "Happy are you when men insult you and persecute you...because you are my followers. Be glad and happy because a great reward is kept for you in heaven (5:11-12)."

This is the same paradox we will soon find in the parables of the Kingdom contained in the third discourse of Jesus (chapter 13). There the disciple is encouraged to sell all he owns in order to purchase the precious treasure of the Kingdom (see 13:44-46).

c. The disciple is received as Jesus, 10:40-42

The missionary discourse began as Jesus called his disciples together and sent them out with his authority. Now the discourse ends with Jesus' words of encouragement for those who receive the disciples sent out in his name.

In verse 40 a double identification is made. First, the disciple is identified with Jesus: "Whoever welcomes you, welcomes me"; secondly, Jesus is identified with his Father: "whoever welcomes me, welcomes the one who sent me (10:40)." The Father extends himself through his Son, Jesus. The Son extends himself to others through his disciples. In this way, Matthew shifts his focus to those who receive the disciples, who are the workers sent by the Father to gather in his harvest (9:38). Those who welcome God's messengers, even if it be the mere giving of "a drink of cold water to one of the least of my followers (10:42)," will share in the reward of those messengers (10:41).

We see in the wording of 10:42 a direct reference to the final judgment scene at the conclusion of the fifth and last discourse of Jesus:

> *You that are blessed by my Father: come! Come and receive the kingdom....I was...thirsty and you gave me drink....I tell you, indeed, whenever you did this for one of the least important of these brothers of mine, you did it for me (25:34-40)!*

Matthew's concluding formula signals the end of Jesus' second discourse:

> *When Jesus finished giving these instructions to his twelve disciples, he left that place . . . (11:1).*

Week Five

In his first ten chapters Matthew has laid the foundations for his account of the Gospel. Following the prologue of the infancy narrative and the introductory passages about the early events in his ministry, Matthew presents Jesus of Nazareth as the Messiah of the Word (chapters 5-7), the Messiah of Mighty Deeds (chapters 8-9), and the Master who commissions his disciples to continue his ministry (chapter 10).

During this week we will study three pivotal chapters of the Gospel. Incomprehensible as it must have seemed to the disciples, Israel does not receive Jesus with open arms. In chapters 11 and 12 Matthew details the growing opposition to Jesus' teachings and ministry. Throughout the rest of the Gospel Matthew will be dealing with the tension between unfaithful Israel and the true Israel which continues in the followers of Jesus.

As always, Matthew writes of past history from the perspective of his own situation. This is particularly evident in the third major sermon of the Gospel (chapter 13). Here Matthew brings together the parables of Jesus, especially those which illumine the mystery of the Kingdom of heaven. Jesus had come and had inaugurated the Kingdom. Why then was it not flourishing? Why was its growth so slow? With his catechetical genius, Matthew applies the teaching of Jesus to these agonizing questions. He helps us to see that the Kingdom is indeed a mystery. Responding to Jesus remains a mystery of God's grace. Although we can't always see it clearly, God is bringing his plan to fulfillment.

The deeds and teachings of Our Lord have much to say to our own situation. You might explore with your group the ways in which these passages speak to you as a diocese.

Daily Study Assignment: Week Five

Day	Matthew	Commentary
1	11:2-30	Pages 131-138
2	12:1-21	Pages 138-142
3	12:22-50	Pages 142-147
4	13:1-35	Pages 147-155
5	13:36-52	Pages 155-159

6—Reflect on Chapters 11 through 13 in light of the reflection questions listed below.

7—STUDY GROUP MEETING

- In 11:4-5 Jesus describes his ministry. In what ways do the powerful deeds of his ministry continue in our personal and parochial lives?

- Our culture glorifies self-reliance and independence. In 11:25-30 Jesus praises the unlearned and offers support to the tired and the burdened. What significance does this teaching have for us? How can the yoke of the Lord be light and easy to carry?

- We have a basic tendency to prefer religious duties to the more difficult demands of concretely loving others; sometimes we allow religious considerations to shield us from the ministry of compassion. How does Jesus' teaching in 12:1-14 apply to our own behavior?

- Which of the parables in chapter 13 is most meaningful to you? Why?

- Which situation of seed and soil in 13:18-23 best expresses your own response to Jesus' message about the Kingdom of God?

- For what treasure would you (literally) sell all you own, as did the protagonists of 13:44-46?

The Mystery of the Kingdom of Heaven, 11:2-13:52

OVERVIEW: ·The narrative section (chapters 11-12) sketches the growing opposition to Jesus and thereby prepares us for the third major discourse of Jesus in chapter 13. In this parable-discourse Jesus turns away from the people, depicted by Matthew as unfaithful Israel, and begins to concentrate on instructing the disciples. Thus the disciples symbolize the faithful remnant of God's people.

The narrative-discourse material in chapters 11-13 constitutes the turning point of Matthew's book. Whereas chapters 1 through 10 concentrated on the identity of Jesus as the long-awaited Messiah, chapters 11 through 28 deal with the refusal of unfaithful Israel and the acceptance and proclamation of Jesus by true Israel, the disciples and their successors.

One of our goals in this diocesan study of Matthew is to bring an end to the inadequate image of Judaism which continues to exist in the Church. It would be accurate to say that important dimensions of this negative image have arisen from Matthew's contrast of true Israel with pseudo-Israel. Over the centuries Christians have read this Gospel without an accurate understanding of the context in which it was written. Particularly in studying the remaining chapters of Matthew's account we should keep in mind these points:

1. When Matthew wrote, there was only the religion of Judaism. While the Church existed as the community of those who followed Jesus, Christianity as a religion was not yet definable. For this reason, those Jews who followed Jesus found themselves opposing and being opposed by those Jews led by the Pharisees.

2. Since both groups of Jews were battling for the one identity of being God's chosen people, i.e., the true Israel, the issues that faced both groups in the 80's could only be resolved by arguing that one group was faithful and the other unfaithful to God. Most of us are familiar only with the line of argumentation in the Christian Scriptures. We also know something of its application by secular rulers to the Jewish people through more than fifteen centuries of European history. If we are sensitive to the teaching of Jesus regarding love of others, we, many of whom are descendants of European ancestors, have the opportunity to set a new attitude in conformity with the mind of Jesus. Instead of seeing Jewish perfidy in their non-acceptance of Jesus, we need to acknowledge the mystery of God's election. In fact, it is correct to say that the Jewish people have been faithful to the God of Abraham, Isaac and Jacob down through thousands of years, often persecuted years, of history.

3. Such a view of Judaism's fidelity to the God of Abraham, Isaac and Jacob, "the God of the living, not of the dead (22:32)," is in complete conformity with the teaching of Vatican II's DECREE ON THE RELATIONSHIP OF CHRISTIANITY WITH THE NON-CHRISTIAN RELIGIONS. In this teaching the Catholic Church recognizes that God has manifested himself in different ways to different peoples. Judaism is a valid religion in its own right. In the working out of God's mysterious providence we might say that the problem of identity disputed by both Matthew's community and the community led by the Pharisees has been resolved. The Church, rooted in Judaism, has become a religion with its own unique identity: Christianity. Judaism remains Judaism. The whole matter is circumscribed by the mystery of God's providential will.

In the final analysis, we cannot judge those Jews who

lived during the time of Jesus and did not accept him. However, we can say something about the norm of judgment. To the extent that their sin led them to reject Jesus, to that same extent they were liable to God's judgment. It is the same for Christians, past and present: to the extent that we reject Jesus by our sin, we are also under God's judgment.

A. Narrative Section, 11:2-12:50

1. *John's Question and Rejection by the People, 11:2-24*

a. The significance of John the Baptist, 11:2-19

The imprisoned John sends his disciples to ask Jesus, "Are you the one John said was going to come (11:3)," the expected Messiah? Did John have second thoughts about Jesus? Perhaps this question reflects the difference between Jesus in his ministry and the rather harsh expectation of the Messiah of Judgment John had preached:

> *The ax is ready...; every tree that does not bear good fruit will be cut down...I baptize you with water...; but the one who will come after me will baptize you with the Holy Spirit and fire...He has his winnowing shovel with him...; he will gather his wheat into his barn, but burn the chaff in a fire that never goes out (3:10-12).*

Jesus did have tough words for those satisfied with the status-quo, for those who have made themselves the norm for justice (the self-righteous), but he was unexpectedly compassionate and merciful towards those whom society often judged to be worthless sinners.

In answering the disciples of the baptizer, Jesus cites the prophet Isaiah. (See Is 26:19; 29:18; 35:5-6; and 61:1.) Not only has Jesus done the messianic deeds described by Isaiah, but he has also done more than Israel had hoped for: "the lepers are made clean...; the dead are raised to life (11:5)." Verses 4-5 thus summarize in a beautiful way the ministry of Jesus. (See 4:23 and 9:35.)

The words of Jesus, "How happy is he who has no doubts about me (11:6)," are words of encouragement for both the disciples of John and for the Church of Matthew's day. Those who do not lose faith in Jesus, those who are not "scandalized," that is, led away from believing in Jesus, will have joy in life. This pronouncement of happiness links us with the beatitudes, i.e., the characteristics of the disciple which Matthew placed in the introduction to the Sermon on the Mount (5:3-11). Recall also the strengthening words of Jesus addressed to the Church of the eighties: "...whoever loses his life for my sake, will gain it (10:39)."

Jesus turns to the crowd and questions them regarding their expectations of John the Baptist (11:7-9). All agree that John is a prophet (a rare event at that time—for centuries Yahweh had not spoken through prophets). Then Jesus declares that Malachi was speaking of John the Baptist in the prophecy that God would send his messenger to prepare a way for the Messiah. According to Malachi 3:23, the messenger preparing the way for God would be Elijah. Therefore, in the logic of faith, John the Baptist is Elijah (11:14).

Nevertheless, the new age to be introduced by Jesus is to be so extraordinary that John the Baptist himself, although he is "greater than any man who has ever lived," is subordinate to the "least in the Kingdom of heaven (11:11)."

The verse regarding the Kingdom of heaven and violence (11:12) is one of the most difficult verses in Matthew. There are many interpretations, none of them fully satisfactory. It is clear that the violent attacks come from the enemies of the Kingdom and make it difficult for others to enter.

The whole of Israel's history of salvation is summed up: "All the prophets and the Law of Moses, until the time of John, spoke about the Kingdom (11:13)." Both the Law and the Prophets, Israel's means of knowing the will of God, have been preparing his people for this ultimate revelation of his reign/rule/Kingdom now taking place in, with, and through Jesus.

However, the initial response to Jesus (4:23-25) is fading. Jesus' comparison of his people with the children in the

market place (11:16-19) is the first indication that Matthew gives of widespread non-acceptance of the teaching of Jesus. The people, seeing the ascetic John fasting in the desert, pronounced him crazy, possessed by a demon (11:18). Jesus, sharing ordinary food and drink with the socially unacceptable people of his day, is ridiculed for being "a glutton and wine-drinker, a friend of tax collectors and outcasts! (11:19)." God's Word comes to the people in John and Jesus, but they refuse to hear either of them.

b. Judgment on the people living near the Sea of Galilee, 11:20-24

Jesus singles out three lake towns whose inhabitants

have marked themselves for judgment by refusing to repent of their sins. Recall the summary of Jesus' message: "Turn away from your sins, the Kingdom of heaven is near! (4:17)." As we saw in chapters eight and nine, the miracles performed by Jesus are signs of the power of the in-breaking Kingdom of God. By undoing all the effects of sin, i.e., separation from God, alienation from each other, illness, possession, the destructive force of nature, and death itself, the miracles proclaim that Satan's hold on the world is coming to an end. By contrasting the response of the three lake towns with the hypothetical response of Tyre and Sidon, Jesus declares that Chorazin, Bethsaida and Capernaum have brought judgment upon themselves by their refusal to repent.

2. *The Father, the Source of Jesus' Authority for Interpeting the Law, 11:25-27*

These verses come from the Q tradition of the sayings of Jesus. Luke places them on the lips of Jesus as the disciples return from their successful missionary journey (Lk 10:19-22). Matthew, however, uses this tradition to show that it is Jesus and Jesus alone who is the authoritative interpreter of God's will. The authority of Jesus is a central theme in Matthew's work:

> *Jesus finished saying these things, and the crowd was amazed at the way he taught. He wasn't like their teachers of the Law; instead, he taught with authority (7:28-29).*

In 11:25-37 Matthew tells us where that special authority comes from:

> *My Father has given me all things. No one knows the*

> *Son except the Father, and no one knows the Father*
> *except the Son, and those to whom the Son wants to*
> *reveal him (11:27).*

Notice how Matthew's "Christology" helps us to understand his message. Since Jesus is God's Son, he is the one who completely knows the Father. Therefore, he is the only one who can truly and authoritatively interpet God's will. Jesus comes as the divine teacher, the proclaimer of God's will: "This is how you should pray: Our Father,...may your Kingdom come; may your will be done on earth as it is in heaven (6:9-10)." According to Matthew, to become a citizen of that Kingdom, one must accept the teaching of Jesus and become his disciple. Since Jesus is the culmination of the Law and the prophets (5:17), he has no need to cite either the traditions of the ancients or the opinions of the Pharisees. Because Jesus is the Father's divine Son, Jesus is greater in authority than all the institutions of Judaism.

The three verses, 11:25-27, connect the previous section, recounting the increasing rejection of his teaching and his miracles, with the coming clash between Jesus and the Pharisees over the interpretation of the Law (11:28-12:21). The unbelief of the lake towns and of those learned in the interpretation of the Law contrasts sharply with the accepting openness of the unlearned (11:25). In chapter two we have seen a paradox similar to this one. Although the chief priests and the teachers of the Law, people privileged and learned, knew from the Scriptures where the Messiah was to be born (2:4-6), they did not care. But the pagan magi with only nature's star to guide them, searched until they found the child born to be king of the Jews (2:2, 9-11).

Humility, gentleness, and thorough-going dependence upon the Father are essential virtues for those who have received the "knowledge of the secrets of the Kingdom of heaven (13:11)." The self-reliant attitude of the wise and well-to-do prevented them from accepting the fullness of God's revelation.

An incident recorded in John clarifies Mt 11:25. Some Pharisees sent the temple guards to arrest Jesus. They came back without Jesus and explained, "Nobody has ever talked the way this man does! (Jn 7:46)." The response of the Pharisees indicates their disdain for the unlearned, the people of the land:

> "Did he fool you too?" the Pharisees asked them. "Have you ever known one of the authorities or one Pharisee to believe in him? This crowd does not know the Law of Moses, so they are under God's curse (Jn 7:47-49)."

Yet it is to the unlearned and the poor that the Father revealed his Son. For such as these Jesus prays in thanksgiving to this Father (11:25-26).

3. Jesus' Interpretation of the Law 11:28-30

"Come to me, all of you who are tired from carrying your heavy loads, and I will give you rest (11:28)." Judging from the context of the entire Gospel, this invitation seems to be addressed to those carrying the burden of poverty as well as those burdened down by legalism. First, consider those who are literally poor. They are the ones who find themselves the most burdened down by life, often working out a mere existence on the very edge of physical survival. Psalm 72 contains this portrait of the messianic ruler. The psalmist prays:

> He rescues the poor who call to him, and those who are needy and neglected. He has pity on the weak and

poor; he saves the lives of those in need (Ps 72:12-13).

Jesus had stressed his commitment to the poor throughout his ministry. His concluding words in his answer to the disciples of John the Baptist were: "...and the Good News is preached to the poor (11:5)." In the Sermon on the Mount, he declared happy are those who are poor in spirit (5:3). Jesus himself lived the life-style of the poorest: "Foxes have holes,...but the Son of Man has no place to lie down and rest (8:20)." To the poor Jesus brought a new dignity, the identity of being children of their Father who

loves them infinitely more than he loves the birds of the air and the lilies of the field (6:25-34). Whereas the well-to-do tended to regard the impoverished, the handicapped, and the uneducated as somehow having brought that condition upon themselves, "...whose sin was it that caused him to be born blind? His own or his parents' sin? (Jn 9:2)," Jesus invited such as these to find new strength and fresh purpose in himself (11:29).

The second group of the tired and weary are those burdened down by legalistic interpretations of the Torah. When Jesus invites others to take his yoke upon them, he is referring to the metaphor, "the yoke of the Law," an expression current in first century Israel. His yoke contrasts sharply with the yoke imposed by some of the Pharisees:

> *They fix up heavy loads and tie them on men's backs, yet they aren't willing even to lift a finger to help them carry those loads (23:4).*

Jesus invited people to follow him and his interpretation of the Torah. It is, he promises, an easy yoke and a light load (11:30). Once again we find the paradox of the Gospel: Jesus makes the most radical demands upon his followers. They must be ready to leave their professions, lose their families and even their lives for his sake (see 4:18-22; 8:20-22; 10:28-29). Nevertheless, the yoke of Jesus is liberating and spiritually enriching. His demand for total commitment opens up to each person the opportunity to go beyond superficial living. Jesus asks his followers to accept and to live out an interpretation of God's will that reaches down into the depths of their being. Jesus' interpretation of the Law claims the person totally—one's thoughts, desires and attitudes (see the antitheses, 5:21-48). Yet it is the acceptance of Jesus and of his interpretation of God's will that enables the believer to experience the fullest development of his or her potential as a human being. Such a person is pronounced "happy" by Jesus (see 5:3-12).

4. Dispute over the Interpretation of the Sabbath Law, 12:1-14

a. Conflict over the disciples eating grain, 12:1-8.
To best understand these conflict passages, let us first glance at the wider historical context. Generations before

Jesus was born, the followers of two famous Rabbis, Shammai and Hillel, were engaged in vigorous debates regarding the interpretation of the Law. The school of Shammai wanted a strict interpretation of the various aspects of the Law. The followers of Hillel favored a more lenient perspective, making allowances and offering interpretations that met both unexpected circumstances as well as the changing needs of everyday life. Opinion was divided among the Pharisees on the question of the lawfulness of picking ears of corn to eat on the Sabbath. The strict interpreters, the school of Shammai, held this action to be contrary to the Sabbath Law. It was this group within the Pharisaic movement which reproached the disciples of Jesus: "Look, it is against our Law for you disciples to do this on the Sabbath! (12:2)."

Matthew, however, is not interested in determining which Pharisaic school would approve of the disciples eating the grain. Jesus has no need to appeal to any school of interpretation because "My Father has given me all things (11:27)." Thus, Jesus, the completion of the Law (5:17), goes to the Law (Nb 28:9-1) and offers his own authoritative interpretation: since the Law commands priests in the Temple to break the Sabbath Law by offering sacrifice on the Sabbath, they break the Law without being guilty (12:5). Jesus declares that he is greater than the Temple (12:6) and then proceeds to criticize the Pharisees for overlooking a far more important expression of God's will: "The scripture says, 'I do not want animal sacrifices, but kindness' (12:7; see Hos 6:6)."

The kindness called for in this case was consideration of the hungry disciples. By citing Hosea, Jesus declares that mercy must always govern the interpretation and application of the Law. If the Pharisees knew the meaning of Hosea 6:6, they would not "condemn people who are not guilty... (12:7)." Matthew ends this conflict story with the

Markan conclusion (Mk 2:28): ". . . the Son of Man is Lord of the Sabbath (12:8)."

b. *Dispute about the man with the crippled hand, 12:9-14.*
This incident is taken from Mark 3:1-6. While Mark

simply states that "Jesus went back to the synagogue," Matthew indicates the distance between Jesus and the Pharisees by stating he "went to one of their synagogues (Mt. 12:9)." Whereas Mark depicts Jesus asking the congregation in the synagogue the question, "What does our Law allow us to do on the Sabbath? (Mk 3:4)," Matthew shifts the initiative to those in the crowd who wanted to accuse Jesus of wrongdoing. (Healing was regarded as working, hence a strict interpretation of Ex. 28:8, the third commandment, would prohibit the action.) Jesus responds to their attempt to entrap him by asking them about the lawfulness of saving the life of a sheep on the Sabbath, another point debated by the different schools of thought among the Pharisees. (Some rabbis held the opinion that the Sabbath Law permitted the saving of the animal from suffocation.)

In this confrontation we have a glimpse of Jesus debating with the rabbis in the synagogue, a situation that probably often occurred during the days of Jesus' ministry during 28-30 A.D. Jesus cites the principle of light matter versus heavy matter. This principle enabled a rabbi to take a principle that applied in a lesser case and then apply it to a more important case. Since the Law permitted the rescue of a sheep even on the Sabbath, Jesus declared:

> *"And a man is worth much more than a sheep! So then, our Law does allow us to help someone on the Sabbath (12:12)."*

Then Jesus cured the man with the crippled hand.

Although neither Matthew, Mark nor Luke indicate it, the healing deed of Jesus would have been praised by many Pharisees of his day. Their reasoning would have been such: a man's crippled hand affected the way he lived his life. According to rabbinical opinion (traditions of the ancients), any law of the Sabbath could be put aside if a human life was at stake. In the heat of debate between Jewish Christians and the Jews led by the Pharisees, the evangelists disregarded the fact that there would have been different responses to Jesus' action. Some Pharisees were bitterly opposed to Jesus. Thus Matthew, writing from the perspective of the conflict situation, tells us that "the Pharisees left and made plans against Jesus to kill him (12:14)."

5. A Summary of the Ministry of Jesus, Mt 12:15-21

Having climaxed the increased opposition to Jesus with the plot to take his life, Matthew tells of Jesus' retreat from that place. While the Jesus of Mark's Gospel often asks those cured to keep the healing deeds secret, Matthew seldom recounts these particular requests of Jesus. However, in 12:16 Matthew does follow Mark's "Messianic secret" theme, using it to declare that the words of Isaiah are fulfilled in Jesus (see Is 42:1-4). Jesus comes to us as God's servant, quiet and compassionate, refusing to rabble rouse in the streets (12:19). Jesus is not an ostentatious wonder worker (a role rejected during the three temptations in the desert, 4:1-11). Rather he comes clothed with the Spirit to proclaim God's judgment, i.e. God's will, to all peoples, Jew and Gentile alike (12:18).

We may interpret this servant's refusal to break off the "bent reed" or to put out "the flickering lamp" (12:20) in terms of Jesus' compassionate concern for sinners and for the poor:

> *"Come to me, all of you who are tired...Take my yoke...and learn from me, because I am gentle and humble in spirit (11:28-29)."*

6. *Jesus and Beelzebul, 12:22-23*

The cure of a possessed man (12:22) becomes the occasion of deciding for or against Jesus, of making the decision to believe or reject his message about the Kingdom of

Heaven. In Matthew's Gospel, we find three types of audience listening to Jesus:

The disciples. At times "disciples" signify the twelve apostles; at other times the disciples are all those who follow Jesus, both during the period of 28-30 A.D. as well as in the period of the 80's.

The crowds. They listen to the teaching of Jesus. The crowds have different responses to Jesus in various parts of the gospel. Here, they are amazed by the curing of the possessed man: "Could he be the Son of David? (12:23)." They are depicted as open to Jesus and his teaching. This portrayal of the crowds on the verge of recognizing Jesus as the Messiah, the Son of David, may well be an indication that Matthew is writing both for those who have accepted the teaching of Jesus, as well as for those who are potential converts. However, the crowd will soon reject Jesus and his message (13:10-13). They will eventually demand his death: "The chief priests and the elders, however, had persuaded the crowd to demand the release of Barabbas and the execution of Jesus (27:20-21)."

Those who formed the leadership structure of first century Judaism. Matthew presents all forms of Jewish leadership as the opposition: Scribes, Sadducees, Pharisees, elders, and chief priests. These groups are depicted by Matthew as scandalizing the people, i.e., leading the people away from Jesus. In 12:24, in response to the wonder of the crowds regarding Jesus' healing the possessed man, the Pharisees attribute the miracle to Beelzebul, the Prince of Demons.

Matthew depicts the Pharisees as interpreting the "signs" that Jesus worked in the most distorted way. Instead of seeing the cure of the blind and deaf man as an indication of the presence of God, the Pharisees claim that the source of Jesus' power is the authority of Beelzebul, the head of Satan's Kingdom. Jesus points out that it is not Satan that brings his own kingdom to ruin but God! The long-awaited rule of God has already risen against the household of Satan (12:28). Satan is the strong man bound up now by God's power acting in Jesus, and even now Satan's possessions are being taken away (12:29)! The healing of the possessed blind and deaf man is a case in point. The person claimed by Satan is taken out of his grip and restored to the physical and spiritual wholeness characteristic of life lived under the reign of God. The Spirit of God is the active power of God working through Jesus; the cures and exorcisms Jesus performs are the signs that God is beginning to reign (12:28).

Therefore, Jesus declares, there is no neutrality about himself. One is either with him or against him (12:30). This statement introduces the difficult verses about the unforgivable sin against the Holy Spirit (12:31-32). Those who attribute Jesus' deeds to diabolical inspiration and power commit such a sin. To "say evil things against the Holy Spirit (12:31)" is to refuse to recognize the divine power by which he acts and, ultimately, to reject God's offer of his love and mercy.

7. A Tree and Its Fruits, 12:33-37

The words one speaks reflect the values and the character of the speaker, just as the tree's fruit manifests the kind of tree it is. Rejection of the works of Jesus by attributing them to the Prince of demons are words that manifest the kind of men these particular Pharisees are. From their bad hearts, bad men bring out that which will bring judgment upon themselves. Notice the parallel between the words of Jesus and the words of John the Baptist (3:7-12). Both John and Jesus call these Pharisees/Sadducees snakes; both John and Jesus mention the tree and its fruit; and both John and Jesus speak of the Judgment Day.

8. Demand for a Miracle, 12:38-42

At first this passage seems unduly harsh on those "teachers of the Law and some Pharisees" who ask, "Teacher, we want to see you perform a miracle (12:38)." Jesus responds by calling them an "evil and godless" people. "Godless" literally means "unfaithful" or "adulterous." Often the relationship between God and his people was depicted by a marriage metaphor. The prophets reminded God's people that by their failure to live out God's will expressed in the covenant they have become guilty of adultery (see Hos 2, Ezek 16). Jesus had expelled demons, cured the sick, and healed the crippled. Perhaps they were asking for the type of miracle Jesus was tempted to perform in the desert (4:1-11), some kind of theatrical display that might astound and entertain, but which would do little to indicate the real meaning of God's reign. Without faith, one cannot "read" the miracle. Jesus answers this request as he had answered Satan in the desert: "No!" Then he alludes to the ultimate sign he will work, the resurrection, by which the Father will attest the whole of Jesus' words and deeds. As the book of Jonah reports the deliverance of Jonah by God after three days in the whale's belly, so will God deliver the Son of Man after three days in death's tomb (12:40).

9. The Parable of the Return of the Evil Spirit, 12:43-45

A parable concludes the series of judgments being pronounced against those who refuse to repent. A man has been exorcized, but he does not act to replace the evil with good. Because he remains empty, the original demon comes back, and, reinforced by seven more demons, retakes possession of the man. He ends up worse than before. Matthew then turns the parable into an allegory, by concluding, "this is the way it will happen to the evil people of this day (12:45)." Hence, the possessed man becomes "this generation" of unbelievers (12:45). The driving out of the evil spirit stands for the ministry of

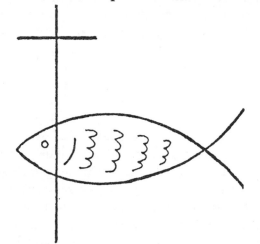

Jesus. The refusal of the people to respond to the message of Jesus calling for repentance is the emptiness of the man. The worse shape of the man "when it is all over" refers to the last judgment.

10. Conclusion: Discipleship and the Family of Jesus, 12:46-50

This scene in 12:46-50 is based on the third chapter of the Gospel according to Mark. However, Matthew makes a significant change in the Markan portrayal of Jesus' family. According to Mark, "When his family heard about this they set out to get him, because people were saying, 'He's gone mad!' (Mk 3:21)." Mark seems to connect this incident with the scene ten verses later: "Then Jesus' mother and brothers arrived. They stood outside the house and sent in a message... (Mk 3:31)." Mark implies that Mary and the rest of Jesus' family have come to take Jesus in tow because they think he's gone insane.

Matthew's knowledge of the tradition about the conception and birth of Jesus permits him to disregard the conjecture about madness (see 1:18-25). Thus, Matthew omits Mark 3:21. Then, Matthew uses the Markan material to make a statement about the larger family of Jesus. His disciples are his family because they seek to do the will of his father in heaven (12:49-50).

There remains the issue of Jesus "mother and brothers." The Greek word for brothers means "kinsmen." It can refer to brothers, cousins or both. Some Protestant Christians interpret "kinsmen" in terms of children born of Mary and Joseph after the virgin birth of Jesus. The tradition accepted by Catholics is that Mary gave birth to no child but Jesus (see Commentary or Mt 1:18-25).

B. The Parable Discourse, 13:1-52

1. *The Setting, 13:1-3*

Again Matthew carefully prepares the setting for an important sermon of Jesus. In keeping with his general structure, he has prepared his readers by introducing or heightening the themes of chapters 11-12: the growth of Jesus'; conflict with his opponents; their increasing hostility to his ministry; Jesus' rejection of unfaithful Israel; the continuation of the true Israel in the community of disciples. All of these themes will be developed in the parable discourse.

As with the Sermon on the Mount, Matthew places Jesus in a regal setting. Due to the size of the crowd, Jesus sits in a boat, while the crowd stands on the shore. (In Rev 7:9-12, God the Father is pictured as enthroned in heaven, surrounded by the standing hosts of saints.) Jesus taught,

Matthew notes, using parables. Of the parables recorded in chapter 13, those of the sower and the mustard seed are also found in both Mark and Luke, while the parable of the leaven is recorded also by Luke. The other four—note that again Matthew has utilized the theological significance of the number seven—are unique to Matthew.

The parable was a familiar type of Jewish teaching. It could take the form of a proverb, a comparison, or a story drawn from everyday life. The parables of Jesus are not unique; similar stories are found in the teaching of the rabbis. Of paramount importance for the hearer of Jesus' parables is the preparation of his heart. For the Master's parables are enigmatic: The disciples hear them and understand, because their hearts are well-disposed. However the crowds—and in particular the scribes and Pharisees—do not comprehend the spiritual meaning of the parables (though the "homey" illustrations would be clear).

In keeping with our use of the tool of composition criti-

cism, we will distinguish two settings in this discourse: (1) the moment of Our Lord's actual ministry, when the parables were told to believer and non-believer alike; and (2) the moment in which Matthew is writing. We can see much evidence—already sketched in Mark but much more pronounced in Matthew—of the community's catechetical use of these parables of Jesus. They are handed on by Matthew in the midst of a bitter conflict of his church with Pharisaic Judaism of the 80's.

They are retold now to encourage a community surrounded by persecution and troubles. Jesus had inaugurated the Kingdom of God in his preaching and healing. Why had the Kingdom not arrived in its full glory? Why is the Church of Jesus embattled on every side? Matthew uses the parables of Jesus to explain to his community the mystery of the Kingdom and the magnificence of God's plan.

Structurally, chapter 13 divides into two parts. In the first half (13:4-35) Jesus continues to speak openly to the Jewish crowds. Matthew here makes a significant adaptation of the Marcan tradition. In Mark, Jesus speaks in parables throughout his ministry. Matthew, however, does not introduce the parable until this moment. Moreover, from this time on Jesus ceases to teach (other than in parables) or preach to the crowds. In the second half of the chapter (13:36-52) Jesus turns away from the crowds and teaches only the inner circle of his disciples. Certainly 13:36 marks one of the important—if not the central—turning points of Matthew's Gospel. By presenting Jesus' use of parables at this point, Matthew informs his readers that the self-righteous Jews are no longer privileged recipients of God's revelation; now they stand under judgment.

2. The Parable of the Sower, 13:4-9

The parable must be understood in the context of Jesus'

ministry. He is the Sower whose word received such a varied response. The key point of the parable is the fate of the seed/word. The Jewish crowds produce little or no fruit, but the disciples represent the fruitfulness of the word of Jesus. Although at first there are set-backs and apparent failures, the success of God's word is certain. Just as the stony and unproductive nature of the Palestinian soil causes the loss of much of the effort involved in sowing, so the hardness of many Jewish hearts creates a minimal response to Jesus' preaching. The Kingdom will come however with an abundant harvest. Note that Matthew reverses (13:8) the Marcan order of fruitfulness (Mk 4:8), perhaps as an encouragement to his hearers to strive for a more abundant harvest within themselves.

3. *The Purpose of the Parables, 13:10-17*

This passage provides another example of the way in which Matthew has altered the text of Mark. Let us compare it with Mark 4:10-12 to see the differences.

Mark 4:10-12	Matthew 13:10-17
(10) When Jesus was alone some of those who had heard him came to him with the twelve disciples and asked him to explain the parables.	(10) Then the disciples came to Jesus and asked him, "Why do you use parables when you talk to them?"
(11) "You have been given the secret of the Kingdom of God," Jesus answered; "but the others, who are on the outside hear all things by means of parables,	(11) Jesus answered, "The knowledge of the secrets of the Kingdom of heaven has been given to you, but not to them.
	(12) For the man who has something will be given more, so that he will have more than enough; but the man who has nothing will have taken away from him even the little he has. (13) The reason I
(12) so that, they may look and look yet not see, they may listen and listen, yet not understand,	use parables to talk to them is this:

they look, but do not see, and they listen, but do not hear or understand. (14) So the prophecy of Isaiah comes true in their case:

'You will listen and listen, but not understand; you will look and look, but not see, (15) because this people's minds are dull, and they have stopped up their ears, and have closed their eyes. Otherwise their eyes would see, their ears would hear, their minds would understand, and they would turn to me, says God, and I would heal them.'

for if they did, they might turn to God and he would forgive them."

(16) As for you, how fortunate you are! Your eyes see and your ears hear. (17) Remember this! Many prophets and many of God's people wanted very much to see what you see, but they could not, and to hear what you hear, but they did not."

In Matthew the disciples do not ask for an explanation of the parables, because they are portrayed as understanding the teaching of Jesus from the beginning. (Remember that they represent the disciples of Matthew's own community.) Instead they ask the purpose of the parables for the others (13:10). By this means Matthew sharply contrasts the Jews and the disciples. To the disciples God revealed the "secrets of the Kingdom." This expression was common in Jewish apocalyptic literature, and simply means God's plan in human history. The saying in verse 12 has parallels in the rabbinic teachings. Matthew places it here to increase the sense of privilege: to the disciples, who understand the Kingdom, more will be given; while those who have not received this revelation will lose even what they have (their privileged status as the true Israel).

Why have the crowds not received the revelation of the

secrets? In 13:13-15 Matthew answers this question, and in so doing makes a significant change in Mark's wording. In Mark, Jesus uses parables from the beginning of his ministry, and he uses them *in order that* they may not perceive the mystery. Mark distinguished two groups: the inner circle who receive the revelation, and those on the outside, whose unfaithfulness to God exclude them from reception of the secret. They are to blame, not for their failure to understand the parables, but for their failure to prepare their hearts to receive the Kingdom.

In Matthew, Jesus teaches the crowds openly. Yet they do not respond. Only at this point in the ministry, then, does Jesus begin to use parables, *because* "they listen, but they do not hear or understand. (13:13)." Thus what Isaiah prophesied about Israel is being actualized in the ministry of Jesus (13:14-15). Israel's hardness of heart has already been foreseen by God; thus Jesus' use of parables is part of the divine plan. The hard hearts of the chosen people will not be penetrated by the teaching of Jesus. From now on he will address them only in parables. The disciples will understand their meaning, but the crowds will be left in the dark. In verses 16-17 Matthew heightens the contrast between faithful and unfaithful Israel. (Note that Luke places this saying of the Lord in a different context. See Lk 10:23-24.) In the entire history of Israel, only the disciples have had the privilege of seeing the Kingdom unfold before their eyes and of hearing its secrets.

4. Explanation of the Parable of the Sower, 13:18-23

The narration of the parable of the sower (13:4-9) was primarily concerned with the time of Jesus' ministry. In the explanation of the parable (13:18-23) we see more influence of the adaptation of Jesus' teaching to the needs and situation of the community. Again a study of the parallel in Mark 4:13-20 is helpful.

Already in Mark we can see the beginning of this adaptation process, but it is much clearer in Matthew. In Mark there is some confusion about the meaning of the seed. In Mk 4:14-15 the seed stands for the word of God. However in verses 16-20 the seed refers to the kind of people who hear it. Matthew clarifies the confusion by dropping all reference to the word of God in order to focus on the hearers. The original parable concentrated on the fate of Jesus' word: the Jews refused it but the disciples received it and bore fruit. In the explanation (which is the early Church's adaptation of the parable) the recipients are all believers; they are already members of the Church. What is at stake is the quality of their hearing of the message.

Those who "do not understand" (13:19) are probably those who have received the teaching of Christ but do not live it. By their refusal to do God's will they lose the precious seed. The second group of hearers (13:20-21) fall victim to the difficulties that inevitably accompany the Christian life. Responding joyfully at first, they are quick to renounce the faith when it becomes burdensome or dangerous. The phrase "give up" in verse 21 has strong overtones of final damnation. Thus Matthew warns his community that even those who belong to the ark of salvation can be lost if they do not persevere. The third group (13:22) do not lose the message; they simply allow it to be choked by worldly interests and the seductiveness of riches. Their expected fruit fails to appear. The seed sown on good soil stands for those who both hear and live out the word, remaining faithful despite the difficulties of discipleship.

Several details in this passage give us an important glimpse into the situation of the early Church. Often we tend to romanticize the lives of the first believers, envisioning them as living trouble-free lives of total love. Matthew's account shows us a suffering community, physically threatened from without by both Jews and Gentiles, and troubled from within by false doctrines, lax morality and even loss of faith. By means of the Church's adaptation of Jesus' parable to a new situation, the Risen Lord exhorts his disciples to hear the word fruitfully and to hold it so faithfully that no affliction or persecution can harm them.

5. The Parable of the Weeds, 13:24-30

In the parable of the weeds Jesus continues to teach that the harvest of the Kingdom will be completed in spite of disappointments. He himself is the sower and the field is Israel. However another sower is also at work, so that the servants discover weeds among the crop. (The wheat represents a people faithful to God's will, as expressed in the teaching of Jesus. The weeds stand for those who refuse obedience.) There was a real risk in pulling up the weeds before the harvest (the Greek word for "weeds" indicates a plant of the wheat family, which was indistinguishable from the wheat before maturity) that some of the immature wheat might also be uprooted.

The owner's reply demonstrates that he is confident of success. The harvest will be successful. Thus it is not for the servants to play the role of the Judge. (The harvest was a familiar Jewish image of the final judgment.) Any premature separation of wheat and weeds would interfere with the Master's plan. He is willing to tolerate the weeds. Judgment belongs to him. The disciples must not lose heart nor grow impatient with unbelieving Israel.

Without doubt Matthew's community would have applied this teaching of Jesus to their own conflict with Pharisaic Judaism. (Some scholars see traces in the parable of Matthew's hand at work. Since we have no parallels with which to compare it, it remains difficult to be certain.) Applied to the situation of the 80's, Jesus' word cautions, "Don't force a separation between Christian Jews and Judaism (i.e., the Jewish community led by the Pharisees). Judgment is not yours, but mine. At the judgment I will separate the faithful from the unfaithful."

6. *Two Parables on Growth, 13:31-33*

The next two parables contrast the humble beginnings of the Kingdom with its final maturity. The mustard seed (13:31-32) was the proverbial smallest seed. Yet it reached a height of ten or twelve feet, large enough to provide a home for the birds. The point of the parable lies in the potential of the seed/Kingdom. Although it has a tiny beginning, its potential is enormous.

We find the same contrast in the parable of the yeast (13:33). There is no comparison between the final amount of dough and the tiny bit of yeast. The Kingdom begins insignificantly. Its growth is silent and secret. (In the Greek, the woman hides the yeast in the flour.) Jesus teaches that the disciples must not become impatient with the slow, silent growth of the Kingdom. Enough to be part of it, for it will inevitably reach its full and glorious maturity.

7. *Explanation of the Parable of the Weeds, 13:36-43*

At this point Jesus makes a decisive shift in the focus of his ministry. Again Matthew communicates this with very few words, using his theological shorthand:

> *Then Jesus left the crowd and went indoors. His disciples came to him and said, "Tell us what the parable of the weeds in the field means (13:36)."*

From this time on Jesus does not teach the crowds except in parables. The remainder of this discourse, as well as those in chapters 18, and 24-25, is intended only for the disciples.

Although the explanation of the parable of the weeds is in continuity with the original parable, there are many indications that Matthew has adapted Jesus' teaching to the needs of his own community. We discover a significant shift in the context of the teaching. While the parable was concerned with the coexistence of good and evil persons in

the Kingdom, the explanation focuses on the harvesting at the end of time. In the parable we meet Jesus in his ministry, sowing in the field of Israel (13:24-30). The explanation, however, presents the exalted Lord of the Church as he presides over the judgment (13:36-43).

Note Matthew's preoccupation with the coming judgment. The language used is highly apocalyptic: images of harvesting, the fiery furnace, reaping angels and weeping and gnashing of teeth (intense distress and rage). In 13:38 we meet the two groups: those who belong to the Kingdom (compare with 8:12) and those who belong to the evil one. The division of people into two radically opposed groups was common in Jewish catechesis. The second group is described in verse 41 as those who "cause people to sin and all other evildoers." We heard of the evildoers in 7:23. They are believers who refuse to do the will of the Father. We will meet them again in 15:5 and 23:23. Those who cause others to sin (or "scandalize" others, in some translations) constitute an important category in Matthew's theology. To cause others to sin is to be an obstacle in their path to salvation, to lead them away from Christ. In one of the strongest passages of the Gospel (16:22-23) Jesus accuses Peter of scandalizing (being an obstacle to) him. Again in 18:6-9 Jesus teaches his disciples the seriousness of causing a brother or sister in the community to turn away from God's will.

Those who belong to the Kingdom are described (13:43) in an image drawn from Dan 12:3. To shine like the sun means that they will partake of God's own glory. "God's people," literally, the "just," is a favorite Matthean term. He uses it some nineteen times in the Gospel.

As in the parable itself, the key to the explanation is the problem of the presence of sinners in the community of the just. In both, the lesson is the same: it is God's business to decide who belongs to his Kingdom. He will reward the just and cast evildoers into the fiery furnace.

8. The Parables of the Hidden Treasure and of the Pearl,
13:44-46

These two parables belong to Matthew's special tradition, and with them he shifts for a moment the emphasis of the chapter. The preceding parables have been concerned with the triumphant growth of the Kingdom in spite of resistance, and with the necessity of patience until the final judgment. In these two similar parables Matthew introduces the themes of (1) overwhelming joy at the unexpected discoveries; (2) the unparalleled value of the Kingdom of heaven; and (3) the willingness of the finder to sacrifice all in order to possess the Kingdom.

As with most of the parables, the opening phrase (13:44, 45) must be understood in a Semitic sense. Thus the Kingdom is not directly compared to a treasure or a pearl; rather, what happens when a man finds a treasure is compared with what happens when a man finds the Kingdom of heaven: he will with joy make any sacrifice necessary to purchase it. A slightly more accurate translation would read: "It is the case with the Kingdom of heaven as with a treasure hidden in a field."

Matthew reminds his community that the Kingdom of God can suddenly and unexpectedly break into one's life. The response of the disciple is total and unconditional. In Matthew, to give up everything for the Kingdom is practically a definition of the disciple. However, the sacrifice is not made grudgingly or from a sense of duty; his great joy makes it impossible for him to do otherwise. In a few words these parables speak volumes about the attractiveness of God's Kingdom.

9. *The Parable of the Net and the Conclusion of the Discourse, 13:47-52*

The final parable returns to the theme of the mixture of good and bad in the Kingdom. It is very similar to the explanation of the parable of the weeds. The situation at the coming of the Kingdom will be like the sorting of a catch of fish. Although good and evil people may be mixed together now, the angels of God will separate them at the end. Again the parable emphasizes that it is God who has the right to judge the quality of the fish. The presence of some bad fish should not act as a hindrance on the casting of the net. It is possible that Matthew understood the net as the church and the fishermen as the apostolic leaders of the community.

In 13:51-52 Matthew brings the parable discourse to a conclusion. Again he emphasizes the understanding of the disciples, contrasted (in an unspoken way) with the failure of the crowds and the Jewish leaders to comprehend the nature of the Kingdom. Teachers of the Law, or scribes, were a powerful group in Judaism. They were experts in the interpretation of the Law, the authorized teachers of Israel. The reference to the scribe who becomes a disciple of (or perhaps better, who is trained for) the Kingdom is not clear. Scholars think that it may refer to the evangelist himself or to a group of Christian scribes. The "new and old things (13:52)" can refer either to the old Law and its new interpretation by Jesus, or to the message of Jesus and its continuing application and interpretation by the Church. In either case they are not opposed to one another. Both together provide for the needs of those who live in the household of the Church.

Week Six

The Fathers of the Church had a beautiful expression: Jesus himself, is the Kingdom of heaven. In the Scripture readings for this week we see that the Kingdom continues to become visible in the person and deeds of Jesus.

Yet these chapters note a difference from the earlier ministry of Jesus. In chapter 13 he made the decisive shift away from the crowds, in order to devote his attention to his small band of disciples. In chapters 14 through 18 we see him preparing the disciples for their future ministry of serving the Church. Thus the community of believers also makes visible the Kingdom of God.

We see clearly in the narrative chapters (14-17) that the disciples' ministry is empty and powerless without the presence of the Master. Yet Peter will be given the keys of the Kingdom of heaven itself (16:19); the disciples will also receive the powers of binding and loosing (18:18). We follow the disciples as they taste both the ecstasy of a mountain-top experience and the disillusionment of their powerlessness to help a tormented boy.

In the fourth major discourse (chapter 18) Matthew gathers the teachings of Jesus about life and relationships in the community of the Church. Humility, concern, compassion and forgiveness must mark out the disciples of Jesus. How well do we measure up to this challenging word of the Lord? With your group you might assess the quality of our parish and diocesan life in the light of this teaching.

Daily Study Assignments: Week Six

Day	Matthew	Commentary
1	13:53-14:36	Pages 163-168
2	15:1-39	Pages 168-172
3	16:1-28	Pages 172-184
4	17:1-27	Pages 184-189
5	18:1-35	Pages 190-201

6—Reflect on Chapters 13 through 18 in light of the reflection questions listed below.

7—STUDY GROUP MEETING

- Matthew's theology of discipleship (14:17) teaches that our ministry is insufficient without the power of Jesus. How can we achieve an appropriate balance between the need for dependence on the Master in all things and the need for personal responsibility in our discipleship?
- What are some of our Catholic rules and practices that could be seen as corresponding with what the Jewish people called "the traditions of the ancestors" (15:1-9)?
- Most Christians do not enjoy the full ministry of Peter which we believe is taught in 16:16-19. How would you express the benefits to the Church of the role of Peter? of the disciples (18:18)?
- What personal examples of "mustard seed faith" (17:20) can you share with the group?
- In what concrete ways is your parish community reaching out to the "little ones" (18:6-14)?
- One might respond that the three-fold process of inviting back a sinner (18:15-17) is an intrusion on personal privacy, the exact thing that busybodies would love to do. What is your response?
- What would be the effects of a parish community's living out the teaching of Jesus regarding unlimited forgiveness (18:21-35)?

The Church: Initial Manifestation of the Kingdom of Heaven, 13:53-18:35

OVERVIEW: In Matthew's arrangement of the Gospel, the Jewish people have rejected Jesus. Therefore, he has turned to instruct his small group of disciples. They will be the faithful remnant continuing to do God's will. Chapters 14 through 17, basically following Chapters 6 through 9 of Mark, portray Jesus laying the groundwork that will enable the disciples to eventually perceive the relation between his death and resurrection. In Chapter 18, the fourth discourse of Jesus, Matthew structures the words of Jesus so that his readers will realize that the authority of those leading the Church comes from Jesus, who shared his authority with Peter and the disciples.

A. Narrative Section, 13:53-17:27

1. Rejection in Nazareth, 13:53-58

Having finished the discourse on the parables of the Kingdom, Jesus returns to his home town of Nazareth. Notice that the discourse of chapter 13 is bracketed by two incidents involving the family of Jesus. In 12:46-50, Jesus had claimed that his disciples, i.e., those who do the will of his Father, are his brother, his sister, and his mother. Now, immediately after his sermon, the people of his home town reject Jesus because they know his family. Just as the Jews, who should have been able to recognize their Messiah, have rejected Jesus, so too, his neighbors also fail to recognize his unique character. Their question, "Where did he get all this?" probably reflects their knowledge that Jesus had not studied with the important rabbinical schools (see

11:25-27). In their eyes, the authority of the prophet, the spokesman of God, accounted for nothing.

Notice the subtle change Matthew introduces into his account: whereas Mark 6:5 states that "He was not able to perform any miracles there...." Matthew declares, "He did not perform many miracles there because they did not have faith (13:58)." Both Mark and Matthew point out that there is an intimate connection between faith and the signs (miracles) Jesus did. Matthew, in changing "was not able" to "did not perform," indicates that it was by his own choice that Jesus did not do "many miracles there." This is in accord with Matthew's thorough appreciation of the divinity of Jesus.

2. *The Death of John the Baptist, 14:1-12*

Matthew shortens Mark 6:14-29 in order to suit his own theological purposes. Descriptive details are omitted in order to make his point: John was murdered as were the prophets who preceded him. Matthew follows Mark in placing the martyrdom of John immediately after Jesus is rejected by his own people in Nazareth.

3. *Jesus Feeds the Five Thousand, 14:13-21*

We find here an account of a miracle with allusions to both past (the account of God feeding his chosen people with manna in the desert, see Exodus 16:13), and future (the institution of the Eucharist at the Last Supper). The setting, "a lonely place" (14:15), suggests the Exodus sojourn. We also find in 2 Kings 4:42-44 an account of the prophet Elijah multiplying food for others. Later on in this narrative section, both Moses and Elijah will be seen bearing witness to Jesus in the account of the transfiguration (see 17:1-13).

Matthew makes several changes in Mark 6:30-44 in order to heighten the status of the disciples. In Mark's account the disciples seem to rebuke Jesus for his suggesting that they feed the people: "Do you want us to go and spend two hundred silver coins on bread in order to feed them? (Mark 6:37)". Matthew omits this inappropriate reference to their purse and has the disciples reply "All we have here are five loaves and two fish (14:17)."

The reply of the disciples in Matthew's account fits precisely into Matthew's theology of discipleship. Without Jesus, what they have is insufficient. In this case, five loaves and two fish are not sufficient to feed the crowds. So the disciples bring the loaves to Jesus. Jesus blesses them, gives them back to the disciples, and they distribute enough for all. Matthew speaks of the proper relationship that must exist between Jesus and his followers. If they rely upon Jesus and his power, they will have what they need to minister to others. It is such dependence upon God that is the basis of the disciples' effective service (see 5:3; 5:5; 6:33). By themselves the disciples are inadequate; together with Jesus, they and their ministry will bear lasting results.

The Greek word for thanksgiving is *eucharistia*. Matthew's allusion to the institution of the Eucharist at the Last Supper is clearly seen by comparing the key sentences:

> *...he took the five loaves and the two fish, looked up to heaven, and gave thanks to God. He broke the loaves and gave them to the disciples, and the disciples gave them to the people (14:18-19)*
> *While they were eating, Jesus took the bread, gave a prayer of thanks, broke it, and gave it to his disciples. "Take and eat it," he said: (this is my body (26:26)."*

MATTHEW 14:22-23

(22) Then Jesus made the disciples get into the boat and go ahead of him to the other side of the lake, while he sent the people away. (23) After sending the people away, he went up a hill by himself to pray. When evening came, Jesus was there alone; (24) by this time, the boat was far out in the lake, *tossed about by the waves*, because the wind was against it. (25) Between three and six o'clock in the morning Jesus came to them walking on the water. (26) When the disciples saw him walking on the water they were terrified. "It's a ghost!" they said, and screamed with fear.

(27) Jesus spoke to them at once. "Courage!" he said. "It is I. Don't be afraid!" (28) Then Peter spoke up. "Lord," he said, "if it is really you, order me to come out on the water to you." (29) "Come!" answered Jesus. So Peter got out of the boat and started walking on the water to Jesus. (30) When he noticed the wind, however, he was afraid, and started to sink down in the water. "Save me, Lord!" he cried. (31) At once Jesus reached out and grabbed him and said, "How little faith you have! Why did you doubt?" (32) They both got into the boat, and the wind died down.

(33) The disciples in the boat worshipped Jesus. "Truly you are the Son of God!" they exclaimed.

Isaiah 41:9-10, 12

"...I called you from earth's farthest corners and said to you, 'You are *my servant*.' I did not reject you, but *chose you. Do not be afraid—I am with you! I am your God—let nothing terrify you!*

I will make you strong and *help you*; I will protect you and *save you*....

I am the Lord your God; I strengthen you and tell you, 'Do not be afraid; I will help you.'"

MARK 6:45-52

(45) At once Jesus made his disciples get into the boat and go ahead of him to Bethsaida, on the other side of the lake, while he sent the crowd away. (46) After saying good-bye to the disciples, he went away to a hill to pray. (47) When evening came the boat was in the middle of the lake, while Jesus was alone on the land. (48) He saw that his disciples were having trouble rowing the boat, because the wind was blowing against them; so sometime between three and six o'clock in the morning he came to them, walking on the water. He was going to pass them by. (49) But they saw him walking on the water. "It's a ghost!" they thought, and screamed. For when they all saw him they were terrified.

(51) Jesus spoke to them at once, "Courage!" he said. "It is I. Don't be afraid!"

(51) Then he got into the boat with them, and the wind died down. The disciples were completely amazed, (52) because they had not understood what the loaves of bread meant, their minds could not grasp it.

4. Jesus Walks on the Water, 14:22-23

The opposite page shows the changes Matthew introduces into Mark 6:45-52. Note also the text of Isaiah 41 which the earliest followers of Jesus perhaps related with the event of Jesus walking upon the water.

Matthew follows the account of Mark rather closely at the start: choppy sea, Jesus walking on water, the terrified disciples, and Jesus' words of encouragement: "It is I. Don't be afraid." Matthew omits a few details and adds a reference to his storm-tossed community (14:24).

Just as he had changed Mark's account of the stilling of the storm into a lesson on discipleship back in chapter 8, so now Matthew changes the entire thrust of the incident by including the scene of Peter walking on the water. Composition criticism, the study of the way an author uses and changes his sources, enables us to see Matthew's point more clearly. Although all the disciples see Jesus walking upon the water, it is Peter who says, "Lord, if it is really you, order me to come out on the water to you (14:28)." Jesus says, "Come," and Peter, the model of the disciple, does what his Master does. He accepts the invitation of Jesus to do the impossible (see 19:26). He follows Jesus walking on the waves.

Often we Catholics read the Christian Scriptures and, coming upon the name of Peter, we think, "first pope." There is no doubt that Peter has been given a unique authority. Peter was the first disciple called (4:18). Peter headed the list of the twelve apostles who were commissioned to heal, exorcise and preach (10:2). Peter will be the first to receive the keys to the Kingdom of heaven (16:19). But Peter is first and foremost the disciple. He was invited to follow and he responded. He saw Jesus upon the water and then asked to be with Jesus even then.

The rest of the account symbolizes the incompleteness of the first disciple's faith. Peter seems to forget about Jesus: "When he noticed the wind, however, he was afraid...." Without completely being open to the presence of Jesus, the disciple is insufficient: "he was afraid and started to sink down into the water (14:30)." His faith was not a total faith. However, being the disciple, Peter turns again to the one he is following: " 'Save me, Lord,' he cried (14:30)." "At once Jesus reached out and grabbed him....(14:31)." There is a promise implicit in this reaching out of Jesus. He is "God-with-us (1:23)." He is the one ready to grant the prayer of the community who recognizes him as Lord. Only after taking Peter by the hand does Jesus rebuke him with the words, "How little faith you have! Why did you doubt? (14:31)"

While in Mark the little crew fails to understand, Matthew ends the scene with a liturgical motif: there in the boat of the Church the disciples worship Jesus as the Son of God (14:33).

5. Conflict: Jesus and the Traditions of the Ancients, 15:1-20

The literary form of these verses is the conflict story. In order to appreciate the original context of such clashes between Jesus and the rabbis of his day, let us examine these "traditions of the ancients." One way to image this is to visualize an unrolled scroll. The Law/Torah of God is written upon this scroll. Its margins are very wide. Through the course of the centuries holy and learned men meditate upon the Law of God. They seek to understand what it means so that the people may be taught how to do God's will. As the Jewish leaders interpret the word of God, they teach it. The teaching becomes a tradition that is eventually written down in the wide "margins" of the scroll.

An example will clarify this. In Deuteronomy 14:21 the Torah reads, "Do not cook a young sheep or goat in its mother's milk." We find the same prohibition in Exodus 23:19 and 34:26. Apparently the Law was aimed at an ancient Canaanite custom that was particularly abhorrent to the Jewish people during the time of the development of the Mosaic code. As the centuries succeeded one another, the culture changed. Nobody cooked kid in its mother's milk anymore, and the prohibition seemed to become obsolete. For the leaders of Judaism, it was unfitting that God's Word be no longer applicable to the life situation of the community. Therefore, they interpreted that prohibition in this way. The young sheep or goat was interpreted to mean all meat; the mother's milk stood for all dairy products. Cooking symbolized all manner of meal preparation. The ancients wrote down this tradition in the wide "margins" near Deuteronomy 14:21, Exodus 23:19 and Exodus 34:26. This is the will of God: separate all meat and dairy products whether in cooking or in serving. To enable you to observe this Law of God, all Jewish homes must have two sets of dishes and pots, one set for meat products, the other for dairy products. Thus, this particular tradition of the ancients has become the basis for the kosher kitchen.

During his public ministry, Jesus clashed with some of those interpretations of the Law. In the case in point, Jesus objects to a particular interpretation which gave human tradition precedence over the Word of God itself. One of the ten commandments states that children must honor their parents (Exodus 20:12), but some Pharisees followed the tradition called Qorban which allowed the legal fiction of vowing property to God, thereby precluding all claims that could be made to that property by one's parents. Jesus bluntly disagreed with this tradition (15:4-5), declaring that the Jewish leaders have lost perspective. We could say that they lost the ability to distinguish between God's

Word at the center of the scroll and the interpretations subsequently written on the margins. Jesus declared:

> *"This is how you disregard God's word to follow your own teachings (15:7)."*

(We know that by 130 A.D. at the latest the Pharisees themselves rejected the practice of the Qorban.)

Jesus' teaching, "It is not what goes into a person's mouth...; rather what comes out of it makes him unclean (15:10)," brings us back to the initial question of the Pharisees and teachers of the Law; "Why is it that your disciples disobey the teaching handed down by our ancestors? (15:2)" The washing of hands was a precaution against tainting oneself with one of the many kinds of ritual uncleanness, designed by the interpreters of the Law to insure the observance of the dietary code. Mark, writing for a Gentile audience, reports this interpretation of the words of Jesus: "In saying this, Jesus declared that all foods are fit to be eaten (Mark 7:19)." Matthew, writing for an audience of mostly Jewish Christians, omits Mark 7:19. It is likely that many Jewish Christians continued to keep the distinction between clean and unclean foods (see Deuteronomy 14:3-21). However, Matthew avoids the issue of distinguishing between clean and unclean foods by presenting the teaching of Jesus in a larger context: fidelity to God is a matter of the heart, a matter of the person's basic attitude towards God and neighbor.

Peter asks for an explanation, and Jesus refers to violations of the fifth, sixth, seventh and eighth commandments. To violate the relationship God wills people to have with each other is to make oneself unclean from inside to outside (15:17-20).

6. *The Faith of the Canaanite Woman, 15:21-28*

As we saw in chapters 8 and 9, faith is essential if the power of Jesus is to be effective. In 13:58 Matthew stated that Jesus did not work many miracles in Nazareth because the people did not have faith. In this incident, the pagan woman comes to Jesus, addressing him by the messianic title, Son of David. Jesus, keenly conscious of his mission to the lost sheep of the people of Israel, ignores her. In Mark's account, the disciples have no role, but Matthew portrays them as intervening, perhaps more on their own behalf than on hers: "Send her away! She is following us and making all this noise! (15:23)". When the woman makes her way into the presence of Jesus, Mark's dialogue indicates that the woman literally talks Jesus into working a miracle on behalf of her daughter. Matthew changes Mark in order to make it clear that it is her faith that makes the healing possible:

> *"You are a woman of great faith! What you want will be done for you." And at that very moment her daughter was healed (15:28, see 8:13; 9:22).*

7. *Summary of Jesus' Healing Ministry and the Feeding of the Four Thousand, 15:29-39*

As we have seen in 4:23 and 9:35, Jesus comes to minister to the sick, the crippled, the blind. These healings, following as they do the cure of the Canaanite woman's daughter and ending with the words, "they praised the God of Israel (15:31)," may have been performed for Gentile people. Furthermore, Jesus began his ministry in the "Galilee of the Gentiles," words Matthew had taken from Isaiah 9:1 and declared fulfilled in Jesus (see 4:12-16). The cures and healings Jesus performed according to 15:31 indicate that Matthew is alluding to the text of Isaiah 35:5-6:

> *The blind will be able to see, and the deaf to hear. The
> lame will leap and dance, and those who cannot speak
> will shout for joy.*

Some scholars think that 15:32-39 is a repetition of
14:13-21, the feeding of the 5,000 people. Whether the feeding of the 4,000 people is or is not another version of the
same event, Matthew seems to have a special purpose in
placing it at this point in the Gospel. It is likely that
Matthew is looking ahead to the eventual entrance of the
Gentiles into the Church. Hence, the crowds of people
following Jesus are those who have been coming with their
lame, their blind, and their crippled (15:30). If the ones
who "praised the God of Israel (15:31)" are Gentiles, it
conforms with Matthew's theme in this second half of the
Gospel: since the Jewish people have largely rejected Jesus,
their status as God's particular chosen people is given to
the true Israel, the Church, consisting of both Jew and
Gentile peoples.

8. The Demand for a Miracle, 16:1-42.

The scene has already been recounted in 12:28-29.
Pharisees and Sadducees ask Jesus to "show them a sign
from heaven (16:2 *Jerusalem Bible*)." There is not a little
sarcasm in Jesus' answer: they ask for a sign in the sky and
Jesus observes that they can predict the weather, but they
cannot "interpret the signs concerning those times (16:3)."
Verses 2 and 3 are missing from the better manuscripts, an
indication that they were added to the Gospel by a hand
other than Matthew's. Nevertheless, the tenor of these
lines is supported by similar Matthean critiques of the
shortsightedness of Jewish leaders. The Pharisees find
fault with the disciples eating grain on the Sabbath, but
they do not know the meaning of the words, "I do not want

animal sacrifices but kindness, (12:7)." The Pharisees disobey God's command and follow their own teachings
(15:3). They are careful to give God even a tenth of the
seasoning herbs, such as mint, dill and cumin, but they
"neglect to obey the really important teachings of the Law,
such as justice, and mercy and honesty (23:23)." Here they
can look at the sky and forecast the weather, but they
cannot see the signs of the inbreaking Kingdom of God
(16:3).

Jesus and the disciples leave the scene of the confrontation via boat. During the trip Jesus warns them to be on
their guard "against the yeast of the Pharisees and Sadducees (16:6)," but the disciples see this warning as a
rebuke for not bringing bread. In Mark, the warning is
against the yeast of the Pharisees and the yeast of Herod
(Mark 8:15); the disciples fail to understand and Mark does
not clarify the teaching of Jesus. In the Gospel According to
Luke, the leaven of the Pharisees is specified as hypocrisy
(Luke 12:1). In Matthew "yeast" signifies the teaching of
the Pharisees and Sadducees (16:11-12). If we can interpret the "yeast" in the light of Jesus' response in 16:1-4,
we can say that their teachings lack a proper perspective:
they cannot read the signs of the times! They cannot see in
Jesus, in his words and deeds, the inbreaking of the
Kingdom of God. If Jesus is the one whose coming affirms
and validates the whole Law (5:17), then the teaching of
the Pharisees is necessarily out of focus. It becomes a
leaven corrupting the whole mass of dough.

9. *Peter's Reception of the Father's Revelation Regarding Jesus, 16:13-20*

Jesus, the Son of Man (see Daniel 7:13-14) asks two
questions about his identity: who do men think he is? who
do his disciples think he is? Regarding the opinion of men,

impressive: John the Baptist, Elijah, Jeremiah, another prophet. Jesus was perceived by his contemporaries as a man who proclaimed God's Word.

But that was not enough. What about the disciples? According to Mark, "Peter answered, 'You are the Messiah' (Mark 8:29)." Luke wrote this: "Peter answered, 'You are God's Messiah' (Luke 9:20)." But Matthew significantly expands Peter's answer:

> *Simon Peter answered, "You are the Messiah, the Son of the living God" (16:16).*

Peter recognizes that Jesus is both Messiah and divine Son of God! Both Mark and Luke follow Peter's declaration of Jesus' messiahship with the first prediction of the passion and resurrection. But Matthew inserts the blessing of Peter and the promises of Jesus to build his church upon Peter (the rock) and to give him the keys of the Kingdom. Only then does Matthew recount the first prediction of the passion, death and resurrection of Jesus.

The blessing of Jesus is the key to this incident:

> *"Blest are you, Simon son of Jonah! No mere man has revealed this to you, but my heavenly Father (16:17,* New American Bible*)."*

Since the response of Jesus to Peter's declaration of faith is so significant, the *New American Bible* translation is used here. The *Good News* translation, "Good for you, Simon," loses much of the impact of Jesus' proclaiming Peter blessed or happy in his reception of the revelation given by the Father.

Matthew stresses that it was not human reasoning (flesh and blood) that led Peter to the insight into the full identity of Jesus, but the Father alone:

*"This truth did not come to you from any human
being, but it was given to you directly by my Father in
heaven (16:17)."*

If we think about this for a moment, this is a surprising
verse. Peter has walked with Jesus now for many months.
He has heard the powerful teaching of the Master and
witnessed the wonderful miracles. It would seem that Peter
could logically conclude that Jesus was the Son of God.
Think, however, of the many thousands who also heard
Jesus teach and saw the miracles, yet did not believe. Faith
is a gift of God, not a conclusion of human reasoning.

From every indication in the Christian Scriptures, the
recognition of the complete identity of Jesus did not come
until after his death and resurrection. What we have here,
then, is an instance in which Matthew reads the post-
resurrection belief of the Church back into the ministry of
Jesus. This recognition that Jesus is the Son of God is the
revelation that makes all the difference between Judaism
and the Church.

There is nothing that should scandalize the twentieth
century readers of the Gospel in this process. We have
seen in chapter 10 that Matthew moves back and forth
between the events taking place in the ministry of Jesus
and the events happening in his own community living in
the 80's. In this account of Peter's confession, Matthew
takes the faith that is the foundation of the Church and
places its manifestation back in the period of Jesus'
earthly life. Matthew does this to demonstrate the continuity between the faith of his believing community and
the faith of the twelve disciples.

This practice of re-arranging chronology in the light of
the Church's post-resurrection faith is referred to in the
teaching of the Second Vatican Council:

Indeed, after the Ascension of the Lord the Apostles

*handed on to their hearers what He had said and done.
This they did with that clearer understanding which
they enjoyed after they had been instructed by the
glorious events of Christ's life and taught by the light
of the Spirit of truth (DOGMATIC CONSTITUTION
ON DIVINE REVELATION, #19).*

Matthew's account of Peter's declaration at Caesarea
Philippi may well be linked with another tradition: that the
risen Jesus first revealed himself to Peter. We find this
tradition in two places. In 1 Corinthians 15 Paul refers to it
as part of the teaching he had received.

*I passed on to you what I received...: that Christ died
for our sins...that he was raised to life three days
later...that he appeared to Peter and then to all
twelve apostles (1 Corinthians 15:3-5).*

The same tradition is found in the Gospel According to
Luke. After the two disciples on the way to Emmaus had
encountered Jesus in the offer of hospitality and the breaking of the bread, they turned back to Jerusalem,

*...where they found the eleven disciples gathered
together with the others and saying, "The Lord is
risen indeed! He has appeared to Simon! (Luke
24:33-34)."*

Taking into account Matthew 16:16, I Corinthians 15:5, and
Luke 24:34, we see that Peter is both the first one to perceive Jesus as the divine Son of God, as well as the disciple
to whom the risen Jesus first manifested himself. Perception of the full identity of Jesus as divine Son of God is
related to faith in the risen Jesus. This faith is a gift. It
comes not from man, but from God.

Jesus responds to Peter's declaration of faith with two promises, both of which deal with the Church. First, Jesus names Peter "rock." Peter, with his faith in the divinity of Jesus, will be the foundation rock of the Church. Secondly, Jesus promises to Peter the keys of the kingdom of heaven.

In interpreting Jesus' first promise to Peter, these verses of Isaiah become very significant:

> *"Listen to me, you that want to be saved, you that come to me for help. Think of the rock from which you came, the quarry from which you were cut. Think of your ancestor Abraham, and of Sarah, from whom you are descended (Isaiah 51:1-2)."*

Isaiah likens Abraham to the rock/quarry from which Judaism has come. In 16:18, Matthew indicates that just as

Abraham's faith can be likened to the rock/quarry that is the foundation/source of Judaism, so also is Peter's faith in the Lord Jesus the foundation of the new community, the Church. The word "Church" comes from the Hebrew *qahal*, meaning the assembly or gathering of the believers. Although 16:18 and 18:17 are the only times the word "Church" is used in all four Gospels, it has become the word that designates the community of men and women throughout history who have followed Jesus. The declaration of Jesus that not even death will be able to overcome the Church to be built upon Peter the rock is perhaps another reference to resurrection. The Greek here reads "the gates of Hades." While this phrase can be understood to mean the gates of hell (the powers of evil), it is preferable in this context to interpret it as the gates of the underworld, the abode of death.

It is faith in the risen Jesus that enables the community to be victorious over death. The gates of death will not be able to imprison the members of Jesus' community. As they have believed in the risen Jesus, they will also share in his resurrection (see I Corinthians 15:16-20). Thus we can say that the Church will overcome death because her faith is related to the faith of Peter, the first disciple to believe in Jesus as the divine Son of God and the first who believed in Jesus risen from the dead. Thus, Peter becomes the foundation stone of the entire community that comes to believe in Jesus as Son of God and risen Savior.

The second promise Jesus makes to Peter, "I will give you the keys of the Kingdom of heaven; what you prohibit on earth will be prohibited in heaven; what you permit on earth will be permitted in heaven (16:19)," has been interpreted in many different ways down through nineteen centuries. The basic meaning of the promise is this: decisions made by Peter (who symbolizes the Church's leadership) will be affirmed by God. The best way to understand the meaning of the keys is to see the promise in terms of the rabbinic practice of first century Judaism. Rabbis had the power to prohibit and to permit (to bind and to loose). They could either impose a temporary excommunication or lift it; they could take certain interpretations of the Torah and make them binding upon the community.

As we have seen, Jesus often opposed some of the interpretations of the Law made binding upon the community by the Pharisees. Jesus invited the people to take his light and easy yoke upon themselves, i.e., an interpretation of the Torah that redeemed rather than oppressed them. The power of the keys given to Peter is clarified by another Matthean passage. Jesus declares:

> *"How terrible for you, teachers of the Law and Pharisees! You hypocrites! You lock the door of the Kingdom of heaven in people's faces, but you yourselves don't go in, nor do you allow in those who are trying to enter (23:13-14)."*

In their use of teaching authority, the Pharisees and scribes have shut the door of the Kingdom in the faces of God's people. Thus, in accord with the thrust of the latter part of Matthew's book, the power held by the leadership of Judaism will be taken away from them and given to others. Matthew might have had a text of Isaiah in mind when he wrote of Jesus' promising the power of forbidding and permitting. Isaiah is called to deliver the word of the Lord to a faithless official named Shebna:

> *"You are a disgrace to the master's household. The Lord will remove you from office and bring you down from your high position.*
>
> *"...When that happens, I will send for my servant Eliakim....I will put your official robe and belt on him and give him all the authority you have had. He will be like a father to the people of Jerusalem and Judah. I will give him complete authority under the king, the descendant of David. He will have the keys of office; what he opens, no one will shut, and what he shuts, no one will open (Isaiah 22:18-22)."*

There are many parallels that could be drawn between Eliakim and Peter. When Israel rejects Jesus, he turns to the band of disciples and instructs them. They become the true Israel. In this true and renewed Israel, Jesus confers the authority for leading the shepherdless sheep upon Peter. Peter becomes the one who has complete authority under Jesus, who is also a descendant of David and a king (Isaiah 22:22). As Eliakim received the keys for opening and shutting, Peter receives the keys of the Kingdom of heaven. Soon the significance of the keys will be placed in a broader context; in 18:18 the entire leadership of the Church will receive the keys.

10. Jesus Speaks of His Suffering and Resurrection, 16:21-28

Matthew returns to the Markan sequence of events. Jesus turns toward Jerusalem and the climax of the Gospel: his death and resurrection. The phrase, "From that time (16:21)," is identical with the wording Matthew used at the very beginning of the ministry of Jesus:

> From that time Jesus began to preach his message, 'Turn away from your sins, because the Kingdom of heaven is near' (4:17).

Recall that Jesus began his ministry immediately after being tempted by Satan to refuse to be the Suffering Servant of God (see 4:1-11). Now, as the full consequences of Jesus' decision to do the will of God manifest themselves, Jesus is once again tempted to take a path other than the one necessary to "save his people from their sins (1:21)."

In popular terminology, "the handwriting is on the wall" for Jesus. We have seen that he was regarded by his contemporaries as a prophet (see 16:14). Some of those in Judaism's leadership positions are plotting to kill him (see

12:14). John the Baptist has been martyred and Jesus has been linked with John:

> *It was at that time that Herod, the ruler of Galilee, heard about Jesus. "He is really John the Baptist, who has come back to life," he told his officials. That is why these powers are at work in him (14:1-2).*

Jesus has alienated himself from other Jewish authorities by challenging their teachings:

> *Then the disciples came to him and said, "Do you know that the Pharisees had their feelings hurt by what you said?"*
>
> *"Every plant which my Father in heaven did not plant will be pulled up," answered Jesus. "Don't worry about them! They are blind leaders; and when one blind man leads another one, both fall into a ditch (15:12-14)."*

In Matthew's account, Jesus has not been near Jerusalem since the time of his birth. But he must go there. It is the center of Judaism's religious life. He must speak of God's Kingdom to God's people even though he will soon say,

> *"Jerusalem, Jerusalem! You kill the prophets and stone the messengers God has sent you! How many times I wanted to put my arms around all your people...(23:37)."*

Jesus speaks "plainly to his disciples (16:21)." He tells them that he must go to Jerusalem to suffer and be put to death. Jesus adds that "on the third day I will be raised to life (16:21)." We know that belief in resurrection was the belief of many Jewish people during the time of Jesus. In Second Maccabees, written about a century and a half before the death of Jesus, we find this account of the martyrdom of the seven brothers by Antiochus Epiphanes:

> One of them, acting as spokesman for the others, said.... "We are prepared to die rather than break the laws of our ancestors.... You may discharge us from this present life, but the King of the world will raise us up, since it is for his laws that we die, to live again forever...."

> When [the fourth] neared his end he cried, "Ours is the better choice, to meet death at men's hands, yet relying on God's promise that we shall be raised up by him . . . (2 Maccabees 7:2-14, Jerusalem Bible)."

The reference to "the third day" may be a citation of the prophet Hosea. In its original context Hosea's words were a critique of Israel's insincere reliance on God:

> "Come, let us return to Yahweh.... he has struck us down, but he will bandage our wounds; after a day or two he will bring us back to life, on the third day he will raise us... (Hosea 6:1-3, Jerusalem Bible)."

God laments the way his people take him for granted,

> "What am I to do with you, Ephraim? ...Judah? This love of yours is like...the dew that quickly disappears. This is why...I slaughtered them with the words from my mouth, since what I want is love, not sacrifice; knowledge of God, not holocausts (Hosea 6:4-6, Jerusalem Bible)."

Again we see hints of the contrast between faithless Israel and the true Israel doing the Father's will. Jesus' love is deep and enduring. Peter is the rock upon which the true and renewed Israel will be built. This ties in with the prophetic critique used by Jesus in his conflicts with the Jewish leaders, namely, "I want love, not sacrifice," (see 12:7; 23:23). The phrase "on the third day" carried the meaning of "in a short time." Jesus does take God's Word seriously. He trusts in him. He tells his disciples three times (16:21; 17:22-23; 20:17-19) that he will suffer and be raised from the dead on the third day. The sign of Jonah (see 12:40-41; 16:4) also refers to the significance of the third day. (Citations were taken from the *Jerusalem Bible* because this translation is more explicit regarding "the third day.")

But Peter, now speaking out of human logic (his pre-resurrection perception) objects to Jesus' plans to go to Jerusalem to suffer and die. "This must never happen to you! (16:22)." Again we see a parallel being drawn with the beginning of Jesus' ministry in 4:1-17. Jesus calls Peter a Satan for trying to prevent him from fulfilling the role of the Suffering Servant. The rebuttal of Jesus,"You are an obstacle in my way, because these thoughts of yours are men's thoughts, not God's! (16-23)," are a marked contrast to Jesus' praise of Peter for his profession of faith (16:17).

Jesus then turns to his disciples and repeats part of the teaching we found in chapter 10: take up your cross if you are to follow me; to gain life you must lose it for my sake.

The words of Jesus, "Will a man gain anything if he wins the whole world but loses his life? (16:26)," suggest Satan's third temptation:

> *"Then the Devil took Jesus to a very high mountain and showed him all the kingdoms of the world. . . . All of this I will give you . . . if you kneel down and worship me (4:8-9)."*

The final two verses of this section are interpreted in various ways. Verse 27 clearly refers to the final judgment (see 13:36-43 and 25:31-46). Verse 28 may refer to the immediate expectation of the end of the world and the Second Coming of Jesus that was common in the first years after the death of Jesus. Or, it may refer to the experience of the glory of the risen Jesus, a faith experience of eleven of the twelve disciples.

11. The Transfiguration, 17:1-13

The first three words, "Six days later," refer the reader to what has come before. It is six days after Jesus first spoke of his passion, death and resurrection (16:23); it is six days after Jesus spoke of the Son of Man "about to come in the glory of his Father" (16:27). In all three synoptic accounts the episode of the transfiguration is placed in this same position: immediately following the prediction of the passion and coming in glory of the Son of Man.

In this manifestation of the divinity (glory) of Jesus, we find an abundance of biblical symbolism, theological statement, and religious experience. It will not do to simply read and re-enact this scene in the eye of one's mind. The passage must be explored in the context of both Judaism and the Gospel itself. The Gospel According to John has no account of the transfiguration. Why? Because John's entire account is written from a post-resurrection perspective. By the end of the first chapter of John, people know who Jesus is:

> "Teacher," answered Nathanael, "you are the Son of God! You are the King of Israel! (John 1:49)."

The whole Gospel According to John is the Transfiguration, the manifestation of the glory of Jesus.

But the three synoptic gospels are written in a way that leads up to the manifestation of his divinity. The humanity of Jesus is clearest in Mark. Matthew tends to stress the importance of the divinity of Jesus.

Jesus leads Peter, James and John up a high mountain. Mountains are often symbols of unique encounters with God. Mountain tops and revelations from God are associated with one another through all of Israel's history. The characteristics of deep religious experience are contained in this account. Jesus' face becomes like the sun, "clothes as white as light (17:2)." In Luke's account we read that "Peter and his companions were sound asleep, but they woke up and saw Jesus' glory and the two men who were standing with him (Luke 9:32)." The deep sleep suggests a form of religious ecstasy, a leaving of the ordinary realm of sense experience in order to share in another kind of knowledge. The change in the countenance and clothing of Jesus suggests the transformation of Jesus after his resurrection, a change which makes it difficult for the disciples and others to recognize him (see Luke 24:16; John 20:14; 21:4). The three disciples perceive Jesus speaking with Moses and Elijah, symbolic figures representing the Law and the prophets. They bear witness to Jesus on the mountain top. Matthew thus brings us back to one of his key themes: Jesus is the completion of the Law (5:17) and the prophets (see 11:13-14; 22:37-40). Moses received the Law on Mount Sinai. Elijah too has an encounter with God on Mount Sinai:

> "Go out and stand before me on top of the mountain," the Lord said to him. Then the Lord passed by and sent a furious wind that split the hills and shattered the rocks—but the Lord was not in the wind....And after the fire there was a soft whisper of a voice.

> *"When Elijah heard it, he covered his face...(1 Kings 19:11-13)."*

The experience of Elijah is modeled on a similar experience of Moses:

> *Then Moses requested, "Please let me see the dazzling light of your presence."*
>
> *The Lord answered, "I will make all my splendor pass before you....I will not let you see my face, because no one can see me and stay alive. . . . When the dazzling light of my presence passes by, I will put you in an opening in the rock and cover you with my hand until I have passed by. Then I will take my hand away, and you will see my back but not my face (Exodus 33:18-23)."*

In the account of the Transfiguration in Mark and in Luke, Peter addresses Jesus as "Master." In Matthew's account Peter says, "Lord (17:4)." Mark and Luke both indicate that Peter does not realize what he is saying: "He and the others were so frightened that he did not know what to say (Mark 9:6; see Luke 9:33)." Matthew, however, portrays Peter calmly saying to Jesus, "if you wish, I will make three tents here.... (17:4)."

The shining cloud (17:5) recalls the theophany (manifestation of God) at Sinai. God spoke with Moses in the midst of thunder, fire and smoke enveloping the mountain peak (see Exodus 19:16-25). In Matthew's account, the voice that speaks from the cloud is also the voice of God. At his baptism Jesus heard a voice from heaven declaring, "This is my own dear Son, with whom I am well pleased (3:17)." These words are repeated in the transfiguration scene. To the words of the baptismal theophany these words are added: "...listen to him (17:5)." The admonition to listen to Jesus prepares us for the next discourse of Jesus in chapter eighteen. Note that the three disciples, Peter, James and John are the persons addressed by the voice from the cloud. These three are in special leadership positions in the early Church. The discourse of Jesus in chapter eighteen, "the community discourse," can also be called "the discourse on the use and abuse of authority."

Thus, in 17:5 the Father, the one who has given Jesus all things (11:27), commands the Church to listen to Jesus. The three disciples are overwhelmed by this astounding revelation and fall to the ground (17:6). Jesus reassures them, "Get up.... Don't be afraid (17:7)." See also 10:26, 28; 14:27; 28:10. Matthew notes that as Jesus spoke, he touched them (17:7).

There are differing interpretations for 17:9. Perhaps the request of Jesus that they tell no one about the vision "until the Son of Man has been raised from death" points to the failure of the apostles to comprehend the relationship of the passion and glorification of Jesus until after they had experienced Jesus risen from the dead.

As Jesus and the three disciples make their way back down the mountain, the disciples ask Jesus about Elijah. They have seen his glory; they know he is the Messiah (16:16). Yet, the prophet Malachi had prophesied that God would send Elijah back before the new age would begin (Malachi 3:23-24). Jesus responds that Elijah has already come but was not recognized. The disciples then understand that Jesus was speaking of John the Baptist (17:13).

12. *Jesus Heals a Possessed Boy, 17:14-21; The Second Reference to his Passion and Death, 17:22-23*

This incident has as its main thrust the centrality of faith. Jesus had already given the power to heal and to exorcise to his disciples (10:1). The disciples fail in their attempt to free the child of his epilepsy (possession). Jesus rebukes them for their lapse in faith. The thrust of this episode is that faith is the crucial condition. The vivid hyperbole, if you have faith as big as a mustard seed, you could move a mountain (17:20), expresses the point Jesus was making. However, it appears that a later hand added verse 21, "But only prayer and fasting can drive this kind out...." This verse is placed in brackets in the *Good News* version and is sometimes omitted in other translations. Prayer and fasting are important works of piety (see 6:1-18), and it is likely that one of the persons transcribing Matthew's work saw the account of the healing as an appropriate time to place this comment. In Mark's account Jesus had said, "Only prayer can drive this kind out...nothing else can (Mark 9:29)."

In Mark's account of the second reference to the passion and resurrection, the disciples do not understand and are afraid to ask for an explanation (Mark 9:32). In Matthew's version, they do comprehend: "The disciples became very sad (17:23)." They comprehend because one of Matthew's primary intentions is to establish the authority of the apostolic Church as a teaching Church (see 28:19). Before they can teach, they must understand.

13. The Payment of the Temple Tax, 17:24-27

This incident is found only in Matthew's Gospel. It indicates that Matthew cares about the relation of the community of believers with Judaism. At the same time, we see the Church being given a certain kind of freedom for itself. The question of Jesus about kings of this world exacting taxes from foreigners and not sons probably refers to the Roman practice of collecting tribute (taxes) from occupied nations while leaving Roman citizens free from sharing the financial burden of supporting the empire. Those who follow Jesus are citizens of God's Kingdom, and therefore they are not obligated to pay the temple tax (which was probably still collected even after the destruction of the temple, in order to support rabbinic schools such as the one at Jamnia).

Reading between the lines again, it is likely that the payment of the temple tax was an issue for Matthew's community. The issue is resolved peacefully: "...we don't want to offend these people (17:27)." In order to avoid the scandal of conflict, Jesus instructs Peter to pay the tax. There is a twist to the payment, though. Instead of paying the tax out of their own pockets, a fish with a coin in its mouth waits for Peter's hook (17-27). It would seem that the incident is more important for its theological statement than it is for its historical accuracy.

Reviewing the narrative section of 13:52-17:27, we see three episodes that present Peter in a special relationship with Jesus. Peter was called to walk on the water with Jesus (14:28-33). It was Peter who received both the Father's revelation regarding the divine identity of Jesus as well as the promise of Jesus that he would be the foundation of the Church and the recipient of the keys of the Kingdom (16:16-19). In the account of the payment of the temple tax, Peter is told to hook a fish with "a coin worth enough for *my* temple tax *and yours*; take it and pay them *our* taxes (17:27)." (Italics added.)

In the entire narrative section, Peter's name is mentioned 16 times. The only other disciples referred to by name are John and James in 17:1.

B. The Fourth Discourse: On the Life of the Ecclesial Community with Emphasis on the use of Authority, 18:1-19:1

OVERVIEW: This discourse is the companion to the

second discourse of Jesus (chapter 10). In the second discourse Jesus had sent out his disciples to carry on his ministry of healing, exorcising and proclaiming the Kingdom. In this discourse Jesus gives instructions about relationships between those who are already members of the believing community. The kindness and care which disciples should show one another, and the necessity of mutual and unlimited forgiveness are the basic concerns of Jesus.

It is not easy to determine the exact audience to which this discourse is addressed. In 18:1 the disciples come to Jesus. Do these represent all disciples (the entire Church) or only the Twelve (only Church leaders)? It is possible to embrace both opinions: Jesus speaks here to all the members of the community, with the twelve as a special focus. Thus, Jesus' teaching in this discourse has a special significance for the Church's leadership.

In 16:16-19 Matthew recounted Jesus' promise to give Peter the keys of the Kingdom of heaven. In this discourse the keys that were promised to Peter are also given to the twelve disciples.

1. Regarding Individuals in the Community, 18:1-14

a. The initial question, 18:1-4

Matthew's point of departure for this discourse is found in Mark 9:33-34. In that account Jesus and the disciples have arrived at a house in Capernaum (Mk 9:33). Jesus inquires about the subject matter of their discussion on the road. Mark tells us:

> But they would not answer him, because on the road they had been arguing among themselves about who was the greatest (Mk 9:34).

Matthew omits the details and simply begins the discourse with the disciples question:

> *At that moment the disciples came to Jesus, asking,*
> *"Who is the greatest in the Kingdom of heaven?*
> *(18:1)"*

Jesus answers the question by calling a child before the group: "Unless you change and become like children, you will never enter the Kingdom of heaven (18:3)." The stakes are high: the gain or loss of salvation. The operative word is "change." Recall the very first words of Jesus at the beginning of his ministry: "Turn away from your sins, because the Kingdom of heaven is near (4:17)." To repent of one's sins is to change. It is to turn back to God, and, at the same time, to re-order one's priorities (see commentary on Mt 3:1-2). Jesus takes the child as the model for the kind of change one must undergo in order to enter the Kingdom:

> *"The greatest in the Kingdom of heaven is the one*
> *who humbles himself and becomes like this child*
> *(18:1)"*

The operative words here seem to be *humbling* oneself and *becoming* like the child. The child is humble in the sense that the child knows that he or she is dependent upon parents. The child is not self-sufficient. A child cannot be independent. Self-reliance is the opposite of the kind of humility that honestly recognizes one's dependence upon another. Thus Jesus teaches that entrance into the Kingdom hinges upon one's trusting the Father. The first beatitude calls blest the person who is spiritually poor, that is, the person who recognizes his or her dependence upon God in all things (5:3).

b. The transition, 18:5
Verse 5 is a transition sentence. We often link this verse

with the preceding because it contains a reference to the child. However, the verbs in the sentence signal the shift:

"And whoever welcomes in my name one such child as this, welcomes me (18:5)."

Jesus is talking now about disciples who have achieved the humility of a child ("one such child"). Disciples are to look on other disciples as on Christ himself. In the act of wel-

coming (receiving, accepting) another disciple, one welcomes Jesus. We have seen a similar teaching at the conclusion of the missionary discourse: "Whoever welcomes you, welcomes me (10:40)."

c. The little ones, 18:6-14

In verse 6 the image of the child shifts to that of the little ones. The little ones are probably a small group within the larger community of Matthew's Church. They already believe in Jesus; yet their faith is weak and faltering. Jesus warns the community about causing "one of these little ones to turn away from his faith in me (18:6)." The verb used here is "to scandalize," that is, to become an obstacle to the faith of another believer. A disciple can become an obstacle by his own sinful conduct (so that another is enticed into evil) and also by a lack of compassion for the weakness of another. In 13:41-42 Jesus taught the seriousness of scandal: "the Son of Man will send out his angels and they will gather up out of his Kingdom all who cause people to sin...and throw them into the fiery furnace, where they will cry and gnash their teeth."

Now he uses another example. If one has the choice between causing another to sin and dying a terrible death, the better choice would be dying the terrible death. The death picture is that of being drowned in the deep sea. The Jewish people feared the sea; for them the sea symbolized the unknown, chaos and destruction. Those who heard the words of Jesus fully realized the terrible evil of scandal.

We have already seen verses 8 and 9 in the context of the Sermon on the Mount (5:29-30). There the radical teaching about separating oneself from whatever caused one to sin primarily related to the individual. Here the teaching has a communal dimension: rather than lead another astray, cut out of your life whatever could cause that to happen! A beautiful example of this concern for the little ones is found in Paul's teaching to the Corinthian community. He writes about the problem of eating meat which has been offered to idols. Mature Christians know that eating such meat does not defile them. Yet their behavior might scandalize a less mature brother or sister. So, he concludes,

> *Be careful, however, not to let your freedom of action make those who are weak in the faith fall into sin...And so this weak person, your brother for whom Christ died, will perish because of your "knowledge"! And in this way, you will be sinning against your Christian brothers and wounding their weak conscience (1 Cor 8:9-12).*

Jesus sums up this section in verse 10: "See that you

don't despise any of these little ones." They are very precious in the eyes of the Father, so important that their angels are in his presence. At the time of Jesus the Jewish people were very interested in angels, believing that God assigned angels to watch over cities and nations, kings and common folk. According to this tradition, not all angels were privileged to see the face of God, only those of the highest rank. Thus, Jesus teaches, these little ones are highly regarded by God; the proof is that he has assigned them the most important and most glorious angels.

We can only guess at the exact identity of the group designated as "the little ones." They may have been the

unlearned, the people of the land. Perhaps they were those on the verge of giving up faith in Jesus. Perhaps they were simply a group of people on the periphery of the community and largely ignored.

But Matthew tells his community: do something about those little ones! Immediately after Jesus stated the high esteem God has for them, Matthew places Jesus' parable of the shepherd who leaves the ninety-nine sheep in order to seek out the one sheep that went astray. The recovery of that one sheep is worth the risk of leaving the 99 percent of the flock. The shepherd "feels far happier over this one sheep than over the ninety-nine that did not get lost (18:13)."

The special interest of Matthew in the little ones is reflected in the way he situates this parable of Jesus. In Luke we see an entirely different context: Jesus was teaching tax collectors and outcasts. "The Pharisees and the teachers of the Law started grumbling, 'This man welcomes outcasts and even eats with them!' (Lk 15:2)." Then Jesus tells the parable of the 100 sheep with this entirely different application:

> "...there will be more joy in heaven over one sinner who repents than over ninety-nine respectable people who do not need to repent (Lk 15:7)."

As the shepherd in the parable acted, so the Father wants the Church to respond:

> "In just the same way your Father in heaven does not want any of these little ones to be lost (18:14)."

Pastoral concern and active service should characterize the whole community, both the leadership and each individual believer. There is great joy in possessing such a shepherd's heart. Note that in Luke heaven rejoices over the repentence of the sinner, while in Matthew's account it is the heart of the shepherd himself which fills with joy.

2. Regarding the Whole Community, with Particular Emphasis on its Leadership, 18:15-35

The *Good News* translation reads, "If your brother sins against you, go to him and show him his fault (18:15)." The more accurate manuscripts read this way: "If your brother sins, go to him. . . ." The later addition of the two words, "against you," has changed the sense of what Matthew intended to communicate. Matthew is painstakingly telling the Church that Jesus intended his community to be a caring community, a loving fellowship of people concerned about one another. Simply stated, Matthew cites Jesus in this sense: if you see another doing something that would lead him away from me, then do all you can to prevent that from happening! First of all, go to that person privately (see Lev 19:17) "and show him his fault (18:15)." If that person receives your correction, you have won him back. The word "won back" is the same word for making a convert. To lead a disciple back to Christ is as important as bringing a person into the Church!

If, however, one does not succeed at first, take two other persons (see Deut 19:15). If that is not effective, then "tell the whole thing to the Church (18:17)." This is the second time Matthew refers to the community by the word Church (see 16:18). In the overall context, telling the Church most likely means telling the leadership of the Church. If the offending person still does not listen, he is to be treated "as though he were a foreigner or a tax collector (18:17)." This is a reference to the "ban," the imposition of a temporary excommunication during which time the community will not associate with the person. The imposition of the ban should not be seen as merely cutting the person adrift. On the contrary, the purpose of the ban was to help the person see the wrongness of his or her action, repent and rejoin the community.

Jesus has been addressing the whole community in the section regarding the situation of the disciple who sins. A three step process of community discipline has been established, beginning with the individual member and ending with "the Church (18:17)," the leadership of the community. In verse 18 Jesus gives this leadership the same powers of prohibiting and permitting (binding and loosing) that he had promised Peter in 16:19.

From our knowledge of the history of the early Church we can read between the lines and see that in chapter 18 Matthew is telling us a great deal about important values in the community of his day. Since Peter had been martyred in the persecution of Nero, at least twenty years before the time Matthew was writing, we can see that for Matthew the continuation of the authority given to Peter (16:17-19) and to the rest of the twelve (18:18) was an issue of great significance. The teaching of Jesus had to be handed on. The words of Jesus needed to be interpreted and applied. The way of life for the community of believers had to be clarified by a discipline. These needs could only be met by authorized leadership.

Thus, Matthew takes the traditions available to him and works them into the Gospel. The authority of Jesus came from his Father (11:25-27). Jesus shared some aspects of his authority with his disciples. They are commissioned to heal, to exorcise and to proclaim the Kingdom (10:1,7-8). Then Peter (16:17-19), and now the rest of the disciples, received the powers needed to oversee the community.

But these powers are to be used compassionately; they are given to the leaders for the sake of the well-being of the community. Those who receive the authority that gives them leadership positions in the community must use it as

Jesus used it. It is an authority not of dominion but of service:

> *Jesus called them all together to him and said, "You know that the rulers have power over the people, and their leaders rule over them. This, however, is not the way it shall be among you. If one of you wants to be great, he must be the servant of the rest; and if one of you wants to be first, he must be your slave—like the Son of Man who did not come to be served, but to serve and to give his life to redeem many people (20:25-28)."*

The understanding of 18:19-20 is best grasped by taking into account its place in the progression of sayings of Jesus. "If your brother sins..." is followed by the three part procedure, ending with the reference to the Church's ability to impose some kind of excommunication upon the sinner (18:17). "And so I tell all of you . . . " is followed by a clarification of the power of the Church's leadership for binding and loosing (18:18). Now Jesus says, "And I tell you more . . . (18:19)."

This phrasing indicates that the situation of two or three agreeing to pray for something is to be seen in the context of the brother who sins. Thus, Jesus teaches that if two or three members of the community come together in agreement to pray for an erring brother or sister, that prayer will be heard by "my Father in heaven." Such prayer will be heard by the Father because Jesus is there, present in the midst of his Community (see 1:23 and 28:20).

Peter's question and Jesus' answer are also best understood in light of the preceding teaching. The sinner can be shown his sinfulness and invited to repent. But Peter, possibly symbolizing the leadership of the Church, asks how many times a sinning brother should be forgiven.

Some of the pharisaic leadership held that one should forgive up to four times. Peter is more generous: "Seven times? (18:21)."

> *"No, not seven times...but seventy times seven (18:22)."*

The norm is the unlimited forgiveness of the sinner. Note the contrast between Jesus' teaching and the unlimited revenge of Lamech, described in Genesis 4:24.

Jesus pictures the Church in chapter 18 as a community of people caring for one another. In chapter 10 the apostles were sent out to proclaim Jesus in spite of the most intense hardships, resistence, and persecution. In chapter 18 the disciples are taught that their efforts to minister to one another must continue without ceasing. They are to care for the little ones. They are to seek those who have strayed. They are to go to the sinning brother at first one by one, then with others, then with the leadership of the Church. If the brother remains unrepentant, they are to meet together and pray for him. Finally, the members of the community must stand ready to forgive without limit.

Jesus then tells a parable that provides the reason why the disciples should forgive without counting the times: "Because the Kingdom of heaven is like a king who decided to check on his servants' accounts (18:22-23)." The gist of the parable is that the king is God, and the servant is the disciple. The servant owed a debt of an incredible amount. It could never be paid back. But the king is a loving king and forgave the enormous debt.

Jesus has proclaimed throughout the Gospel that people are called to repentance because the Kingdom of God is at hand. God has taken the initiative in reconciling and forgiving. The conclusion of Jesus' interpretation of the Law ends with the mandate: "You must be perfect—just as your

Father in heaven is perfect (5:48)." The norm for the response of the disciple is the perfection of God himself. This is also the point of the parable. The servant refused to forgive his fellow servant as the King had first forgiven him:

> "You worthless slave!...I forgave you the whole amount you owed me, just because you asked me to. You should have mercy on your fellow servant, just as I had mercy on you (18:32-33)."

The conclusion of the parable is a judgment scene:

> "The master was very angry, and he sent the servant to jail to be punished until he should pay back the whole amount (18:34)."

The message is clear. The servant is cast out, "sent to jail." The jail symbolizes eternal damnation, for the worthless servant must be punished there until "the whole amount" is paid back, and that is an impossibility. As the description of the final judgment will again declare, salvation depends on the deeds of kindness and mercy done for others (see 25:31-46).

The words of Jesus, "In just the same way your Father in heaven does not want any of these little ones to be lost (18:14)," concluded the first half of the discourse. In the same fashion Jesus concludes the second half: "That is how my Father in heaven will treat you if you do not forgive your brother, everyone of you, from your heart (18:35)." These two conclusions summarize the teaching of the fourth discourse: outgoing and tender concern for all, especially the little ones, and the merciful forgiveness of another as many times as forgiveness is needed.

Week Seven

With the conclusion of Jesus' discourse on the Church, Matthew turns now to Jesus' Judean ministry. According to Matthew's account, Jesus has not returned to Judea since he fled Bethlehem as an infant. As he makes his way, inexorably, toward Jerusalem, Jesus continues to make clear to his followers the demands of discipleship (chapters 19 and 20).

In chapter 21 Jesus enters Jerusalem, a messianic moment which inaugurates the great events of our redemption. He acknowledges the acclamation of the crowds, yet he rides on a donkey. He is not the Messiah that met Jerusalem's expectations.

Chapters 21 and 22 focus on the authority of Jesus. In a symbolic gesture, reminiscent of the prophets of old, he purifies the Temple, House of God and center of Israel's worship. He teaches clearly that those whom God had specially chosen are proving themselves unworthy of such trust; the Kingdom will be offered to others.

The Jerusalem ministry is controversial. While the simple pilgrims and children welcome the Son of David with praise and joy, the leaders of the people greet him with chilling hostility. Thus he begins his final great discourse with a lengthy lamentation over the failure of Israel's leadership. There is a terrible sadness in Jesus's unreturned love for Jerusalem. How faithfully have we responded to God's overwhelming love and grace?

Daily Study Assignments: Week Seven

Day	Matthew	Commentary
1	19:1-30	Pages 205-210
2	20:1-34	Pages 211-214
3	21:1-46	Pages 214-224
4	22:1-46	Pages 224-230
5	23:1-39	Pages 231-236

6—Reflect on chapters 19 through 23 in light of the reflection questions listed below.

7—STUDY GROUP MEETING

- How can the Church give witness to Jesus' teaching on the permanence of marriage and at the same time respond with pastoral compassion toward those in a second marriage?

- What changes would occur in the Church if we understood Christian marriage to be a calling as graced as that of Christian celibacy?

- What things must you "sell" (19:21) in order to follow Christ more perfectly?

- The world's estimation of greatness is radically challenged by the teaching of Jesus in 20:26-28. How can we live this teaching, both within our parish communities and in service to the world?

- Who are the prophets and wise men (23:34) of our own day who have been and are persecuted because of their faithfulness to the will of God?

- In what ways do we as a parish community or as a diocese fall under Jesus' critique of hypocrisy, pride and blindness (23:2-33)?

- What do the parables of the Two Sons, the Tenants, and the Wedding Feast (21:28-22:14) have to say about a smug confidence in our salvation?

The Approaching Advent of the Kingdom, 19:1-23:39

OVERVIEW: In his sixth major division Matthew again introduces a sermon of Jesus (chapters 23-25) with a narrative section (chapters 19-22). The narrative section is already looking toward the Passion. It includes: an insistence on the demands of following Christ; the entrance of the humble Messiah into Jerusalem; and various parables and controversy situations in the Temple area. Matthew presents the discourse in two parts: the first is a condemnation of the teachers of the Law and the Pharisees; the second is a teaching about the end of time and the last judgment. In this week we will study the narrative section and the first part of the sermon (19:1-23:39).

A. Narrative Section, 19:1-22:46

1. *Teaching on the Permanence of Marriage, 19:1-12*

In 19:1 we meet again one of the special phrases with which Matthew concludes the great discourses of Jesus. At the conclusion of his "community" discourse Jesus leaves Galilee and sets out for Judea. In 16:21 the Master had explained to his disciples the necessity of his journey to Jerusalem. Now he begins that journey, which will conclude with his death. This verse is another example of Matthew's theological geography. Matthew does not mention, as does Luke, the presentation in the Temple (Lk 2:22-38) or a boyhood visit to Jerusalem (Lk 2:41-50); nor does he narrate other visits to the Holy City, as does John (Jn 2:13-25; 5:1-15; 7:10-10:39). According to Matthew,

Jesus will be entering Jerusalem for the first time. As the Master moves south into Judea, great crowds follow him, and he continues to heal them. Note, in comparison with Mark 10:1, that Matthew emphasizes both the following of the crowds (Mark has "came flocking to him") and the healing ministry of Jesus (Mark mentions only that Jesus taught).

We postponed a discussion of the teaching of Jesus on divorce, which appeared as the third antithesis (5:31-32), until now, for here Matthew again introduces it. We find an expanded context, which provides us with a glimpse into Matthew's rabbinic mind.

By changing the question of the Pharisees as posed in Mark ("allow a man to divorce his wife"), Matthew shifts the context to that of a contemporary rabbinic dispute. The question thus asks Jesus to decide between the stricter school of Shammai (which allowed divorce only for adultery) and the more liberal school of Hillel, which permitted divorce for the most trivial reasons. Jesus refuses to side with either one of the schools. Instead he cites Genesis 1:27 and 2:24 as the authentic expression of the will of God. In turn the Pharisees cite the command of Moses in Deuteronomy 24:1 regarding a divorce notice. Jesus corrects their interpretation of Moses: he did not encourage divorce, but permitted it because of the unteachableness (literally, hardness of heart) of God's people. Again Jesus affirms the creation or paradise-will of God: divorce and re-marriage do not conform to the Father's will for his people.

In 19:9 Matthew creates a difficulty for interpreters by adding the phrase "and she has not been unfaithful." At first glance this addition, which is not found in the parallel texts in Mark and Luke, seems to establish an exception to the teaching of Jesus. Catholic scholars would not agree. By comparison with its companion text in 5:32 it becomes clear that re-marriage is not at issue, but only a separation. Moreover, much depends on how the Greek word *porneia* is translated. It can mean marital unfaithfulness, as the *Good News* translation has it. It can also refer, as in Acts 15:28, to marriage within a degree of kinship forbidden by Jewish law. Thus to marry a first or second cousin would constitute *porneia*. We prefer to interpret 19:9 in this way, since it does not weaken the teaching of Jesus. Given Matthew's care to present the truly radical teaching of Jesus, it does not seem likely that he would introduce an exception unknown to the other evangelists. 19:9 then should be translated like this: I tell you, then, that any man who divorces his wife—I am not talking about pagan converts who have married within the forbidden degrees and now must separate—commits adultery if he marries some other woman.

Matthew places a high priority on interpreting the Law so that God's will is clear and undiminished. However he also realizes the equally important demands of compassion and love. For many centuries the Church has interpreted Jesus' teaching on the indissolubility of marriage almost entirely in terms of Law. Recently members of the Church have asked whether we can approach it from a more pastoral perspective. (It might be helpful to recall that the other five antitheses—5:21-48—carry equal weight in Jesus' teaching, and yet have always been approached from a pastoral viewpoint.)

The basic question is this: without denying the teaching of her Lord, can the Church recognize that in fact a marriage has totally failed? If so, could the Church, without denying the teaching of Jesus, permit either or both partners to enter into a second marriage? The first question can be answered with a yes. The second question is more complex. The Church must always proclaim clearly the teaching of her Lord that remarriage after divorce does not conform to the expressed will of God. However, it seems that in some pastoral situations the Church could recognize a second marriage of evident durability and permit the partners to receive the sacraments.

In 19:10 the disciples are surprised at the severe teaching of their Master. If God's will is so strict, it is better not to marry at all. The phrase "this teaching" in verse 11 is ambiguous. It can refer to Jesus' teaching on divorce (19:9), or it can look forward to his teaching on abstaining from marriage for the sake of the Kingdom of heaven (19:12). We are accustomed to the latter interpretation. Thus Jesus is saying that voluntary celibacy is a special gift of God.

It would be fruitful to apply "this teaching" also to Jesus' words on the durability of the marriage relationship. Understood in this way, Christian marriage becomes as much a gift of God as celibacy. Thus, both of the Christian "states-of-life" are graced; both are the result of God's gift.

2. The Children, 19:13-15

Following Mark, Matthew next adds the account of Jesus' blessing the children. In the time of Jesus it was common for parents to bring their children to rabbis, to be blessed by the laying on of hands. By rebuking the people the disciples again manifest that they misunderstand Jesus' mission. The children are to have free access to the Master, because to "such as these (19:14)" the Kingdom belongs. In 18:3 Matthew has already quoted the saying (which Mark places here, its more probable setting) about becoming like children in order to enter the Kingdom.

3. Possessions and the Kingdom, 19:16-30

As the reaction of the disciples in 19:10 highlights the perfection of the teaching of Christ, so Jesus' discussion with the rich young man emphasizes the perfection of Christian discipleship. Matthew makes several small changes in the Marcan account (Mk 10:17-31) which highlight his usual theological approach. Note his shift of the word "good" from "Good Teacher" (Mk 10:17) to "good thing (19:16)." As we have seen several times, Matthew changes any wording in Mark which might lead to a misunderstanding of Jesus' divinity or mastery over a situation. Eternal life is life approved by God, life which provides access to the Kingdom (both present and future). Matthew emphasizes the importance of doing God's will. Mark's "you know the commandments" (Mk 10:19) now

reads, "Keep the commandments if you want to enter life (19:17)." In addition Matthew adds the command of loving one's neighbor (19:10) to the commandments listed in Mark 10:19. The reason for this becomes clear in verse 21. After the young man's reply that he has observed all these commandments, Matthew makes another important change in the Marcan tradition. Mark's "You need only one thing (Mk 10:21)" becomes "If you want to be perfect, sell...give...then come and follow me (19:21)." As we saw in 5:48, being perfect is the goal of the disciple, and is best expressed in imitation of the outgoing love of the Father. Matthew's twofold condition ("if you want to enter life" and "if you want to be perfect") does not envision two kinds of Christians, the ordinary and the perfect. The demand of perfection is addressed to all disciples of Jesus. Moreover 19:23 shows that wealth is an impediment, not to a special position in the Kingdom, but to entering it at all. It is best to understand this teaching as another expression of the radical demand which Jesus makes upon his disciples. The point of the renunciation of wealth is not so much self-denial but total generosity toward others and perfect freedom in following Jesus.

Material poverty is not demanded of every believer, but it is asked in those cases in which earthly possessions form a stumbling block to discipleship. In this case the price of discipleship is too high and the rich man departed in sorrow. This occasions Jesus' remarks about the difficulty with which a rich person enters the Kingdom. As we saw in 6:19-34, earthly wealth not only can distract the believer's attention with many cares and anxieties, but also can corrupt the heart itself.

The example in 19:24 seems to have been common in oriental cultures. Parallels can be found in Indian literature which speak of an elephant passing through the eye of a needle. The disciples correctly grasp the impossibility and ask, "Who can be saved, then? (19:25)." Jesus' response means the same as his answer to the disciples in 19:11; without God's power neither the lifelong fidelity of a married person nor the salvation of a rich person is possible.

The reward of the disciple of Jesus is clearly promised in a brief appendix to the story of the rich young man (19:27-30). As befits its leaders, the apostles will join their Master in ruling the new Israel. All other disciples, by definition those who have sacrificed possessions or family in order to follow Christ, will receive a hundred times more, and in addition, eternal life. Note that Matthew omits Mark's hundredfold "in this age" (Mk 10:30); for him the final judgment is the time of reward and punishment.

4. The Workers in the Vineyard, 20:1-16

This parable, unique to Matthew, was probably placed here as an explanation of 19:30. The saying is repeated in 20:16. The parable form is similar to the parables of the Kingdom in chapter 13. Since the time of Isaiah, the vineyard was a familiar image of Israel. (See Is 5:1-7). The working conditions of the parable—unemployment, hiring of extra laborers, the silver coin as a day's wage—are true to Palestinian life of Jesus' day. The precise wage is agreed upon only with the first group. The later workers are promised only a fair wage. It is important to the parable that the last to be hired are paid first, a full day's wage. Thus the original laborers expect to be paid more. When they receive only what was promised, they begin to grumble against the owner.

The parable declares the sovereign grace and generosity of God, which welcomes (in the person of Jesus) latecomers into the Kingdom. It is addressed to those who criticized Jesus for receiving despised outcasts and sinners into God's mercy. The original workers are not wrong in expecting their wages. It is in comparing themselves to others (who have not worked as hard) that they part company with the mind of Jesus. The challenge is to learn from Jesus how to see things with the eyes of God and not with their own evil eye. (In the Greek, the phrase in verse 15 which is translated "Are you jealous?" reads "Is your eye evil?")

The key to the parable is the generosity of the owner and the complaints of the original workers. Its original context must have been a scene such as that of 9:10-13. Jesus welcomes sinners, and those who for years have observed the Law object that they are being treated unfairly. The incomprehensible goodness of God can become a stumbling block to the person who clings to human ideas of justice and merit. How long and faithfully we serve God is not important but only that we have been called and will receive a just reward.

5. *The Way to Greatness, 20:17-34*

Intending to set out for Jerusalem, probably to celebrate one of the feasts, Jesus takes aside the twelve (from the larger group of pilgrim disciples), in order to explain to them what is going to happen. In this third mention of the Passion (see 16:21 and 17:22-23), Jesus becomes more explicit, mentioning the Gentiles (Romans), mockery, scourging and crucifixion. It is difficult to understand the Good Friday behavior of the disciples, if they had already heard three such clear and detailed predictions of the Passion and Resurrection. Most scholars would hold that the details of the three accounts have been affected by the actual events. There is no doubt however that Jesus understood himself as the Suffering Servant of God and tried to

prepare his disciples for his death. In the Greek text, 17:20 indicates Jesus' firm resolve to face the future, with its enormous cost.

As in 16:24, Jesus again explains that his followers must share in his suffering. The disciples still failed to understand that participation in the Kingdom meant sharing in his suffering. Obviously James and John had eyes only for a share in Jesus' glory. Note how again Matthew protects the reputation of the disciples (20:20). In Mark 10:35 James and John themselves approach Jesus to ask the favor. Here it is their mother who seeks the best seats of honor. The plural of "You don't know what you are asking" confirms that Mark's version is the original.

The "cup" in verses 22-23 is a figure of God's punishment and retribution (see Is 51:17). By his death Jesus will drink the cup of God's wrath, that is, he will take upon himself the punishment for sin deserved by God's people. By promising that the brothers will share his cup, Jesus is not necessarily predicting their martyrdom, but promising that they will share in the suffering and renunciation which attend the life of any genuine disciple.

The anger of the other disciples, probably prompted by jealousy, provides the Master with yet another occasion for a teaching on greatness in his Kingdom. Jesus reminds them that in the community of his disciples greatness will not be manifested in terms of power and authority (as among the Gentiles), but will be measured in terms of service. Rank in God's dominion does not depend on ambition and talent but on the quality and whole-heartedness of one's service.

The model for such behavior is that of the Master himself, who came to serve others and to give his life as a ransom for many. The phrase "many people" does not mean that some are expected but is a Semitic way of expressing all. Thus the death of Jesus will be the means of liberating all of God's people from captivity to the slavery of sin. The idea of the life of a martyr being offered as a ransom for others was already present in 2 Mac 7:37-38. In addition Jesus may have had in mind the Suffering Servant theology of Is 53:12

As they leave Jericho, Jesus pauses to restore sight to two blind men. As already mentioned in week four, most scholars hold that this is the same miracle as that narrated in 9:27-31, but told from a different catechetical viewpoint.

Here we glimpse a twofold significance: (1) despite the fact that he goes to Jerusalem to suffer, Jesus is the Son of David (favorite title for the Messiah); and (2) despite the importance of his mission, Jesus stops to help two blind men. This son of David has come not to be served but to serve. The large crowds of pilgrims continue to accompany Jesus on his way to Jerusalem. The episode with its loud and repeated cries to the Son of David is a beautiful preparation for the entry into Jerusalem. Rather than the threefold "sir" of the *Good News* version (20:30, 31 and 33), we would prefer that the Greek *kyrie* be translated "Lord." In the first place, the text shows the influence of the Church's liturgy. The Greek reads: "Lord, have mercy on us, Son of David!" which is already an attempt to preserve the liturgical prayer form at the expense of good grammar. Secondly, the men, once healed, "follow" Jesus, a verb which is used only of disciples in Matthew. Of the evangelists, Matthew alone mentions Jesus' compassion and describes his reaching out to touch their eyes.

6. *The Entry into Jerusalem, 21:1-11*

Jesus begins his Jerusalem ministry with a solemn entry and the purification of the Temple. Although presented as a unit by the synoptic evangelists, the Jerusalem ministry is probably a collection of events which took place over a longer period of time. For example, the green branches and chants from Psalm 118 indicate that the feast for which Jesus and his disciples went up to Jerusalem was probably the Feast of Dedication (a winter feast) or that of Tabernacles, which occured in the fall). Yet only a few "days" later—26:2—it is the time for the Passover (a spring feast).

Jesus enters Jerusalem from the east (see Ezek 43:1-9). On the road from Jericho, Bethpage is the last village before the valley of Kedron. Zechariah 14:4 pictures the Mount of

Olives as a place of messianic judgment. (Rarely does Matthew provide this much geographical detail.) In a comparison with Mark's account (Mk 11:1-10), we notice that Matthew heightens the Messianic significance of the entry.

In Matthew Jesus declares his Messianic dignity and lays claim to the homage of God's people. The style of the entry also declares Jesus' understanding of his Messiahship. Matthew brings this out clearly by his fulfillment quotation in verse 5. Actually the quotation combines two texts, part of Is 62:11 and the beautiful prophecy of Zech 9:9:

> *Rejoice, rejoice, people of Zion!*
> *Shout for joy, you people of Jerusalem!*
> *Look, your king is coming to you!*
> *He comes triumphant and victorious,*
> *but humble and riding on a donkey—*
> *on a colt, the foal of a donkey (Zech 9:9).*

By the use of this text Matthew highlights the sense of excitement and joy which accompanied this dramatic moment. Where Mark speaks of "many" or those "in front and those who followed behind," Matthew notes that great "crowds" accompanied Jesus. Another Matthean touch, in verse 10, is the mention that "the whole city was thrown in an uproar." The reader cannot help but remember the turmoil of Herod and all Jerusalem upon hearing of the birth of the king of the Jews (see 2:3). In both cases Matthew pictures all Jerusalem as affected by Jesus' presence.

By quoting Zechariah Matthew makes clear that Jesus acted in deliberate fulfillment of the prophet's words. But Matthew has deliberately omitted the words "triumphant and victorious," since he wants to emphasize the gentleness and humility of the Messiah. The gentleness/ humility/meekness of Jesus was emphasized in 11:29 and encouraged as a quality of every disciple in 5:5. His care to demonstrate the fulfillment of the prophecy explains also the confusing picture in which Jesus seems to be riding both the donkey and the colt. Semitic poetry frequently uses parallels to speak of one object. Thus Zechariah's donkey and colt refer to only one beast.

The reaction of the crowds in 21:8-9 is typical of the reception of a king (2 Kg 9:13) or a military hero (1 Mac 13:51 and 2 Mac 10:7). The acclamation of the crowds is taken from Psalm 118:25-26, traditionally used at the great feasts. The "Hosanna!" ("Praise!" in the *Good News* translation) was originally a cry of help (Lord, save us!), but in time it became an acclamation of praise and joy. The crowds acclaim Jesus as the Son of David and the Lord's representative. It is probable that by the time Matthew wrote the Gospel these acclamations had already become part of Christian liturgy. In verse 11 Jesus, who fulfills the prophecies of the Hebrew Scriptures, is himself welcomed

as a prophet. Like earlier prophets he will die in the city he
has entered.

7. *The Temple and the Fig Tree, 21:12-22*

Matthew's account of the purification of the Temple is
highly dramatic. Immediately after his entry Jesus goes to

the Temple and, by symbolically purifying it, inaugurates
the final Messianic era in Jerusalem itself. Two texts from
the Hebrew Scriptures illuminate the significance of this
event:

> *The LORD Almighty answers...*
> *"Then the Lord you are looking for will suddenly*
> *come to his Temple. The messenger you long to see*
> *will come and proclaim my covenant."*
> *But who will be able to endure the day when he*

> *comes? Who will be able to survive when he appears?*
> *He will be like strong soap, like a fire that refines*
> *metal.... As a metalworker refines silver and gold, so*
> *the LORD's messenger will purify the priests...(Mal*
> *3:1-3).*

> *When that time comes, there will no longer be any*
> *merchant in the Temple of the LORD Almighty (Zech*
> *14:21).*

Thus the purification of the Temple formed an important part of Jewish expectations for the coming of the Messiah. By this action Jesus clarifies the revelation of himself as Messiah which began with his entrance into the Holy City. In 12:6 he had asserted: "There is something here greater than the temple." Now he symbolically claims that supremacy.

The moneychangers were engaged in the task of changing Greek and Roman coins into the standard Temple currency, while the pigeon sellers provided the sacrifices used by the poor for purification ceremonies. Jesus' action is not so much directed against the immorality of the businessmen as it is against the whole sacrificial practice of Israel. Sacrifice was acceptable to God only insofar as it expressed the genuine faithfulness of Israel to the covenant. The Temple cult should have been an expression of true worship; instead, the moral bankruptcy of much of Israel's leadership renders it unsatisfactory (see Amos 5:22-27 and Is 1:11-17). By his action Jesus proclaims the imminence of a new order: true worship of God will no longer take place in the Temple but in the person of the Messiah. Jesus justified his radical action by quoting two texts of the Scriptures, Is 56:7 and Jer 7:11. The latter text, in particular, helps us to understand Jesus' prophetic action:

"Look, you put your trust in deceitful words. You steal, murder, commit adultery, tell lies under oath, offer sacrifices to Baal, and worship Gods that you had not known before. You do these things I hate, and then you come and stand in my presence, in my own Temple, and say, 'We are safe!' Do you think that my Temple is a hiding place for robbers? I have seen what you are doing (Jer 7:8-11)."

The healing of the blind and the crippled strengthens the Messianic dimensions of this moment. An ancient ruling of David excluded them from the Temple area (2 Sam 5:8), but the Son of David welcomes them and restores their wholeness. This is the only healing in Jerusalem recorded by the synoptic evangelists; thus it must have carried a special importance for Matthew. The text highlights the incongruity of the event: the "wonderful things (21:15)" provoke two very different reactions. The chief priests and scribes notice only that Jesus is taking the Law into his own hands. (We have already seen in chapter 12 that for Jesus compassion is the prime value; a legalistic approach to the Law can mask the demands of compassion, and thus be displeasing to God.) While the Temple officials are angry, the children are responding to the wonderful deeds of Jesus with the Messianic cry, "Praise to David's Son!" Thus Matthew contrasts the official representative of Judaism, who should have received the Messiah, with the children, who receive him with joy. How often have we seen in Matthew that it is the children, the little ones, whose hearts are open and responsive to God's design!

The Jewish leaders fail to recognize the Messiah at the crucial moment. This provides the clue for interpreting the strange episode of the cursing of the fig tree (21:18-19). Frequently the prophets performed symbolic gestures, dramatic actions which expressed what was happening in the covenant relationship. (See, for example, Jer 13:1-11 and Ez 4:1-3.) Israel is represented by a fig tree, from which God seeks fruit in vain. The concept of sterility and the absence of fruit is a favorite Hebrew image in describing the sinful state of God's people (see Jer 8:13). The fruit that Jesus seeks is fidelity to God's will.

Prophetic actions are symbols, and symbols can be interpreted in many ways. It could be said that the fig tree symbolized Judaism itself, being condemned to barrenness because it did not accept Jesus as Messiah and Lord. Mark's account of this incident relates the fate of the fig tree more to the barrenness of worship in the Temple. In Mark's account Jesus arrived in Jerusalem and went to the Temple late in the day. There he "looked around at everything (Mk 11:11)." He left the Temple, spent the night at Bethany and, early the next morning, started out for the Temple again. On the road to the Temple Jesus searches a fig tree for figs, and, not finding any, says, "No one shall ever eat figs from you again! (11:14)." Then Jesus goes to the Temple, purifies it by driving out the buyers and sellers, leaving the city at nightfall (Mk 11:15-19). On the following day the disciples find the cursed fig tree "dead all the way down to its roots (Mk 11:21)." Judaism has been without the Temple for nineteen centuries.

However, even without its Temple, the Jews are still a people, "most dear to God." The teaching of the Second Vatican Council states:

> As holy Scripture testifies, Jerusalem did not recognize the time of her visitation (cf Lk 19:44), nor did the Jews in large numbers accept the gospel; indeed, not a few opposed the spreading of it (cf. Rom 11:28). Nevertheless, according to the Apostle [Paul], the Jews still remain most dear to God because of their fathers, for He does not repent of the gifts He makes

nor of the calls He issues (cf. Rom 11:28-29). DEC-LARATION ON THE RELATIONSHIP OF THE CHURCH TO NON-CHRISTIAN RELIGIONS, #4.

Most scholars think that verses 20-22 were connected to the cursing of the tree by later tradition. Note that in Mark they are separated by the cleansing of the Temple (Mk 11:12-14, 20-24), with the result that the withering of the tree is not discovered until the following day. In both synoptic writers, however, the discussion of the meaning of the withered tree has nothing to do with the original prophetic action of Jesus. The tradition has focused on the miraculous power of Jesus, and thus the explanation becomes a teaching on the importance of expectant faith in prayer. We have already seen the essence of this teaching in 17:20. Here the emphasis is on the opposition between doubt and faith. If disciples do not doubt, they will share in the miraculous power of the Master. The teaching is not an invitation to a magical approach toward prayer, but a reminder that Christian prayer flows from a boundless confidence in the Lord and a total openness to his designs in human history.

8. *The Authority of Jesus and its Rejection, 21:23-22:14*

Jesus' actions have shocked the Jewish leaders. On his return to the Temple they challenge the basis of his authority: does it come from God, from men or from himself? The account is recorded in a form common to Jewish religious debates. Thus, Jesus answers by asking another question. If the elders cannot discern about the authority of John the Baptist (whether from embarrassment or fear), then they are not competent to pronounce judgment on Jesus.

With this challenge Matthew introduces a long series of

controversies about the authority of Jesus. In this section we will discuss the three parables with which Jesus responds to the Jewish leaders. Only Matthew records all three. He has arranged them in an ascending order: (a) the two sons (the present situation of Jesus' day); (b) the wicked tenants (judgments on Israel within history, fulfilled in the destruction of Jerusalem); and (c) the wedding feast (final fulfillment of the end-time, from which the old Israel has been excluded).

a. The parable of the two sons, 21:28-32

In this parable Jesus contrasts two reactions within Israel to God's will. The "sinners" at first refused to do God's will, that is, they ignored the Law and the teachings of the rabbis. Later, however, they repented through the preaching of John and Jesus, opening their hearts to God's design. The righteous, on the other hand, said "yes" to God by meticulously following the Law. In fact, however, they did not do what God really wanted.

This parable is unique to Matthew, and the presence of many of his literary characteristics and favorite theological themes (i.e., the will of God, the kingdom of God) indicate that he was the first to hand on the tradition in written form. It has many similarities with the parable of the two sons in Luke 15:11-32. Both probably originated in a setting such as that of 9:10-13, in which the ministry of Jesus to outcasts was challenged.

b. The parable of the tenants in the vineyard, 21:33-46

In this second parable of the trilogy, Jesus confronts the Jewish leaders with their failure to bear the fruit expected of them. Scholars dispute the exact nature of the original parable told by Jesus. Certainly as Matthew hands it on here it evidences the post-Easter reflection of the Church.

The parable provokes the Jewish leaders to an even more

determined resistance to Jesus. They could not mistake that it was directed at them, since the vineyard is clearly Israel—verse 33 is almost a quotation from Is 5:1-2—and they are the official stewards of Israel's heritage. The parable takes the form of an allegory, in which the landowner is God, the two groups of slaves refer to the prophets of Israel, and the son is Christ himself. Comparison with Mark 12:1-12 shows that Matthew emphasizes the sequence of events as an exact outline of redemptive history. The Marcan account of three individual slaves becomes two groups of slaves (the earlier and later prophets), who are stoned, the classic death of a prophet (see 2 Chron 24:21 and Mt 23:37). The son is killed outside the vineyard, as Jesus was crucified outside Jerusalem. In addition Matthew emphasizes (21:41, 43) that the vineyard will not only be taken away from its original tenants but will be given to those who will produce the expected fruits.

In verse 42 Jesus emphasizes the conclusion already drawn by the elders: by their own choice they have put themselves outside of God's wonderful plan. Attention is now drawn away from the past (vineyard and tenants) and focused on the new building (the Church) of which Christ is the cornerstone. Luke adds here a quotation from Is 8:14, which found its way into some texts of Matthew. The more reliable manuscripts of Matthew's Gospel do not contain this quotation. That it is probably not original is indicated by the brackets around verse 44.

Thus Matthew shifts the focus of the parable from the unworthiness of the original tenants and the killing of the son to the transference of the Kingdom from Israel to the Church. Jesus' own mission is to the Jews alone; he is the hope of Israel. Yet she rejects her Messiah and thus proves unfaithful to her privilege as God's chosen nation. From this time on, entry to the Kingdom will not follow from merely belonging to the chosen people, but will take place, for both Jew and Gentile, through faith in Jesus as Messiah and Son of God.

c. The parable of the wedding feast, 22:1-14

Matthew here has probably united two separate parables, one which again reaffirms that salvation is passing from Israel to others (22:1-10), and a second which warns that, even for Christians, membership in the Church without the fruits of discipleship is not sufficient (22:11-13). A comparison of the parable as Luke records it reveals the freedom of the evangelists in handing on the oral tradition. Matthew adds many details to the first parable, thereby adapting it to his theological purposes. A list of the most important adaptations follows:

Luke 14:16-24	Matthew 22:1-14	Theological Purpose
a man...a great feast (16)	a king...a wedding feast (2)	Dramatizes the significance of the parable; the messianic times were often pictured as a wedding feast (see Is 25:6-7).
they all began...to make excuses (18)	they did not want to come (3) the invited guests paid no attention, grabbed the servants...and killed them (5-6)	Although more effort is expended, the guests deliberately refuse; they mistreat God's servants; a harsher picture of Israel.
	The king...sent his soldiers, who killed those murderers and burned down their city. (8)	This could represent the later addition of the Church, symbolizing the Roman destruction of Jerusalem in 70 A.D.

| 'Hurry out to the streets...and bring back the poor'...(21) | 'the people I invited did not deserve it. Now go...invite to the feast as many people as you find.' (9) | In Luke the invitation passes from the Jewish leaders to the poor. In Matthew from the Jews to the Gentiles. |

The presence in the banquet hall of both good and bad (22:10) prepares the way for the subsequent parable. These verses (22:11-13) are unique to Matthew, and many scholars consider that it was added by the evangelist himself, the fruit of his reflection on the teaching of Jesus. In chapter 13 Matthew has insisted that the Church consists both of good and bad, and that the time of separation will arrive only at the final judgment (see 13:36-43; 47-50). The wedding clothes represent the faithful obedience which is expected of disciples.

Although the members of the Church have entered the Kingdom of heaven, this in itself is no guarantee of a favorable judgment. Without the wedding garment of obedience to the Father's will, even Christian believers will be cast outside at the judgment. Verse 14 could be paraphrased in this way: all are invited, but not all qualify for admission (see 7:21-23, 13:40-43).

9. The Authority of Jesus Vindicated, 22:15-46.

Matthew follows the three parables (four parables if one holds 22:1-10 and 22:11-13 to be two separate parables) with four moments of controversy between Jesus and the Jewish leaders. Each event adds to the picture of the final division between the Hope of Israel and its official leaders.

a. The question about payment of taxes, 22:15-22
Matthew paints a darker picture of the intentions of the Pharisees than that of Mark 12:13-17. Their concern is to

trap Jesus, either into disfavor with Rome (if he objected to the taxes) or into unpopularity with the people, who bitterly resented the taxes. The debate involves a poll-tax levied on all male inhabitants of Palestine in 6 A.D. It was paid directly to Rome, using a silver denarius which was specially minted for the tax. As Roman loyalists, the Herodians would have favored the tax, while the Pharisees probably joined the people in opposing it.

The question carries civil implications, but its more important dimension is theological: is it permissible according to the law to pay the tax? As usual, Jesus' reply cuts to the heart of the question. Some scholars have proposed that Jesus' answer is based on a passage from Ecclesiastes 8:2, which reads in part: "Observe the precept of the king, and in view of your oath to God, be not hasty to withdraw from the king." "King" in this text could refer, at different levels, both to the earthly ruler and to God. Jesus' answer then means: obey the Emperor in matters of civil government (where the Law makes no demands), for this is also obedience to God himself. But where God has spoken through the Law (and particularly if there should arise a conflict between the Law and the demands of the Emperor), God alone is to be obeyed.

Jesus' reply thus shows a positive appreciation of the role of the state, which is not incompatible with the demands of the Kingdom of God. However this saying of the Lord cannot provide the basis for a theology of politics. Jesus definitely does not intend to divide up the world into areas belonging to Caesar and to God. He makes no attempt to define whether Caesar has a right to rule or exactly what belongs to him. What is clear is that a person's entire life belongs to God, and that obedience to the state which does not compromise this prior demand is legitimate.

b. The question about rising from the dead, 22:23-33

The Sadducees (see commentary on Mt 3:7-12) were theological conservatives and refused to accept belief in an individual life after death, which had entered Jewish theology during the time of the Maccabees. Their question seeks to reduce such belief to an absurdity. In addition they probably hoped to further alienate Jesus from the Pharisees.

The Mosaic teaching cited in the example is taken from Deut 25:5-6 (see also Gen 38:6-8). By producing children of his deceased brother's wife, the living brother continued his name and family, and thus a certain kind of immortality. This practice arose long before belief in external life developed in Judaism.

Jesus' answer is twofold: (a) the Sadducees' understanding of the resurrection life is too materialistic; it will not be just an extension of the good life of the present world; (b) moreover they fail to understand the Scriptures. The quotation from Ex 3:6 points to the resurrection, since God speaks to Moses as if the patriarchs were contemporaries with one another and with Moses. Yahweh proclaims that he is not the God (that is, the unceasing protector) of the dead, but only of the living. Matthew concludes the episode by mentioning once again that the crowds were amazed at Jesus' teaching.

c. The question about the great commandment, 22:34-40

Again Matthew portrays the Pharisees as the leading opponents of Jesus (as they also were of the early Church). He notes that "they came together (22:34)," wording which foreshadows their plotting against Jesus in the Passion narrative. One of their party, who is also learned in the Law, attempts to trap him. The rabbis distinguished 613 separate commandments to the Law, which were divided into greater (heavy) and lesser (light) commandments. The question posed was normal in rabbinic discussion; often rabbis attempted to sum up the spirit of the entire body of Jewish law.

In answer, Jesus quotes Deut 6:5, which formed part of the *Shema,* the prayer and profession of faith recited daily by devout Jews. Love of God must involve heart, soul and mind, that is, the totality of the person. Another commandment, he adds, is equally important, equally central. (The *Good News* translation could be misleading; the second commandment, cited from Lev 19:18, is not second in importance, but a second which is of equal gravity.) Love of neighbor is not identified with love of God, but one is as urgent as the other.

On these two commandments, Our Lord adds, the entire Law and the prophetic writings depend, that is, hang as a door on its hinges. All the commandments and the prophetic teachings flow from these two as their basis. The newness in Jesus' response does not lie in his bringing together these two commandments (note that Luke places them on the lips of the Jewish lawyer, Lk 10:27) but in making them equally "heavy" and the foundation of all other commandments. Thus Our Lord cut through the tangle and confusion which 613 commandments created, to show that there is no fulfillment of the Law which is not, at root, loving obedience to God or loving service to neighbor. Here Matthew clearly underlines the fundamental difference between legalism and the teaching of Jesus. God's will is not fulfilled if a legalistic observance of particular commandments shields us from the "weightier" matters of love and compassion. The duty of the disciple is to seek the greater faithfulness which Our Lord speaks of in 5:20.

Before concluding, we should notice how the situation of Matthew's community has colored the account of this controversy. We have already noted that the Pharisees are pictured as trying to trap Jesus. In Mark 12:28-34 this polemical atmosphere is not present. The scribe there is pleased with Jesus' answer to the Sadducees about the resurrection and is delighted with Jesus' response to his own question and makes the answer his own. What was a genuine question in Mark becomes in Matthew a snare in which to trap Jesus. This again demonstrates the freedom which the early community felt in adapting the tradition to their own catechetical needs. Moreover Matthew strengthens the position of the two "hinge" commandments. In Mark 12:31 Jesus says, "There is no other commandment more important than these two." Matthew aligns the response with the theological position he has repeatedly taken in the Gospel (see 5:43-48; 7:12; 9:13; 12:7-13; 19-19; 23:23; and 25:31-46): "The whole Law of Moses and the teachings of the prophets depend on these two commandments (22:40)."

d. *The question about the Messiah, 22:41-46*

In this last of the four controversies, Jesus himself poses a question for the Pharisees. The title, Son of David, is important for Matthew. He devotes the first passages of his account of the Gospel to demonstrating that Jesus, in spite of the virgin birth, is the true Son of David. "Have mercy on us, Son of David" is a frequent cry in the Gospel (see 9:27; 15:22 and 20:30-31), and it accompanies the Messianic entry into Jerusalem (21:9,15). Throughout his account Matthew has insisted that Jesus' mission was first to the lost sheep of the house of Israel (see 9:36; 10:6; 15:24); it was not a lack of faithfulness on God's part that accounted for the failure of many first century Jews to recognize Jesus as the Messiah.

Matthew is also aware that Jesus' significance extends beyond Israel, and that he has a transcendent dignity which earns him also the title of David's Lord. Thus this first verse of Psalm 110 became a favorite passage of early Christian liturgy and literature. Just as Jesus is greater than

John, Solomon and the Temple, so he is greater than David.

In verse 46 Matthew emphasizes the impotence of the Pharisees to make any reply. Jesus has emerged victorious in this period of controversy with the Jewish leaders. The stage is now set for the condemnation of the Jewish leaders in chapter 23.

B. The Fifth Discourse, Part One: Warning Against the Jewish Leaders, 23:1-39

OVERVIEW: This section serves both as a conclusion to the long controversy between Jesus and the Jewish leaders (chapters 21 and 22) and as the opening part of the final discourse. Through a comparison with the parallel passages in Mark (Mk 12:38-40) and Luke (Lk 11:39-51; 13:34-35; and 20:45-47), it becomes evident that again the sermon format is the product of Matthew's catechetical genius. He has gathered sayings of the Lord from various moments of his ministry and ordered them into a unit. Another evidence of this is provided by the diversity of audiences in this chapter: Jesus speaks to the crowds (verses 2-7), to the disciples (verses 8-12), to the scribes and Pharisees (verses 13-33), and to the entire population of Jerusalem (verses 34-39).

In interpreting this chapter we must again recall the twofold level on which Matthew composes his account. The two groups mentioned in 23:1 represent not only the historical crowds and the original disciples of Jesus' ministry but also Pharisaic Judaism (the crowds) and the Matthean church (the disciples) of the 80's. This explains the intensity of the warning against the Jewish leaders. Matthew's young community is fighting for its very survival against a Judaism which, after the destruction of the Temple in 70 A.D., seeks to preserve its traditions through strict regulations. Thus the extreme bitterness of this chapter does not spring from the attitudes of Jesus during his ministry but from the fact that Matthew remembers the controversies of Jesus' ministry from the perspective of the bitter struggle of his own day.

1. Attitude of the Disciples to the Scribes and Pharisees, 23:1-7

In verses 2-3 the authority of the Jewish leaders is recognized; they are "the authorized interpreters of Moses' Law (23:2)," and so must be obeyed. This approval of their teaching is surprising. In 5:21-48, 15:1-20 and 16:11-12 Jesus has rejected the way in which the Jewish leaders interpet the Law of God. We catch here a glimpse of the tension within the young Christian community. Some Christians wanted to remain totally faithful to the Law of Moses; others wanted to break free from it. Jesus here does not condemn the Pharisees' authority to teach but the fact that they do not follow their own teachings.

Many of them interpreted the Law in ways which suited their own lifestyle but which were burdensome for the average person (23:4). In verses 5-7 Jesus criticizes their desire to be seen as pious and to enjoy a place of honor in the community. The "containers with scripture verses (23:5)"—usually quotations from Exodus or Deuteronomy—were worn as a literal fulfillment of Ex 13:9 and 16. The "hems of their cloaks (23:5)" had been commanded by Num 15:37-41. Jesus himself wore such fringes, but some of the Pharisees lengthened them in order to demonstrate that their fidelity to the Law was greater than that of others.

2. Warning to the Community, 23:8-12

In this section we hear an application of 23:7 to the

Christian community. It was possible that some Christian leaders had begun to take on the lordly airs which Jesus had warned against. The Christian community is a body of disciples, of brothers and sisters; there is only one Teacher, one Father, and one Leader.

This teaching objects not so much to the use of titles as to the relationship which underlies them. A Jewish teacher or rabbi (which literally means "my great one") was often held in such great reverence that he became an obstacle to the believer's direct dependence on God as the unique Teacher and Father. While the sayings of the rabbis were held in great honor and passed on from generation to generation, early Christian writings contain no sayings of the Apostles; Christ is the only authority, and all teaching flows from him alone. Thus the Christian leader is called to humble service (23:11-12).

3. The Seven Lamentations, 23:13-33

These denunciations are not curses, as has often been supposed, but lamentations. They do not call down God's anger upon the scribes and Pharisees; rather Matthew is convinced that God has already pronounced judgment upon his people, and particularly upon her spiritual guides. Matthew again has made use of the theological significance of the number seven. Not counting verse 14, which is not found in the most reliable manuscripts, Matthew shapes the teaching of Jesus into seven lamentations.

First Lamentation (23:13)—Entry into the Kingdom is the goal of every believer. What a terrible indictment of their ministry, to say that the religious leaders of Israel prevent God's people from entering the Kingdom! During the ministry of Jesus, this charge probably meant that by their teaching the leaders obscured the really important issues. In the situation of the 80's, the charge has become more serious. The Kingdom has already been inaugurated by the preaching of Jesus. The Pharisees refuse to believe, and try to prevent others from believing in Jesus as Messiah.

Second Lamentation (23:15)—There is evidence of vigorous Jewish missionary activity during the first century, at least until the 70's. A convert not only accepted belief in the one God but also accepted circumcision. The phrase "twice as deserving of going to hell" reflects the situation of the 80's. Gentile converts to Judaism were probably even more opposed to belief in Christ and to the Christian community than their teachers.

Third Lamentation (23:16-22)—In this section we glimpse the intricacies of scribal rulings on the Law. Jews of this period were reluctant to swear by God's name, and so would swear by the altar or the Temple. Over a period of time some tried to void an oath on the grounds that the Temple did not represent God but was merely a building. Thus the rabbis sought formulas which would make such equivocation impossible; one could swear by the gold in the temple or the gifts on the altar. We have already seen a similar example of this legalistic approach to the Law in the practice of the Qorban (see 15:3-9). Jesus cuts through the legalism with a single stroke: all oaths ultimately call upon God for their verification, and thus all are equally binding. His own position on oaths is more radical: do not swear at all (5:33-37).

Fourth Lamentation (23:23-24)—Deuteronomy 14:22-23 commanded the tithing of crops. Some of the Jewish leaders extended the obligation even to the smallest garden herbs. Yet they neglected "the really important teachings of the Law (23:23)." Again and again we have heard this accusation. Many Pharisees give scrupulous attention to unimportant matters, which inevitably results in a loss of perspective. The triad of justice, mercy and honesty is consistent with the earlier teaching of Jesus: the greater faithfulness of 5:20; the golden rule of 7:12; the kindness of 9:13 and 12:7; and the two great commandments of 22:37-40.

Fifth Lamentation (23:25-26)—Jesus takes up the accusation of the prophets (see Is 1:10-17 and Amos 5:21-6:7) that ritual observances without love and justice were empty and a mockery of God. The scribes and Pharisees are careful to wash their dishes in conformity with the laws of ritual cleanliness. Yet the food some of them eat from such clean vessels is the result of greed and exortion. It is justice that makes one's eating "clean" (see 15:10-20).

Sixth Lamentation (23:27-28)—During Passover the tombs around Jerusalem were whitewashed, so that pilgrims would not accidently make themselves unclean by touching one. The tombs glistened in the spring sunlight, but within were dark and full of decay. This, Jesus laments, is the spiritual condition of the religious leaders of Israel.

Seventh Lamentation (23:29-31)—Although hostility to the prophets and their stinging indictments goes back to the origins of Israel, the picture painted here is excessive; there are few instances in Hebrew literature of the murder of prophets. The reasoning used in verses 29-31 is rabbinical and difficult to follow. Perhaps some of the Jewish leaders thought that by building monuments over the tombs of the prophets they atoned for their ancestors' murders. However their present conduct proves them to be true sons of their fathers.

Conclusion (23:32-36)—With verse 32 the style changes to that of the apocalyptic literature. Verse 33 recalls the preaching of John the Baptist in 3:7. The opportunity to escape from God's wrath has now passed. As the Christian prophets and wise men and teachers arrive, the unrepentant Jewish leaders will have the opportunity to complete the work which their ancestors have begun. The murdering of the prophets, John the Baptist, Jesus himself and the early Christian missionaries constitutes one continuous process. (There is no evidence that Christian missionaries were crucified; the phrase "nail others to the cross" in 23:24 may have been added after Matthew's times.) Matthew understood the "punishment for all these (23:36)" as fulfilled in the destruction of Jerusalem.

4. *The Lament over Jerusalem, 23:37-39*

This climactic moment of the discourse pictures Jesus' love for God's people and his desire to draw Jerusalem to himself. The Hebrew Scriptures had compared God's care

for his people with that of a mother for her child (see Is 49:15) or of a bird sheltering her young (see Deut 32:11; Ps 17:8; Ps 36:7). Now we find Jesus speaking the metaphors that those Scriptures have used to describe God's solicitude for his people. Jesus laments Jerusalem's rejection of his message and his person. This passage concludes the section which began with chapter 19 and which included the enthusiastic welcome of the son of David by Jerusalem

(21:8-11). The "home" of verse 38 refers to the Temple, which symbolizes the entire people. We hear echoes of earlier prophetic words such as those of Jer 12:7 and Ez 10:18-19, in which Yahweh is pictured as leaving the Temple. The event predicted in 23:39 is not totally agreed upon by the evangelists. In Luke it could look forward to Jesus' messianic entrance into Jerusalem (see Lk 13:35). However in Matthew's account that event has already occurred. It might refer to a later coming of Christ, probably his advent as Judge at the end time. Some scholars have seen in verse 39 the possibility of an eventual conversion of Israel, such as that foreseen by Paul in Romans 11:25.

Week Eight

Our study of this final week is divided into three parts. In the first part we conclude the final discourse of Jesus, in which he speaks of the end of time and the coming in glory of the Son of Man. The communities of Paul and Mark had expected the second coming within a few years after the ascension of Jesus. By the time that Matthew writes it has become evident that Jesus' coming might lie in the distant future. How, then, can the disciples avoid complacency? Matthew responds by emphasizing the necessity of watchfulness, of preparedness for the Lord's coming, of faithful service until that time.

In the second part we will study the narrative of Our Lord's passion and death (chapters 26-27). This narrative formed the heart of the early preaching of the apostles and was the first part of the Gospel tradition to be written down. In the passion we reach the culmination of the life and ministry of Jesus. What strikes us is the brevity and soberness of the account. Matthew does not try to stir up our emotions or to produce an artificial sense of tragedy. His perspective for remembering these events is the resurrection of Jesus. Thus, even here, Jesus is majestic, is in control, is the Lord.

We conclude our study program with Matthew's account of the resurrection of Jesus, the appearance to the disciples in Galilee and the solemn commissioning of the disciples to continue the work of Jesus Christ himself (chapter 28).

Chapters 26 through 28, dealing with death, resurrection and new beginnings, parallel chapters 1 through 4, which recount the birth of Jesus and the beginnings of his public ministry. Many of the themes of the first four chapters of the Gospel will find their conclusion in the last three chapters. The hostility of Herod, the Pharisees and the scribes to the inquiry of the magi about the child born king of the Jews finds its terrible consummation in the trial and death of Jesus. As Jesus recognized his calling to be the obedient Suffering Servant of God in chapters 3 and 4, he suffers ridicule and crucifixion in chapters 26 and 27. As God's providential care saved Jesus from the murdering soldiers of Herod, so God watches over his crucified Son, raising him to life on the third day.

Matthew wants to teach us that Jesus is fulfilling the Father's plan. Through the Hebrew Scriptures the Father had foretold all these events. Nothing happens outside the scope of his power. With your group explore how the power and providence of the Father continue to guide the disciples of Jesus.

Daily Study Assignments: Week Eight

Day	Matthew	Commentary
1	24:1-51	Pages 241-251
2	25:1-46	Pages 251-260
3	26:1-75	Pages 262-273
4	27:1-66	Pages 273-284
5	28:1-20	Pages 285-293

6—Reflect on Chapters 24 through 28 in light of the reflection questions listed below.

7—STUDY GROUP MEETING

- Many Christians try to relate current social and political events to the biblical prophecies about the end of time. What response do you think Matthew would give to such endeavors?

- What are your own feelings about the second coming of Jesus? Is it an important doctrine in your life?

- Several times Matthew speaks of the surprise of those who expected to enter the Kingdom but were refused entry (7:22-23; 25:11-12, 24:30; 25:44-46). How can we apply this teaching to our own lives? In what ways can we apply the teaching of 25:31-46 in our parish life?

- Matthew brackets the account of the institution of the Eucharist with Jesus' knowledge of Judas' betrayal and the prediction of Peter's denial (26:17-35). How do we sometimes re-enact this pattern?

- Which event of the passion narrative speaks most strongly to you?

- What is the significance of the resurrection in your own life?

- Some scholars see in the solemn commission of the risen Jesus (28:16-20) a summary of Matthew's entire Gospel. Which words express major themes of his theology?

The Final Discourse Concluded, the Passion and Resurrection of Jesus, 24:1-28:20

A. The Fifth Discourse, Part Two: Ultimate Realities, 24:1-25:46

OVERVIEW: We have divided the fifth discourse of Jesus into two parts, the first part of which we studied at the end of the seventh week. We begin our eighth week with the second part of this discourse which is addressed to the disciples on the Mount of Olives overlooking Jerusalem. This part of the discourse is basically written in the style of a farewell address, the final thoughts of a great man shared with his intimate friends. The subject matter is Jesus' answers to three questions: the question regarding the end of the world, the question about the destruction of Jerusalem, and the question about the coming of the Son of Man in glory. This section of the gospel is often referred to as the "apocalyptic discourse" because it employs the conventional imagery of cosmic upheaval associated with God's final intervention in the history of the world. The answer to the third question is followed by seven parables (24:32-25:46), the last of which (25:31-46) is more a scenario of the final judgment than a parable. Matthew's teaching is clear: the Church must be alert and faithful lest the final coming of Jesus find them unprepared.

1. The Disciples's Questions, 24:1-3

Leaving the area near the Temple, Jesus predicts the Temple's destruction. Arriving at a place on the Mount of Olives, the disciples ask Jesus:

"Tell us when all this will be, ... and what will

happen to show that it is the time of your coming and the end of the age (24:3)."

2. The Answer to the Question About the End of the Age, 24:4-14

Jesus begins speaking about the third part of the disciples' question, regarding the end of time. Note that for both the disciples of Jesus' own day as well as the members of Matthew's community, the subject matter of these verses concerns the future. Although the earliest followers of Jesus expected the end of the world and the glorious coming of Jesus to come shortly after his death and resurrection, by the time Matthew writes it is clear that an indefinite period of history stretches out before the Church and the world.

Matthew's concern is to provide his community with the assurances of Jesus so that turmoil within the community can be avoided. Jesus says, "... do not let anyone fool you. Because many men will come in my name, saying, 'I am the Messiah!' (24:4-5)." These false Messiahs might point to the events of history as they make their false claims, saying that wars and battles are evidence of the end. Jesus tells his community not to be troubled, because such events "must happen, but they do not mean that the end has come (24:6)."

The traditional apocalyptic symbols of the world's end: wars, famines, earthquakes, images of cosmic catastrophe, are put in a different context by Jesus. The life of the disciple is a life of continued faithfulness, not a series of external repentings triggered by each natural or historical disaster.

The more reliable signs regarding the end are those that affect the community: persecution, hatred by others, the stress of persecution that leads some to give up their faith, and the false prophets (see 7:21-23; 13:41-42) who lead others astray. Finally, the love that should characterize the life of the disciple "will grow cold (24:9-12)."

In verse 13, the tone of this section shifts to one of hope: "But whoever holds out to the end will be saved (24:13)." It is a theme characteristic of Matthew's proclamation of Jesus; salvation is not complete until the end. We saw the same teaching of Jesus applied earlier to the community of the church in the 80's (10:22). In the garden of Gethsemane Jesus will encourage the disciples to pray and be watchful, lest they fall away at a time of testing (26:41). Only after "this Good News about the Kingdom" is preached through all the world will the end come (24:14).

3. The Answer to the Question about the Destruction of Jerusalem, 24:15-22

Keep in mind that these verses, dealing with the fall of Jerusalem during the Jewish-Roman war of 66-73 A.D., describe an event that lay in the future from the point of view of Jesus. From the point of view, however, of Matthew's community, these verses describe an event that has already happened.

"The Awful Horror" mentioned in the book of Daniel probably referred to the statue of the Greek god, Zeus, which Antiochus Epiphanes set up in the Temple in 168 B.C. (see Daniel 9:27 and Daniel 12:11). In this context it could refer to the Roman presence in the Temple or its destruction by the Romans. The entire section of 24:15-22 is clearest when understood in the context of the events of the Jewish war. Fighting broke out in 66 A.D. After the Romans were driven out of Jerusalem by the Zealots, there were periods of civil war within the city itself. In 70 Titus laid seige to Jerusalem and the suffering of the inhabitants was terrible. There was a lack of food and water, as well as all the human tragedy associated with the irrational destruction of war.

There is a report that Christians had left the city prior to 68 A.D. and fled to Pella in Perea. If so, there is likelihood that the prophecy of Jesus regarding Jerusalem influenced their decision to flee the city. Keep in mind that Jerusalem had been under seige before, and that the first Temple built by Solomon had been destroyed by the Babylonians in 586. Jesus knew the writings of the prophets. He knew of God's message delivered by Jeremiah," And now, since you have committed all these sins...I will treat this Temple that bears my name, and in which you put your trust...just as I treated Shiloh (Jeremiah 7:13-14)." Jesus knew of Ezekiel's foretelling of the siege of Jerusalem:

> "...I mean to destroy the stock of bread in Jerusalem; in their distress they will eat bread strictly weighed; in terror they will drink water grudgingly measured...; they will all pine and waste away as a result of their sins (Ezekiel 4:16-17)."

Foreseeing the eventual clash between the Jewish people and the Roman Empire's occupation forces, Jesus told his disciples that when the sign spoken of by Daniel again appears, "The Awful Horror," they are to flee for their lives because the terrible time, the time of trial will soon follow. The absolute urgency of immediate flight is sketched in terms of daily life in first century Israel. If one is on the rooftop, one must not even stop to enter the house in order to carry away any belongings (24:17). If ploughing in the field, one must not even return to the edge of the field to pick up one's cloak (24:18). The compassion of Jesus is striking—he thinks of the difficulty of pregnant and nursing refugees and grieves over their suffering (24:19). He instructs his followers to pray that the time of flight will not have to be during the winter, the rainy season in Israel (24:20). Concerned for the importance of the Law, Matthew adds the phrase "or on a Sabbath" to his Markan source. Flight would entail more than a Sabbath day's permitted journey so the community is asked to pray that they would be spared the need to break the Sabbath Law.

The description of "the trouble at that time" being "far more than any there has been (20:21)," alludes to Jeremiah's lamentation over destroyed Jerusalem:

> "Look at me, Lord," the city cries..."No one has ever had pain like mine...(Lamentation 1:11-12)."

Verse 22 signals a new hope; God mercifully shortens this period of terrible trial: "For the sake of his chosen people, however, God will reduce the days (24:22)."

4. The Answer to the Third Question (24:23-31)

These nine verses speak of a future event both from the view point of Jesus and the view point of Matthew's community. Since the coming of the Son of Man in glory is linked in some ways with the end, we find some correspondence between this section and the section regarding the end of the age (24:4-14).

As we saw in 24:5 and 24:11, the community is warned against false prophets claiming to be the Messiah (24:23-24). The reference to the power of these false prophets in performing great signs and wonders ties in with the ending of the Sermon on the Mount:

> *"When that Day comes, many will say to me, 'Lord, Lord! In your name we spoke God's message, by your name we drove out many demons and performed many miracles!' Then I will say to them, 'I never knew you. Away from me, you evildoers!' (7:22-23)."*

In the context of chapter 24, these false prophets are not only the lawless, but they also seek to scandalize others with their signs and wonders, "deceiving God's chosen people if possible (24:24)."

Jesus tells his people to disregard all rumors concerning his coming. When the Son of Man does come, his arrival will be as manifest as lightning in the sky (24:27). As vultures are the obvious sign of an animal's carcass, the coming of Jesus will not be able to be mistaken (24:28).

The words, "... after the trouble of those days (24:29)," refer either to the turmoil caused by the false prophets or to the terrible events of the Jewish-Roman war. Apocalyptic imagery, i.e., images of cosmic upheaval heralding God's final intervention in human history, is used to describe the final coming of Jesus (24:29). Finally, after the sun darkens and stars fall, Jesus comes:

> *Then the sign of the Son of Man will appear in the sky; then all the tribes of earth will weep, and they will see the Son of Man coming on the clouds of heaven with power and great glory (24:30).*

Matthew has used the Messianic title, the Son of Man, some thirty times in the Gospel. This title has many associations with apocalyptic literature written in the century or two prior to the death of Jesus. Matthew's use of the title is clearly related to this passage in the book of Daniel:

> *One like a son of man coming on the clouds of heaven; When he reached the Ancient One and was presented before him, He received dominion, glory, and kingship; nations and peoples of every language serve him. His dominion is an everlasting dominion that shall not be destroyed (Daniel 7:13-14* New American Bible).

In the context of the book of Daniel the Son of Man designates a mysterious person who is brought into God's presence. Just prior to the appearance of the Son of Man, Daniel has described the Babylonian, Median, Persian and Alexandrian empires in the imagery of four beasts (Daniel 7:1-7). The Son of Man seems to symbolize God's chosen people in contrast to the kingdoms of this earth. Thus, by contrasing the animal forms with the human form, Daniel dignifies God's people, a people destined to receive everlasting dominion over the world.

Just as Jesus adapted Isaiah's image of the mysterious Suffering Servant of God, symbolizing either a unique individual or a special community, so also Jesus used the title of Son of Man, another symbolic individual representing God's people. Only Matthew includes the vision of the earth weeping at the glorious coming of Jesus (24:30). This verse has several possible meanings. Abraham had received from God the promise that "through you I will bless all the nations (Genesis 12:3)." Thus, Matthew may mean that when Jesus comes in glory, all the tribes of the earth will repent and find salvation in him, thus finding themselves blessed through Abraham's descendant, Jesus (1:1).

The reference to the weeping/contrite tribes could also refer to the final recognition of Jesus by the Jewish people. In the writings of the prophet Zechariah we find a reference to the pouring out of God's blessings upon his people through the sufferings of an unknown person, a person similar to the Suffering Servant described in Isaiah (52:13-53:12). In a portrayal of the repentance and restoration of Jerusalem, Zechariah spoke this Word of God:

> But over the House of David and the citizens of Jerusalem I will pour out a spirit of kindness and prayer. They will look on the one whom they have pierced; they will mourn for him as for an only son, and weep for him as people weep for a first-born child (Zechariah 12:10, Jerusalem Bible).

5. The Parable of the Fig Tree, 24:32-36

The original setting of this teaching is not clear. The lesson of the fig tree could refer to the coming of Jesus in glory (24:23-31) or to the events surrounding the destruction of Jerusalem (24:15-22). The reference to the summer conveys the image of harvesting, a symbol of judgment. Thus, the greening of the tree seems to speak of the glorious coming of Jesus and the gathering of the chosen. However, the warning of Jesus, "All these things will happen before the people now living have all died (24:34)," indicates that the parable of the fig tree refers to the coming destruction of Jerusalem.

The Jewish people looked upon the Torah as something eternal because it was the expression of the will of God. Jesus, the ultimate interpreter of God's will, makes a similar claim for his teaching (24:35), which, as we have seen, completes and affirms the Law (5:17).

Verse 36, dealing with Jesus' lack of knowledge regarding the time and the hour of the end can be understood as a reference to the limitations of Jesus' human knowledge.

6. *The Parable Based on the Days of Noah, 24:37-41*

At this point Matthew takes his departure from Mark. In the Markan account, the reference to the unkown day and hour is followed by the concluding parable of a man going on a journey after putting his servants in charge. Mark concludes with these words of Jesus:

> *"Watch, then, because you do not know when the master of the house is coming—it might be in the evening, or at midnight, or before dawn, or at sunrise. If he comes suddenly, he must not find you asleep. What I say to you then, I say to all: Watch! (Mark 13:35-37)."*

While Mark stresses watching, Matthew emphasizes being prepared and being faithful. The difference reflects the change in perception that has taken place since the time Mark wrote. Mark and the believers of his day still expected Jesus to return in glory very soon. Matthew no longer expects an immediate return, and therefore, instead of watching, Matthew stresses living the faith so that one is always prepared for Jesus' second coming.

The saying of Jesus regarding the days of Noah is also found in Luke, and hence probably was taken from the Q source of Jesus' sayings. In the days of Noah, people were going about the ordinary human activities of eating and drinking and marrying. There is no reference to moral corruption. Then the flood comes and normal life is swept away. The point is simple: the end will come swiftly and suddenly. Noah was saved because he was ready. The two

men working in the fields and the two women grinding
meal are seemingly alike, engaged as they are in similar
activities. But their inner attitudes were different. On the
basis of their inner preparedness, one is taken and the
other is left.

Being taken and being left can be best understood in
light of the description of the final judgment in 25:31-46.
There are six parables positioned by Matthew between
Jesus' words about his coming in glory and the final judgment scene. Four of these parables speak of judgment as a
separating process: those prepared by fidelity to Jesus,
teaching are received into the glory of the Kingdom, and
those who are not prepared are cast out or left behind.
Verses 40 and 41 indicate such a judgment.

7. The Parable of the Burglar, 24:42-44

The point is clear: "...you also must always be
ready...(24:44)." A generalized readiness is not enough.
Jesus specifically states that "the Son of Man will come at
an hour when you are not expecting him (24:44)." The
disciple must be always alert and prepared, displaying the
same kind of preparedness as a householder would manifest if he knew the time when the burglar would strike.

8. The Parable of the Two Servants, 24:45-51

The parable of the fig tree and the beginnings of this
parable have been taken from Mark. Matthew has expanded the number of Marcan parables about the coming
of Christ from two to seven, because, by the 80's, it was
obvious that the immediate coming of Jesus has not only
been delayed, but that it may not even come at all during
the life-time of Matthew's generation. Matthew seems to
have been very sensitive to the danger of becoming a

complacent Church, settling down into a routine and institutional existence. To guard against this possibility, Matthew intensified the emphasis on being faithful to the teachings of Jesus, thereby keeping prepared for his return whenever that would be.

These concerns of Matthew express themselves in the contrast of the two servants. The "faithful and wise servant," probably the symbol of the leader in the community, is placed in charge of the other servants. He provides for their needs (24:46) and is happy when the master comes home and finds him ministering as he should (24:47).

On the contrary, the unfaithful servant does not carry out his master's will. He neglects and mistreats his fellow servants, and indulges himself in such material comforts as eating and drinking in the company of other self-centered companions. He symbolizes, perhaps, the person who thinks that the delay of the coming of Jesus will go on indefinitely. Unexpectedly, the master returns. He will punish him severely, which is the just punishment of hypocrites, those persons who believe but who do not do the deeds required by faith (the lawless; see 7:21-23; 13:41-42; 24:12). In the knowledge that his own hypocrisy brought him to this end, the unfaithful servant "will cry and gnash his teeth (24:51)."

9. The Parable of the Bridesmaids Awaiting the Bridegroom, 25:1-13

This is the fifth parable about the end-time. Again Matthew stresses the need for alertness during that indefinite period of time before Jesus' coming in glory. The parable concerns the coming of the Kingdom. All the elements of the parable—the ten bridesmaids, the supplies of oil, the delay and then the arrival of the bridegroom, the wedding feast—help to express what the Kingdom will be like on "that day (25:1)," i.e., judgment day, the day of the coming of the Son of Man. The ten girls represent two types of believers. The Church is a community of those who hope for the coming of Jesus. Thus, the ten girls are "waiting" to meet the bridegroom. When the bridegroom arrives at his home, the task of the ten girls is to greet him and then escort him to the wedding feast (the banquet of the Kingdom).

The bridegroom delayed and the night wore on. When he finally approaches, the sleeping girls wake and five of them realize that they have used up their oil. While they are searching for the oil dealer, the bridegroom arrives! Judgment follows the scene of separation:

> *"The five girls who were ready went in with him to the wedding feast and the door was closed (25:10)."*

Later, the five unprepared bridesmaids arrive, but it is too late. Compare the words of the bridegroom with the teaching of Jesus given in the Sermon on the Mount:

"When that Day comes, many will say to me, 'Lord, Lord! . . .' Then I will say to them, 'I never knew you. Away from me, you evildoers!' (7:22-23)."	"Later the other girls arrived. 'Sir, sir! Let us in!' they cried. 'But, I really don't know you,' the bridegroom answered (25:12)."

Judging from the context of the parable and its relationship with the teaching of Jesus in the Sermon on the Mount, the oil symbolizes the deeds of mercy and love that ought to characterize the life of the disciple. Merely acknowledging that Jesus is Lord, merely belonging to the Church is not sufficient. Being prepared means doing the deeds that express faith in Jesus; his words must be heard and then lived out (see 7:24-27). To be prepared with the deeds of faith is to be heedful of Jesus' teaching: "Watch out, then, because you do not know the day or hour (25:13)."

10. *The Parable of the Three Servants, 25:14-30*

The sixth parable of the series is also about judgment day. It teaches that preparedness for the day involves faithfulness to the responsibilities of disciples. We are familiar with this parable in terms of the "talents," a large sum of money. To see the point of this parable clearly, keep in mind that Matthew pairs (symmetrically balances) this discourse with the first discourse of Jesus in chapters 5-7. Of particular interest to us is the teaching of Jesus in 5:20:

> *"I tell you, then, that you will be able to enter the Kingdom of heaven only if you are more faithful than the teachers of the Law and the Pharisees in doing what God requires."*

Being a disciple of Jesus demands a thorough-going commitment to do the will of God in all things. The disciples must be more faithful than the Jewish leaders in doing what God requires. This might well be a reference to a common rabbinic outlook regarding the final judgment. It was held that a person would be saved if on the day of judgment the person's good actions totaled more than his bad actions. Thus, in this bookkeeping view of judgment, a person whose bad actions totaled 4,999 would be saved if his good actions totaled at least 5,000.

The point of the parable of the three servants contradicts this accountant's view of judgment. It is not enough merely to do one's appointed tasks and come before God with things evened out. God requires initiative in doing good. The servant who returned the same thousand dollars he was given has not taken initiative in doing good. Instead, as he says, "I was afraid, so I went off and hid your money in the ground (24:25)." The hiding of the money could well be related to another of Jesus' teachings in the Sermon on the Mount. Because "a city built on a hill cannot be hid," the disciples being the salt and light of the world, are told to let the light of their good deeds shine before all people in order to "give praise to your Father in heaven (5:13-16)."

Further light on the guilt of the bad servant is shed by the parable about the king who decided to check on his servants' accounts (18:23). At the conclusion of the parable, the unmerciful servant is condemned to punishment because he did not forgive the debt of his fellow servant, even though he was first forgiven an enormous debt by his master.

We can understand the parable in this way: the three servants have received the "property" of love, kindness, and forgiveness from the hand of God. In light of Jesus' teaching—"You must be perfect—just as your Father in heaven is perfect (5:48)"—the servants must do for others the deeds God (their master) has first done for them. The master's response is the same to each of the servants who have been faithful:

> *"Well done, good and faithful servant!...You have been faithful in managing small accounts, so I will put you in charge of large accounts. Come on in and share my happiness! (25:21, 23)."*

These servants have been faithful—their deeds (the increase of the money) have been the practice of their faith. The words of the master, "Come on in and share my happiness (25:21, 23)," invite the servants into the joy of the Kingdom. Note the similarity of the invitation with the last judgment scene soon to follow:

> *"Then the King will say to the people on his right, 'You that are blessed by my Father: come! Come and receive the kingdom which has been prepared for you ever since the creation of the world. I was hungry and you fed me, thirsty and you gave me drink...'* (25:34-35)."

On the other hand, the servant whose laziness and indifference prevented the deeds that should flow from faith is told:

> *"As for this useless servant—throw him outside in the darkness; there he will cry and gnash his teeth (25:30)."*

Notice the parallel of this servant's fate with those on the King's left in the last judgment scene:

> *"Away from me, you that are under God's curse! Away to the eternal fire...I was hungry but you*

> *would not feed me, thirsty but you would not give me drink...(25:41-42)."*

11. The Final Judgment, 25:31-46

In six parables, Matthew has illustrated the necessity of the Church to be prepared for the coming in glory of the Son of Man. Now he presents a scene which is more than a parable. It is a summation of the last discourse of Jesus; it is a summation of the entire teaching of Jesus. The death and resurrection of Jesus is presupposed; the living out and the completion of the long epoch of the Church is presupposed. These lines take the reader beyond the answer of Jesus to the question of the disciples, "tell us...what will happen to show that it is the time for your coming...(24:3)." These sixteen lines, lines found only in Matthew, sketch what lies beyond the ultimate horizon. The scene is one of universal judgment:

> *"When the Son of Man comes as King, and all the angels with him, he will sit on his royal throne, and all the earth's people will be gathered before him (25:31-32)."*

The teaching is divided into two parts: the first describing the blessing of the righteous, the second dealing with the punishment of evildoers. The imagery parallels that of Ezekiel:

> *"Now then, my flock, I the Sovereign Lord, tell you that I will judge each of you and separate the good from the bad, the sheep from the goats (Ezekiel 34:17)."*

The entire Gospel has been preparing the reader for the criteria of judgment given here: deeds of love, compassion, mercy, and forgiveness.

Nevertheless, there is a surprising feature in this description of the final judgment. The Son of Man has identified himself with his followers. Those who were hungry and who were fed, those who were strangers and who were received into homes, these were the disciples of Jesus sent out as missionaries. The disciples of Jesus were the ones hungry, sick, thrown into prison and in need of clothing. Recall the instructions Jesus gave to his apostles as he commissioned them to share in his ministry (10:5-15). They were sent out without money, without an extra shirt, even without shoes (10:9-10). They were told to stay in the homes that welcomed them and to move on if they were not received (10:13-14). Jesus issued a severe warning concerning people who would refuse to listen to them: "On Judgment Day God will show more mercy to the people of Sodom and Gomorrah than to the people of that town! (10:15)" Now that day of judgment has come. Jesus had said that his missionaries would be arrested and taken to court (10:17). Those who visted them in prison, visited him (25:36). Finally, in that missionary discourse Jesus identified himself with his missionary-disciple:

> *"Whoever welcomes you, welcomes me....Whoever welcomes God's messenger because he is God's messenger will share in his reward....Whoever gives even a drink of cold water to one of the least of these my followers, because he is my follower, will certainly receive his reward (10:40-42)."*

Returning to the Final Judgment, the righteous are surprised:

> "When Lord, did we ever see you hungry and feed
> you...? When did we ever see you a stranger and
> welcome you in our homes, or naked and clothe you?
> (25:38-39)."

As the King answers, notice the parallelism between the
words of Jesus in chapter 10 and the words of the King in
chapter 25:

> "Whoever gives even a drink of cold water to one of
> the least of these my followers, . . . will certainly re-
> ceive his reward (10:42)." "I tell you, indeed,
> whenever you did this for one of the least important
> of these brothers of mine, you did it for me! (25:40)."

On the other hand, those on the King's left are told:

> "Away from me, you that are under God's curse!...I
> was hungry but you would not feed me...; I was sick
> and in prison but you would not take care of me
> (25:41-43)."

Those on the King's left also express surprise. The King
makes the same identification between himself and the
brethren who are his disciples:

> "I tell you, indeed, whenever you refused to help one
> of these least important ones, you refused to help me
> (25:45)."

Matthew tells us that all the people of the world, whether
Christian, Jew or Gentile, will be judged on the basis of how
each person responds to the needs of the disciple-
missionary of Jesus! Audacious. Incredible. Yet that is
what Matthew teaches and it is in complete harmony with

his entire account of the Good News of Jesus. Matthew sees every believer as a disciple, and every disciple is seen as a missionary. Matthew has reported the words of Jesus:

> *"What I am telling you in the dark you must repeat in broad daylight, and what you have heard in private you must tell from the housetops (10:27-28)."*

He has placed this teaching of Jesus at the beginning of the Sermon on the Mount:

> *"You are like salt for all mankind ... You are like light for the whole world. A city built on a hill cannot be hid ... In the same way your light must shine before people, so that they will see the good things you do and give praise to your Father in heaven (5:13-16)."*

Matthew will conclude his work with the great commission of Jesus;

> *"Go then, to all peoples everywhere and make them my disciples: baptize them in the name of the Father, the Son and the Holy Spirit, and teach them to obey everything I have commanded you (28:19-20)."*

Matthew envisioned the Church as an active, energetic and loving community of disciples. If the disciples were to be ready at the coming of the Son of Man, they would be preparing themselves by lives that expressed their faith in living deeds. Matthew probably expected a rapid spread of the Good News of Jesus to the world known by the people of his day, the Mediterranean world, for the most part. The peoples of the Gentile nations had been redeemed by Jesus of Nazareth, "a descendant of David ... a descendant of

Abraham (1:1)." It was to Abraham that God had promised:

> "All the tribes of the earth shall bless themselves through you (Genesis 12:3)."

The missionary Church was seen by Matthew as the means of enabling the nations to receive that promise through Jesus Christ.

Those who had refused to respond "will be sent off to eternal punishment; the righteous will go to eternal life (25:46)." The last verse declares that the righteous, those who do the Father's will, will enter into the joy of the Kingdom forever. As we have seen in each of the five discourses of Jesus, a judgment scene serves as the conclusion. In the Matthean formula signaling the close of the discourse we find a new word, "all":

> When Jesus had finished teaching all these things, he said to his disciples, "In two days . . . it will be the feast of Passover, and the Son of Man will be handed over to be nailed to the cross (26:1-2)."

B. The Passion Narrative, 26:1-27:66

OVERVIEW: With the conclusion of the final discourse Matthew begins the narration of the passion. Matthew recounts it as a drama, and indeed it is the drama of our salvation. Scholars agree that this part of the tradition about Jesus was the first to be written down. No other part of the life of Jesus has been handed down to us with such detail. The passion account, coupled with the proclamation of the resurrection, was the focal point of the early preaching of the apostles.

In Mark's Gospel we are closest to the early preaching of the Church. Fully one-fifth of his account is devoted to the passion narrative. Since Matthew has included much of Jesus' teaching in his version of the Gospel, the proportion devoted to the passion is not as large, but it still remains a notable portion of his Gospel.

In Matthew's use of his Marcan source he has followed the passion narrative more closely than he has followed any other section of Mark's book. Consistent, however, with his usual approach, Matthew added details which greatly enhance the power and significance of his account. Two things should be noticed: First, in Matthew Jesus is more evidently in control. In the passion a twofold process,

similar to that which we saw in the miracle section of chapters 8 and 9, is evident: Matthew abbreviates the details in Mark in order to highlight the majesty of Jesus. He knows what is going to happen and permits it. Secondly, Matthew makes it clear that these events were decreed by God from the beginning. The evangelist accomplishes this through the use of quotations from or allusions to the Hebrew Scriptures. The need for this must have been occasioned by the early preaching of the Church. Many of the Jewish people were potential believers in Jesus. How could they possibly believe in a Messiah who had undergone the ignominious death of crucifixion? Matthew's answer is clear: all this happened in fulfillment of the will of God. Indeed, for those who have eyes to see, it was already foreshadowed in the psalms and prophetic writings of Israel. In this way Matthew illumines for us the love and power of the Father. His love expresses itself in the total gift of his beloved Son; his power transforms the sin that brought Jesus to the cross into a source of life.

What immediately strikes us about the passion narrative (in all four Gospels) is its sobriety. In addition, there is less theologizing on the death of Jesus (i.e., interpreting the meaning of his death) than we find in the letters of Paul and Peter. In the Gospel we hear simply the powerful proclamation of the great saving act of God, the culmination of his wonderful deeds on behalf of his people.

1. The Plot Against Jesus, 26:1-5

Jesus solemnly announces his death (26:2). The feast of Passover is near, and Jesus specifically links his death to this Jewish feast. Even while they plot against Jesus, the leaders of the people are bringing to fulfillment the plan of God (see Ps. 2:2). With heavy irony, Matthew notes that the leaders are frustrated even in their timing. They desired to postpone Jesus' death until after the Passover festival (26:5).

2. The Anointing at Bethany, 26:6-13

Although Jesus died a criminal's death and received a criminal's burial, he was spared an unanointed death. The importance given in Jewish spirituality to the anointing of the dead probably explains the prominence given to this passage. (Note that in Matthew's account of the resurrection the women do not come to anoint the body of Jesus, as they do in Mark.) The disciples (Judas in John 12:4-5) complain about the waste, for the perfume used was very expensive. Jesus accepts the gesture as an act of love and relates it to his imminent death. Hers is the only action in the Gospel that is promised a universal and lasting memory (26:13). Jesus' reply to the disciples (26:11) distinguishes between the good work of giving alms to the poor, a work which Deut 15:7-11 teaches must always be done, and the particular act of love done for him now, immediately preceding his death.

3. *Judas' Agreement, 26:14-16*

Judas plays a major role in the passion narrative. Yet none of the evangelists explain his motivation. Popular presentations of the passion in our own day (*Jesus Christ Superstar* and *Godspell*) view Judas' actions from the perspective of disappointment. Judas expected Jesus to be a political messiah, liberating Palestine from Roman domination. Many scholars think that the name Iscariot links Judas with the Zealots (Palestinian Jews who supported liberation by means of violent rebellion against Rome), which would add weight to this theory.

Only Matthew mentions the agreed price. The thirty silver coins (26:15) probably alludes to Zech 11:12. It was a small amount and, according to Ex. 21:32, it was the price to be paid for the accidental killing of a slave. The context of the text from Zechariah is significant. In 11:4-17 the prophet is instructed to take responsibility for the sheep (Israel) whose leaders are no longer concerned about them. But the prophet is ignored; the leaders will not hear the Word of Yahweh through him. His request for wages earns him thirty pieces of silver, which he takes as a sign of the leaders' contempt for his ministry. Matthew seems to underline both the tiny amount for which Judas was willing to betray the Master and the lack of significance which Jesus' ministry had in the eyes of the Jewish leaders. Thus Judas unknowingly fulfills the Scriptures in accepting the thirty coins.

4. *The Passover Meal, 26:17-25*

Matthew simplifies the Marcan account of the Passover

preparation, again in order to heighten the sense of Jesus' mastery. We can notice many similarities with Matthew's earlier account of the preparations for the entrance into Jerusalem in 21:1-9. Verse 18 is particularly striking. In the Greek, Jesus' "hour" (26:18) signifies a decisive moment, one crucial to his destiny. The wording in Matthew is very solemn: my hour is at hand; at your house I keep Passover with my disciples (present tense in the Greek). Perhaps Matthew is intentionally drawing a verbal parallel between Judas' looking for an opportunity (*eukairian*) to betray the Master (26:16) and Jesus' hour (*kairos*).

The dating of the Last Supper is debated by scholars. John places it one day earlier, in order to link Jesus' death on the cross with the slaughter of the Passover lambs. There is no doubt, however, that this last meal was interpreted by the synoptics as a Passover celebration.

During the solemn meal Jesus shares the heaviness of his heart: one of the disciples will betray him (26:21). The disciples are dismayed, and surprisingly uncertain of their own commitment: "Surely you don't mean me, Lord? (26:22)." The meal was served in common bowls, from which each participant served himself. To share the same bowl heightened the sense of fellowship which was an integral part of the Passover celebration. Note the irony of the sign: Judas' betrayal shatters the fellowship which his sharing of the common bowl symbolizes. Note also the contrast between Judas' "Teacher (26:25)" and the disciples' "Lord (26:22)."

The condemnation of Judas is the most severe in the Gospel. His role is necessary in order to fulfill the Scriptures. Yet his action is free; this does not excuse him. A similar relationship between the necessity of God's design and free will is found in 18:7.

5. Institution of the Eucharist, 26:26-30

Matthew's account of the pivotal moment of the paschal meal presupposes that the reader is familiar with the Passover theology, for Jesus' action takes its significance chiefly from its paschal context. This is the first moment of his great sacrificial action, which will reach its fulfillment with his death on the cross. The account reflects the use of this text in the liturgy of the early Church.

Prior to the prayer of thanksgiving and the breaking of the bread (26:26), Jesus and his disciples remembered and celebrated Yahweh's wonderful deed in liberating his people from their slavery in Egypt. Down through the centuries the Jewish people entered into that mystery of their salvation by eating the bread of Passover. Jesus divides the bread, passes it to the disciples, and adds a new dimension: "This is my body." Now the disciples participate in the mighty saving deed which God is about to accomplish in the death of his Son.

Then Jesus took the cup and again gave thanks. (The blessing prayers over the bread and wine used at the presentation of gifts in our Eucharist echo the thanksgiving blessings of Passover.) The cup which seals God's covenant is poured out for the remission of sins (26:28; see 1:21). The blood of the covenant is a clear allusion to Ex 24:8 where blood is sprinkled both on the altar (symbolizing Yahweh) and on the people, as a sign of the covenant God made with his chosen people at Sinai. Note that Matthew does not speak of a *new* covenant, as do Luke and Paul, who record Jesus' reference to the new covenant prophesied by Jeremiah (see Jer 31:31-34; I Cor 11:25; Lk 22:20). Instead, Matthew refers to the blood of Jesus as that "which seals God's covenant (26:28)." Matthew emphasizes the continuity in God's saving work. God invites all those who believe in Jesus into the providential design for human history.

Note that Matthew records a phrase not found in the other accounts of the Last Supper: "for the forgiveness of sins (26:28)." This phrase clearly expresses the significance of Jesus' death, thus linking the death of Jesus with another one of Matthew's key themes. Recall that Jesus has received his name ("Yahweh saves") because he has come to set God's people free from their sins (1:21). Jesus is God's Suffering Servant who takes upon himself the pain and burdens of God's people (see 8:17 and 12:18) and who gives his life to redeem them (20:28).

As the letter to the Hebrews teaches us:

> For if the blood of goats and bulls and the sprinkling of a heifer's ashes can sanctify those who are defiled so that their flesh is cleansed, how much more will the blood of Christ, who through the eternal spirit offered himself up unblemished to God, cleanse our con-

sciences from dead works to worship the living God!
(*9:13-14*, New American Bible).

Jesus' blood is poured out "for many," a Semitic expression that means for all without restriction. Thus, we find another reference to the final Suffering Servant song of Isaiah:

> *Because he surrendered himself to death and was counted among the wicked; And he shall take away the sins of many, and win pardon for their offenses* (*53:12*, New American Bible).

Verse 29 anticipates the messianic banquet of the Kingdom. The unity of Jesus and his disciples, symbolized and sealed in the Eucharistic meal, cannot be broken even by death. The *Hallel* was sung during the Passover celebration. The first part (Ps 113, 114) preceded the blessing of bread and wine; Our Lord and his disciples sang the second part (Ps 115-118) before they left for the Mount of Olives.

6. *Announcement of Peter's Denial, 26:31-35*

Matthew places the Last Supper between the announcement of Judas' betrayal and Jesus' words about the fragile commitment of the disciples. His words are more accurately translated in the *New American Bible*: "Tonight your faith in me will be shaken (26:31)." Again we meet the "scandal" of 13:41, 16:23 and 18:7. The disciples' will stumble and doubt because of the disappointment of their messianic hopes for the coming of the Kingdom in this world. They will be helpless when they lose the Master. Yet, Jesus says, all this has been foreseen by the prophet Zechariah. Matthew alters the text so that it is God himself who strikes the shepherd; it is God's plan that is being carried out. Jesus affirms this (26:32) by declaring to the disciples that they will again see him and be together with him in Galilee (see 28:7).

Once again Peter takes a role of leadership (26:33). But Jesus responds that Peter's pride will lead him into a more serious fall than that of the other disciples. They will stumble in faith, but he will disown the Master, and that three times! In verse 35 Peter and the others re-affirm their loyalty.

The disciples did not spare themselves, as they humbly told and re-told the momentous events of this night. The memory of their stumbling must have remained very strong in their minds, proof that infidelity is possible for any disciple.

7. The Prayer of Jesus in Gethsemane, 26:36-46

In this passage we enter into the mystery of Jesus' struggle to be faithful to the Father's will. At no other place in the Gospels do we so clearly encounter the incomprehensible union of his divinity and his humanity. In his anguish Jesus sought the support of his chosen friends. In a special way he invites Peter, James and John—who had been the witnesses of his transfiguration (17:1-8)—to enter into his sorrow: " 'Stay here and watch with me' (26:38)." (This pericope seems to have been used by Matthew's community in catechesis on vigilance and on prayer.) But they are unable to stay awake.

As he frequently does, Matthew alters Mark in order to enhance the majesty of Jesus. In verses 37 and 39 he softens Mark's wording (Mk 14:33,35) slightly. In his humanity Jesus shrinks from the death that awaits him. Yet his sorrow is tempered by the obedience of a son. In 20:22-23 Jesus had spoken of the cup which he was about to drink.

The cup in Jewish theology was a symbol of God's wrath and punishment; here it refers to the suffering and death which await Jesus. Verses 41 and 42 contain two allusions to the Our Father. The temptation (26:41) which the disciples are to pray that they avoid alludes to Jesus' words, "Do not bring us to hard testing...(6:13)." And in verse 42 Matthew shapes the second prayer of Jesus so that he repeats the words of 6:10: "your will be done." It is possible that Matthew intentionally relates the threefold affirmation of obedience (verses 39, 42 and 44) to the triple rejection of Satan's temptations in 4:3,5 and 9). Now, in the Father's design the "hour has come for the Son of Man to be handed over to the power of sinful men (26:46)." Judas has found his opportune time and is there to betray the Master.

8. The Arrest of Jesus, 26:47-56

The betrayal of Jesus is familiar to all. Both in the last supper scene ("Surely you don't mean me, Teacher?") and in the betrayal scene ("Peace be with you, Teacher") Judas only acknowledges Jesus by the title of "Rabbi" or "Teacher" (see 26:25; 26:49). Matthew thus indicates that Judas lacked faith in Jesus as Messiah and Lord.

The crowd sent by the chief priests and the Jewish elders

(26:47) are probably the Temple police. The incident in which one of the disciples struck the servant of the High Priest is recorded by all four evangelists, but only Matthew has these words of Jesus:

> *"Put your sword back in its place, because all who take the sword will die by the sword. Don't you know that I could call on my Father for help and at once he would send me more than twelve armies of angels? But in that case, how could the Scriptures come true that say it must happen in this way? (26:52-54)"*

These words of Jesus re-focus several Matthean themes. First, Jesus lives out his own teaching given in his Sermon on the Mount:

> *"But now I tell you: do not take revenge on someone who does you wrong. If anyone slaps you on the right cheek, let him slap your left cheek too....*
>
> *"But I now tell you: love your enemies, and pray for those who persecute you, so that you will become the sons of your Father in heaven (5:39, 44-45)."*

Jesus tells his disciple that violence is not the way (26:52). We may see in this a reference to the seventh beatitude,

> *"Happy are those who work for peace among men; God will call them his sons! (5:9)"*

Secondly, Jesus refers to the angels his Father could provide, thus recalling the scene of his temptation in the desert in chapter four. There, angels ministered to Jesus after he rejected Satan's suggestions that he refuse to be the obedient Suffering Servant of God (see 4:1-11). Finally, there is the theme of Jesus fulfilling the Scriptures, particularly the prophecy of Isaiah:

> *He was treated harshly, but endured it humbly; he never said a word. . . . He was put to death for the sins of our people (Is 53:7-8).*

Jesus spoke three times on the occasion of his arrest. First, there were the brief words for Judas, followed by his words for his disciple regarding the futility of violence. Finally, Jesus addresses the crowd. His reference to their coming for him as if he were "an outlaw" (26:55) is a critique of their distorted perception of the one who sat and taught in the Temple. His words also look ahead to the choice that Pilate will present to the crowd, the choice between Barabbas, the outlaw of violence, and Jesus, the man about to suffer violence out of redeeming love for his people.

The disciples then desert him as he had predicted during their last meal together (26:31).

9. *Jesus Before the Council, 26:57-68*

Matthew follows Mark, making a few changes in the account of the trial of Jesus before the Jewish Council (the seventy-two members of the Sanhedrin). We need to keep in mind that we are not reading a stenographer's courtroom transcript in these twelve verses. We have in this account a combination of historical memories, some indication of the reason why Jesus was condemned, and a profession of the Christian community's belief in the divinity of Jesus, all of which are placed in the dramatic framework of a night trial that violated Judaism's own procedures of just process.

As the narrative reads, the charge against Jesus was that

of blasphemy, i.e., his reference to himself as the one sitting at the "right side of the Almighty (26:64)," a reference that identified him with God. However, the words of the High Priest, "... tell us if you are the Messiah, the Son of God (26:63)," are more representative of the Church's faith in Jesus (see 16:16-19) than indicative of a Jewish official's accusation.

The more likely charge against Jesus would have been his words against the Temple, a charge alluded to by the testimony of the two men in 26:61. Jesus had been likened to Jeremiah the prophet (see 16:14). Jesus had repeated the words of Jeremiah as he drove buyers and sellers from the Temple (see 21:13; Jer. 7:11). Jeremiah had delivered this "word" of the Lord to the people of Jerusalem some six centuries before:

> *"I, the Lord, have said that you must obey me by following the teaching that I gave you....If you continue to disobey, then I will do to this Temple what I did to Shiloh...(Jer 26:4-6)."*

A trial follows Jeremiah's prophecy, in which the leaders of Judah gather to hear the testimony. Notice the similarity of the wording:

"Then the priests and the prophets said to the leaders of the people, 'This man deserves to be sentenced to death because he has spoken against our city. You have heard him with your own ears (Jer 26:11)."

At this the High Priest tore his clothes and said, "Blasphemy! We don't need any more witnesses! Right here you have heard his wicked words! What do you think?" They answered, "He is guilty, and must die (26:65-66)."

Jeremiah was acquitted: "This man spoke to us in the name of the Lord our God; he should not be put to death (Jer 26:16)." Jesus, however, is delivered up to Pilate:

> *Early in the morning all the chief priests and the*
> *Jewish elders made their plan against Jesus to put him*
> *to death. They ... took him, and handed him over to*
> *Pilate, the Roman governor (27:1-2).*

10. Peter Denies Jesus, 26:69-75

Peter, the first to be called by Jesus and the first to respond to his call, Peter, the symbol of the disciple, fails and fails completely. His threefold denial of Jesus contrasts with Jesus' threefold affirmation of his Father's will: "My Father, if this cup cannot be taken away unless I drink it, your will be done (see 26:39-44)."

Matthew stresses the totality of Peter's denial. To Mark's account of Peter's denials, Matthew adds the phrases "in front of them all (26:70)," and "I swear that ... (26:72)." In the light of Jesus' teaching in the missionary discourse, "But whoever denies publicly that he belongs to me, then I will deny him before my Father in heaven (10:33)," it may well be that Matthew is holding Peter up as one who has gravely sinned and abundantly received the forgiveness of Jesus in the manner of seventy times seven (see 18:22). Even though Peter denied Jesus before all, even though he swore he did not know Jesus, even though he vowed that he did not know Jesus, nevertheless, Peter repented, weeping "bitterly (26:75)," and implicitly received the forgiveness of Jesus.

11. The Death of Judas, 27:3-10

None of the other evangelists speak about the death of Judas. There is another tradition about Judas in Acts 1:18-19, indicating that he himself bought a field with the money he received for betraying Jesus. In that field he died by a fall. The tradition with which Matthew is familiar lent itself to his theological purposes: the declaration of the innocence of Jesus and an emphasis on the guilt of the chief priests and the elders (26:4-6).

12. *Jesus and Pilate, 27:11-14*

Pilate's question, "Are you the king of the Jews? (27:11)," recalls another question, the question of the magi about the baby born to be the king of the Jews (2:2). Three more times during his passion Jesus will be mockingly referred to as the King (27:29, 37, 42). Jesus says nothing about the charges made against him, his silence suggesting Isaiah's description of the Suffering Servant of God:

He was treated harshly, but endured it humbly; he never said a word. Like a lamb about to be slaughtered, like a sheep about to be sheared, he never said a word (Is 53:7).

13. Jesus Barabbas Or Jesus Called the Christ?, 27:15-26

Our text reads, "At that time there was a well-known prisoner named Jesus Barabbas (27:16)." The oldest manuscripts read "Jesus Barabbas," and the theological purpose of Matthew indicates that he clearly wanted to stress the choice that lay before the Jewish people. The name "Jesus" meant "God (Yahweh) saves." Barabbas means "son of the Father." Pilate asked the crowd:

> "Which one do you want me to set free for you? Jesus Barabbas or Jesus called the Christ? (27:17)"

Barabbas is an insurrectionist. The choice between Barabbas and Jesus seems to be one between the advocate of saving ourselves through violence and the teacher of redemptive non-violence. Barabbas, the son of the father is contrasted with Jesus, the true and obedient Son of the Father. They choose Barabbas. Although Pilate was the one ultimately responsible for the unjust condemnation of the innocent Jesus (there is no real charge, only accusation), Matthew tries to heighten the responsibility of the whole population of Jerusalem, both leaders as well as the com-

mon people. Thus Matthew includes several incidents that present Pilate in a more favorable light. The account of the dream of Pilate's wife contrasts a Gentile's pleading for Jesus' life with the Jewish leaders' asking for his death. Matthew links this event with another incident that is unique to his narrative, Pilate's washing of his hands as a symbol of his lack of responsibility for the death of the innocent Jesus. Thus, the stage is set for transferring responsibility for the death of Jesus to the entire population of Jerusalem.

> "I am not responsible for the death of this man! This is your doing!" The whole crowd answered back, "Let the punishment for his death fall on us and on our children! (27:24-25)"

As no other evangelist gives an account of Pilate's self-absolution, so also no other evangelist records the self-damning words, "Let the punishment for his death fall on us and on our children (27:25)." We must ask why Matthew wanted to so exaggerate the guilt of the people of Jerusalem. Perhaps Matthew softened Pilate's role in the crucifixion of Jesus lest a negative image of a Roman ruler prove to be a hindrance in proclaiming the Gospel to the Gentile wor.d. Or perhaps the answer is related to Matthew's theological interpretation of the destruction of Jerusalem by the Romans in 70 A.D. The punishment (the blood of Jesus) the Jews called down upon themselves and their children could very well be the suffering of the people of Jerusalem during the war and the final destruction of Temple and city. If so, Matthew was utilizing his faith in Jesus as an aid in explaining why an event as terrible and tragic as the devastation of the beloved city of God's beloved people could happen. Matthew, in accord with a thousand years of the prophetic tradition, was declaring what the prophets had always declared: the tragic events experienced by God's people happened because they had sinned, and because God wanted them to repent of their sin and come back to him! It is probable that Matthew so stressed the responsibility of the people of Jerusalem for the death of Jesus so that they could, in Matthew's eyes, recognize their sin in rejecting their Messiah, and thus contritely turn back to God and find the salvation Jesus has come to bring his people:

> "She will give birth to a son and you will name him Jesus—because he will save his people from their sins (1:21)."

We have seen Jesus lamenting,

> "Jerusalem, Jerusalem! You kill the prophets and stone the messengers God has sent you! How many times I have wanted to put my arms around all your people. . . . Now your home will be completely forsaken. From now on you will never see me again, I tell you, until you say, 'God bless him who comes in the name of the Lord' (23:37-39)."

This lament is followed by the discourse in which Jesus speaks of the destruction of Jerusalem, a destruction so terrible, so filled with loss of life, that God himself intervened for the sake of his chosen people (24:21-22).

It is true that, in the heat of the sometimes bitter debate with the Jewish people of his day, Matthew has painted both the opponents of Jesus and the opponents of his community with very dark strokes. However, it is difficult to perceive Matthew's being so motivated by vengeance that he deliberately stressed the guilt of the Jewish people in order to bring them pain and harm. It is likely that

Matthew had known and had loved the city of Jerusalem. It is even more likely that he loved his people and probably considered the worst sufferings for their rejection of Jesus to have ended with the close of the Jewish-Roman war. It is a fact that Matthew loved God's Torah and Jesus' interpretation of that Torah. Matthew had both learned and lived the teaching of Jesus regarding love of all, enemies included, and regarding forgiveness, exemplified by Jesus' living and dying as God's Suffering Servant.

Unfortunately, the course of history took a very different track. The acceptance of Matthew's account as if it were a strict historical record that condemned the Jewish people has led to outbursts of anti-Semitism down through the history of western culture. The Second Vatican Council deemed it necessary to clarify the matter:

> *True, authorities of the Jews and those who followed their lead pressed for the death of Christ (cf. Jn 19:6), still, what happened in His passion cannot be blamed upon all the Jews then living, without distinction, nor upon the Jews of today. Although the Church is the new people of God, the Jews should not be presented as repudiated or cursed by God, as if such views followed from the Holy Scripture (DECLARATION OF THE RELATIONSHIP OF THE CHURCH TO NON-CHRISTIAN RELIGIONS, #4).*

Returning to the passion narrative, Pilate bows to the wishes of the people:

> *Then Pilate set Barabbas free for them; he had Jesus whipped and handed him over to be nailed to the cross (26:26).*

The people of Jerusalem have made their choice. In the

span of years between 30 and 70 A.D., they and their children will experience Jerusalem's destruction, which Matthew sees as the consequence of that choice. And yet, in God's mysterious providence, their rejection of Jesus is the instrument through which salvation will be offered to the whole world, the world of both Jew and Gentile, in the new age of the Church.

14. *The Soldiers Ridicule Jesus, 27:27-31*

The soldiers have their cruel sport with Jesus, giving him a crown of thorns, a robe suggesting the imperial color, and a stick for a scepter. They mockingly kneel before him, acclaiming him as "the King of the Jews! (27:29)" The irony is that Jesus is truly the King. The reader of the Gospel knows this. But the reader knows that Jesus is not the kind of King the soldiers are mocking. Jesus has rejected the trappings of power and domination since the time of his temptation in the desert. He did not want to possess "all the kingdoms of the world (4:8)." He chose to be the Suffering Servant prophesied by Isaiah:

> *I bared my back to those who beat me. I did not stop them when they insulted me, when they pulled out the hairs of my beard and spit in my face (Is 50:6).*

The irony of this scene is more than matched by its paradox. Jesus seems to have been utterly defeated, yet his disfigurement heralds his glory:

> *The Lord says, "My servant will succeed in his task; he will be highly honored. Many people were shocked when they saw him; he was so disfigured that he hardly looked human. But now many nations will marvel at him, and kings will be speechless with*

*amazement. They will see and understand something
they had never known (Is 52:13-15)."*

15. *Jesus Nailed to the Cross, 27:32-44*

Matthew almost follows Mark word for word in these
verses. The reference to "the written notice of the accusa-

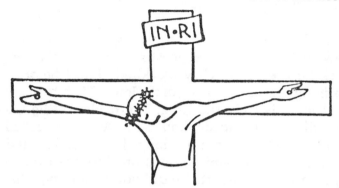

tion against him: 'This is Jesus, the King of the Jews'
(27:37)" is very likely the charge for which the civil authority sentenced Jesus to death. Crucifixion was a
punishment reserved for slaves, brigands and insurrec-
tionists, since its particular horror was thought to deter
people from committing those crimes that seriously un-
dermined the society of that day. That Jesus was crucified
along with two other bandits (27:38) also indicates that
Jesus was falsely sentenced for rebellion.

The offering of wine mixed with gall to Jesus (27:34)
suggests Psalm 69: "When...I was thirsty, they offered me
vinegar (69:21)." The casting of dice for his clothes and the
taunting by the bystanders recall Psalm 22:

*A gang of evil men is around me; like a pack of dogs
they close in on me; they tear at my hands and*

feet....My enemies look at me and stare. They gam-
ble for my clothes and divide them among themselves
(Ps. 22:16-18).

Finally, there is the last temptation of Jesus:

"He saved others but he cannot save himself! Isn't he
the King of Israel? If he will come down off the cross
now, we will believe in him! He trusts in God and says
he is God's Son (27:42-43)."

The language and the sense of these words echo the wording of Satan's temptations of Jesus just prior to the beginning of his Galilean ministry.

The first temptation and the temptation to introduce
himself to the people by a miraculous descent from the
tower of the Temple began with the words, "If you are
God's Son...(4:3, 6)." Now Jesus is mockingly challenged
to verify that he is God's son by a miraculous descent from
the cross (27:42-43). As we have seen in the desert temptations as well as throughout the ministry of Jesus, the issue
is this: what kind of Messiah is Jesus? Does he come to
benefit himself or to manifest the love of the Father for his
people? Does he come to be the glorious Messiah leading
Israel into prosperity or is he come to be the Suffering
Servant of God showing that the way to satisfy the human
heart is through the paradox of losing one's life for the sake
of others (see 10:38-39)? The demand that Jesus perform a
special sign, a miracle, is rejected by Jesus as he had done
before (12:38-39; 16:1-4).

Luke's account of the passion has many poignant scenes
that are not found in Matthew: the words of Jesus for the
Daughters of Jerusalem, his forgiving his executioners, the
dialogue between the two thieves, and Jesus' promise of
Paradise to the repentant thief (see Lk 23:27-43).

16. *The Death of Jesus, 27:45-56*

From noon until three Jesus suffers the agony of crucifixion. Matthew follows Mark, who has passed on the earliest tradition of the passion. That tradition records only one sentence spoken by Jesus on the cross:

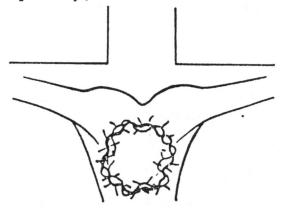

"Eli, Eli, lema sabachthani?" which means, "My God, my God, why did you abandon me? (27:46)"

This one sentence has a signififance that cannot be measured. It is not a cry of despair, it is the prayer of a dying and faithful Jew whose trust in God is expressed in terms of hope and praise even in the midst of the most despairing circumstances. The words of Jesus are the opening words of Psalm 22. The rest of the Psalm is both prayer and prophecy:

> *My God, my God, why have you abandoned me?...Our ancestors put their trust in you; they trusted you and you saved them....*
>
> *All who see me make fun of me;...."You relied on the LORD," they say, "Why doesn't he save you?..."*

*I have relied on you since the day I was born, and you
have always been my God....*

*O Lord, don't stay away from me! Come quickly to
my rescue!...
I will tell my people what you have done;
I will praise you in their assembly:
"Praise him, you servants of the Lord!
...Worship him, you people of Israel!..."*

*Future generations will serve him; men will speak of
the Lord to the coming generation. People not yet
born will be told: "The LORD has saved his people
(Ps 22:1-31)."*

Bystanders, hearing the Hebrew word for God, *Eli*, mistakenly think Jesus is calling upon Elijah (27:47-49).

Having prayed the twenty-second Psalm, Jesus gave a "loud cry, and breathed his last (27:50)." The splitting of the temple curtain and the other apocalyptic events of verses 51-53 seem to be more theological than historical in intent. The tearing of the Temple curtain probably indicates that God's special sanctuary, the Holy of Holies, has passed from the temple to Jesus (see 12:7). The phenomenon of splitting rocks, opening graves and earthquakes are associated with the Day of Yahweh, the day of God's great intervention in history. Only Matthew includes these symbolic happenings. In Mark, the Roman centurion is moved to profess "Truly this man was a son of God! (Mark 15:39)" because of the manner in which Jesus died. In Matthew, the earthquake and everything else that happened so terrified the army officer and the soldiers that they said, "He really was the Son of God! (27:54)." In contrast to Peter and the other male disciples of Jesus, "There were many women there, looking on from a distance, who had followed Jesus from Galilee and helped him (27:55)." Since these women "had followed Jesus," they are singled out as disciples who courageously kept close to Jesus to the very end. Two of the women named in verse 56 will be the first to experience the risen Jesus (see 28:1, 9-10).

17. The Burial of Jesus, 27:57-61

Another disciple steps forward, Joseph of Arimathea (27:57). As Jesus lived without a place to lie down and rest (8:20), so he dies without a grave. The disciple Joseph gives his own tomb for the burial of the body of Jesus, an incident which early believers saw foretold by Isaiah:

> "...he was buried with the rich, even though he had never committed a crime or ever told a lie. (Is 53:9)."

Jesus has obediently completed his mission. The words of the Father, heard by Jesus after his baptism by John, have been consummated:

> "This is my own dear Son, with whom I am well pleased! (3:17)."

18. The Guard at the Grave, 27:62-66

This section is found only in Matthew. His manifest intention is to provide a defense against the refusal of some to believe in the resurrection of Jesus on the grounds that the body of Jesus was stolen from the tomb by the disciples. The only solid conclusion that we can draw from these verses and from 28:11-15 is that both the Jews and the disciples knew that the tomb was empty by the third day after the death of Jesus.

C. The Resurrection of Jesus and The Great Commission, 28:1-20

OVERVIEW: In applying redaction or composition criticism to the accounts of the resurrection, we notice that there are many more differences between the evangelists here than there are in the passion accounts. This indicates that the resurrection accounts were not as fully established in the oral tradition as the passion narrative.

One substantial difference in the resurrection accounts is the location of the appearances of the risen Jesus to the eleven. Mark, Matthew and the twenty-first chapter of John indicate that Jesus appeared to the eleven not in Jerusalem, but in Galilee. Luke and John (chapter 20) place the resurrection appearances of Jesus in Jerusalem.

The older of the two traditions is probably the one contained in Mark and Matthew. We may conjecture that after the disciples fled (26:56), they returned to Galilee. There, in the place where Jesus spent most of his ministry, the disciples encountered the risen Lord. Whatever the divergences in the resurrection accounts, all the evangelists are in agreement on one central point: Jesus of Nazareth is risen! He has been seen by the disciples!

1. The Two Women Encounter the Risen Jesus, 28:1-10

As we have done several times, let us compare Matthew's account with the earlier version of Mark:

Mark 16:1-8	Mt 28:1-8
(1) After the Sabbath day was over, Mary Magdalene, Mary the mother of James,	(1) After the Sabbath, as Sunday morning was dawning, Mary Magdalene and the other Mary went to look at the grave.

and Salome bought spices to go and anoint the body of Jesus. (2) Very early on Sunday morning, at sunrise, they went to the grave. (3-4) On the way they said to one another, "who will roll away for us the stone from the entrance to the grave?" (It was a very large stone.) Then they looked up and saw that the stone had already been rolled back.

(2) Suddenly there was a strong earthquake; an angel of the Lord came down from heaven, rolled the stone away, and sat on it. (3) His appearance was like lightning and his clothes were white as snow. (4) The guards were so afraid that they trembled and became like dead men.

(5) So they entered the grave, where they saw a young man sitting at the right, wearing a white robe—and they were filled with alarm. (6) "Don't be alarmed," he said. "I know you are looking for Jesus of Nazareth, who was nailed to the cross. He is not here—he has been raised! Look, here is the place where they placed him. (7) Now go and give this message to his disciples, including Peter: 'He is going to Galilee ahead of you; there you will see him, just as he told you.' "

(5) The angel spoke to the women. "You must not be afraid," he said. "I know you are looking for Jesus, who was nailed to the cross. (6) He is not here; he has been raised, just as he said. Come here and see the place where he lay. (7) Quickly, now, go and tell his disciples, 'He has been raised from death, and now he is going to Galilee ahead of you; there you will see him!' Remember what I have told you."

Until this point, (Mk 16:1-7 and Mt 28:1-7) there are only minor divergences. Mark has three women who come for the purpose of anointing the body; they wonder about how they will open the tomb. Matthew has two women merely going to visit the grave, perhaps because Jesus was anointed for burial at Bethany (26:6-13). Then an angel appears, there is an earthquake and the guards are terrified. Now Matthew significantly changes the original ending of Mark's account:

(8) So they went out and ran from the grave, because fear and terror were upon them. They said nothing to anyone, because they were afraid.

(8) So they left the grave in a hurry, afraid

and yet filled with joy, and ran to tell his disciples.

From this point, the material in Matthew has no parallel in the other evangelists. It is unique to Matthew.

On their way, the women are met by Jesus. Matthew is not interested in the resurrection appearances as such. By the 80's belief in the risen Lord is well established. Matthew wants to focus attention on the message of the risen Jesus. Thus, Jesus appears to the women, giving them his peace and commissioning them to deliver the message they had already been given by the angel:

> "Go and tell my brothers to go to Galilee and there they will see me (28:10)."

Matthew's account of the Gospel is swiftly moving towards the climactic meeting between Jesus and his disciples upon the Galilean mountain top.

2. Matthew's Refutation of the Claim that the Disciples Stole the Body of Jesus, 28:11-15

This incident, together with its preparation in 27:62-66, in which the Jewish leaders asked Pilate for soldiers to guard the tomb, are events recounted by Matthew alone. From what we can gather, the Jewish community explained away the empty tomb (which was taken by many of the first believers as evidence of Jesus' resurrection) by asserting that the disciples came and stole the body of Jesus. Matthew refutes this argument by first placing it on the lips of the chief priests and Pharisees when they see Pilate and request soldiers to guard the tomb (27:64). Then, in 28:11-15, Matthew offers an explanation of how the calumny about the disciples' stealing their master's body began in the first place: the chief priests and elders bribed the guards to spread this lie (28:13).

3. The Climax of the Gospel: Jesus Commissions His Disciples, 28:16-20

At the very beginning of Jesus' public ministry Matthew declared as fulfilled the words of the prophet Isaiah:

"Land of Zebulun...Galilee of the Gentiles! The people who live in darkness will see a great light. On those who live in the dark land of death the light will shine (4:15-16)."

Then Jesus began to preach his message, "Turn away from your sins, because the Kingdom of heaven is near! (4:17)." Now, on a mountain top in Galilee, there is a new beginning. The place is significant. On a mountain Jesus gave his first discourse, interpreting for his disciples the will of the Father. On a mountain top Jesus was transfigured, and his divinity was manifested to Peter, James and John. On the Mount of Olives Jesus taught his disciples how to be prepared for the sudden coming of the Son of Man. Now, on this mountain in Galilee, Jesus will give his disciples the fullness of his power and send them out to make disciples of all peoples (28:18-19). The disciples, who are the salt of the earth and light of the world, are themselves sent to "those who live in the dark land of death (4:16)," empowered with the full authority of the risen Jesus.

a. The eleven arrive, 28:16-17

In the context of foretelling Peter's denial and the desertion of the disciples, Jesus had said, "But after I am raised to life I will go to Galilee ahead of you (26:32)." The disciples have followed the instruction given them by the women (28:7). Because the words of Jesus are of the greatest significance, Matthew gives only the briefest statement regarding the resurrection appearance: "When they saw him they worshipped him, even though some of them doubted (28:17)." The reference to the doubting is puzzling. Perhaps it reflects the same difficulty in recognizing the risen Jesus that we find in other resurrection appearances, such as that found in the account of the two disciples journeying to Emmaus (Lk 24:16); perhaps it reflects the doubts expressed later by disciples who were not present (see John 21:24-29). It is not surprising that there should be some hesitation and questioning, since the death of Jesus had shattered their expectation of what kind of Messiah he would be.

b. The authority of Jesus, 28:18

Throughout the entire Gospel, the authority of Jesus was a central Matthean theme. He did not teach like "their teachers of the Law; instead, he taught with authority (7:29)." He has given the disciples authority to heal, exorcise and proclaim the Kingdom (10:1, 7). He has stated, "My Father has given me all things (11:27)." Now Jesus claims the fulness of authority:

> "I have been given all authority in heaven and on earth (28:18)."

This claim of Jesus, soon to be coupled with his command to teach the whole world, is best understood in the context of the description of the Son of Man given by the prophet Daniel. As the Son of Man received "dominion, glory, and kingship (Dan 7:13-14)" from the Ancient One, so Jesus, obedient unto death and risen from the dead, has received from his Father "all authority in heaven and on earth (28:18)." As the Son of Man received dominion, glory and kingship so that "nations and peoples of every language serve him (Dan 7:14)," so Jesus shares his fullness of power with his disciples so that "all peoples everywhere (28:19)" will become his disciples, serving him by obeying "everything I have commanded...(28:20)." As Daniel had foretold that the Son of Man's "dominion is an everlasting dominion that shall not be taken away, his kingship shall not be destroyed (Dan 7:14)," so Jesus has established his

Church which "not even death will be able to overcome (16:18)." He, the Lord, will be with his Church "always, to the end of the age (28:20)."

c. Discipleship: baptism, teaching his commands, 28:19-20

Here the missionary thrust of Matthew's theology of discipleship comes to its fullest expression. The disciples now receive the authority to be the light that shines on heathen Galilee and on the rest of the world.

Before Jesus rose from the dead, the disciples were instructed to limit their ministry to "the lost sheep of the people of Israel (10:6)." Now, endowed with the fullness of the power of Jesus, they are sent to the whole world in order to make disciples of "all peoples everywhere (28:19)." They are to accomplish this task in two actions. First, they must baptize others in this way:

> *"...in the name of the Father, the Son, and the Holy Spirit (28:19)."*

We should note a remarkable aspect about this baptismal formula. It indicates that the first step in becoming a disciple is initiation into the Church (the community of believers) through the baptismal rite. As we have seen, Matthew's community was engaged in a struggle with Judaism regarding the issue of self-identity as the true Israel. Here we see that the individual's identity is related to the community's identity. The community is composed of those who have received through Jesus the new revelation that God is Father, Son and Holy Spirit. The trinitarian profession of faith has become, even as early as the 80's, the entrance rite into the Church!

Secondly, the eleven disciples are commissioned to

> *"...teach them to obey everything I have commanded you (28:20)."*

In this verse the theme of the teaching of Jesus comes to its climax. This is the very first time that Jesus sends forth his disciples to teach. Until now, Jesus was the teacher, and they were the disciples being taught. Jesus had shared with his disciples the authority to heal, exorcise and proclaim the Kingdom. Now, having experienced Jesus risen from the dead, they are at last ready to teach.

They are to teach people "to obey everything I have commanded you (28:20)." Matthew's entire account might be seen as a commentary on this mandate of the risen Lord. The disciple is above all one who *obeys*. In all things he desires to do the will of God, as fully and perfectly as possible. The disciple is to obey *everything*. He does not pick and choose, deciding which teachings are compatible with his personality or lifestyle. Moreover, the disciple obeys what is *commanded*. More than the other evangelists, Matthew presents Jesus as the one who makes clear the will of God. But the will of God makes demands upon us. The disciple is eager to do all that God requires.

d. Jesus is with his Church always, 28:20

That which is most significant for Matthew and for his community is proclaimed in the last sentence of the Gospel:

> *"And remember! I will be with you always, to the end of the age (28:20)."*

This promise of Jesus to be present to his community always is the fourth and final mention of universality in the concluding two verses of the Gospel. Jesus has received *all* authority; Jesus commissioned his disciples to go to *all* peoples everywhere, teaching them to obey *all* that he has taught them; finally, Jesus will be with them *always*, "to the end of the age." Jesus, by his promise to be actively present in the community, completes the prophecy given to Joseph at the very beginning of the Gospel (1:23):

> "...he will be called Emmanuel," (which means, "God is with us").

Here begins, in Matthew's theology, the era of the Church. Strengthened by the dynamic presence of the risen Lord, empowered by his authority, the disciples go out to continue his mission.

Glossary

Apocalyptic writing: a form (genre) of writing that tries to put into words the effects of God's final eruption into human history. This apocalyptic form was common between 200 B.C. and 200 A.D. In it God's intervention in history is described in terms of cosmic upheaval, e.g., stars falling from the sky, earthquakes, etc.

Christian Scriptures: term used to designate The New Testament. The commentary uses the terms, Hebrew Scriptures, Christian Scriptures, in order to emphasize the unity and continuity of the Word of God contained in the Bible. The customary terms, Old Testament, New Testament, often placed too great a division between the Scriptures written before and after the death and resurrection of Jesus. Furthermore, the adjectives old and new sometimes convey the false idea that the covenant God has made with his chosen people, the Jews, has been nullified. If God is ever-faithful, then both covenants, the Mosaic covenant and the covenant made with both Jew and Gentile in Jesus, are eternally valid.

Didache: an early second century writing containing a portrait of Christian life in the areas of moral precepts, ecclesial organization and instructions for liturgical functions. The full title of the *Didache* would read "The Lord's Instruction to the Gentiles through the Twelve Apostles."

Form criticism: a branch of literary science that singles out the different literary forms used by an author in a particular work, e.g., the parable, the miracle account.

Hebrew Scriptures: the term used to designate what is more commonly known as The Old Testament. See "Christian Scriptures."

Jewish midrash: a rabbinic technique of interpreting the Scriptures by means of meditating upon the Word of God and then creating stories that have as their point the elucidation of a particular text of Scripture.

Literary criticism: a branch of literary science that looks at a work of literature as a whole and seeks to understand the way in which the author has constructed his work.

Orthopraxy: derived from *ortho,* meaning "correct," and *praxis,* i.e., making or doing. Othropraxy refers to action that is in conformity with established norms of Christian living. "Orthodoxy," correct teaching, is the companion of orthopraxy.

Pharisees: usually rabbis (not priests) who studied and interpreted the Hebrew Scriptures. The men who constituted this movement were divided into several schools, of which the school of Shammai (favoring strict interpretation of the Law) and the school of Hillel (favoring a more flexible interpretation) were the most influential at the time of Jesus.

Source criticism: a branch of literary science that analyzes a particular work in terms of the sources used by the particular text.

Symbol: a word or sign that points beyond itself to a larger reality. Many of the symbols encountered in Scripture point to realities that can never be adequately described in human language, e.g., the Kingdom of God.

Synoptic Gospels: the Gospels written by the three evangelists, Matthew, Mark and Luke. Literally, synoptic means to look at several columns of writing at the same time. Matthew, Mark and Luke can be arranged in parallel columns because of their similarity in content.